Advanced Manufacturing and Supply Chain with IoT

Revolutionizing Industries through Smart Technologies and Connectivity

Ameya Deshpande
Bidyut Sarkar
Deep Dave
Ravi Dave

www.bpbonline.com

First Edition 2024

ISBN: 978-93-xxxxx-xxx

LIMITS OF LIABILITY AND DISCLAIMER OF WARRANTY

www.bpbonline.com

Dedicated to

Our family members and mentors for their unwavering support and guidance throughout our journey.

About the Authors

- **Ameya Deshpande**, a seasoned professional with over eight years of experience, has cultivated a deep understanding of the intricate dynamics that drive complex supply chains and manufacturing systems. His journey at the forefront of innovation, working within organizations such as Google, Cummins, and Lyft, has provided him with a unique perspective. Ameya's strong educational foundation, which includes a Master's degree from Purdue University and a Bachelor's degree in Mechanical Engineering from the University of Pune, has been instrumental in shaping his expertise. Throughout his career, he has meticulously observed the transformative shifts within the consumer electronics and automotive sectors.
- **Bidyut Sarkar** is an IT professional specializing in the Life Science and Industrial Manufacturing industry. Over his 20-year career at IBM, he has developed a blend of industry experience, a comprehensive understanding of AI and Analytics, and strategic solutioning skills. His work has impacted large pharmaceutical companies and industrial manufacturing industries, particularly in the United States. He has been part of efforts to provide IT solutions against counterfeit drugs and implement AI/ML-powered predictive demand and automated replenishment capabilities. Through AI-driven technologies, he has contributed to solutions that enhance cybersecurity and guarantee the authenticity and safety of medications worldwide. His professional experience has taken him to various parts of the world, including the USA, Netherlands, Saudi Arabia, Brazil, and Australia. This multicultural experience has given him insights into global organizational challenges, reinforcing his commitment to addressing critical issues.
- **Deep Dave** is an esteemed digital transformation and IT system reliability expert specializing in Industrial IoT (IIoT) and digital strategy. His achievements include pioneering digital initiatives that have transformed manufacturing processes, enhancing operational efficiency and patient care. As a tech influencer, Deep has extended his impact beyond the confines of his immediate professional circle. He has been a voice of authority and inspiration in the digital transformation community, sharing his insights and experiences through various platforms. His passion for knowledge extends to research and academia. He has authored multiple research papers on pivotal topics such as digital transformation, neural manufacturing, industry 4.0 and 5.0, IT system reliability, IoT, and human-robot collaboration.
- **Ravi Dave** is an accomplished supply chain expert in orchestrating SAP global rollouts, specializing in customized solutions for purchasing, inventory management, and warehousing. With over 12 years of invaluable global supply chain and logistics experience, Ravi's distinguished career has been marked by a relentless commitment to driving digital transformation across various industries, including retail, distribution, consumer goods, manufacturing, automotive, and textiles. As a digital transformation leader, Ravi is profoundly committed to propelling the frontier of innovative technologies. His passion lies in recognizing and harnessing the transformative potential of cutting-edge advancements such as AI, IoT, blockchain, and automation.

About the Reviewers

- **Balaji M** is a Microsoft Azure IoT Specialty-certified IoT engineer with a Bachelor's in Electronics and Communications Engineering. He has a significant amount of experience in the end-to-end processes of both the hardware and software sections of IoT. His area of expertise is in consumer electronics and automation. Quite recently, he expanded his horizons by stepping into Industry 4.0. His areas of interest include but are not limited to wireless technologies, safety / integrity of systems, low-power devices, data analytics, and ML on edge.

- **Nishant Krishna** is an entrepreneur, writer, and inventor who loves exploring and using new ways to solve complex problems in cybersecurity, cyber forensics, system programming, cognitive computing, and product scaling to hyper-scale levels.

  In his software development career of 23+ years, he has created many products from scratch, working in various technical roles in Architecture, Cybersecurity, API Development, Anti-Counterfeiting Technologies, Cloud and Virtualization, the Internet of Things, and Machine Learning.

  In his consulting role, he advises many companies in product development, threat surface reduction, cyber forensics, database, and application scalability, using standard processes for delivering high-quality products.

  As an adjunct faculty member in many prestigious educational institutes, he tries to find innovative and hands-on ways to teach complex concepts as part of his teaching assignments.

Acknowledgements

We would like to express our sincere gratitude to the families and friends whose unwavering support and encouragement has been the cornerstone of the creation of this book. We greatly appreciate the professionalism and dedication of BPB Publications, which played a pivotal role in bringing this book to fruition. Their professionalism and dedication are indispensable to its success.

The development of this book has significantly benefited from meticulous reviews, technical insights, and editorial expertise. We extend our heartfelt thanks to all the reviewers for their thoughtful contributions, substantially strengthening this work.

Lastly, we extend our gratitude to all the readers who have shown interest in our book and have supported its realization. Your encouragement has been invaluable to us, and we deeply appreciate your continued support.

Preface

In an era defined by connectivity, data-driven decision-making, and unprecedented technological advancements, this book delves into the pivotal role of the Internet of Things (IoT) in revolutionizing how we conceive, produce, and distribute goods.

This book presents an in-depth study of the interaction between advanced manufacturing and IoT, providing priceless insights and useful consulting advice to transform the industrial manufacturing sector.

The principles of IoT in manufacturing, real-world case studies, difficulties and solutions, and the potential of IoT in supply chain management are just a few of the many subjects covered in this book.

Throughout the book, readers will gain a thorough understanding of how IoT improves operational efficiency, enables predictive maintenance, optimizes production planning, ensures quality control, and transforms the supply chain.

This book also equips manufacturing professionals with its pragmatic approach and forward-thinking viewpoint to use IoT to unlock new levels of productivity, competitiveness, and creativity in the constantly changing field of advanced manufacturing.

Chapter 1: IoT Fundamentals, Architecture, and Protocols - The book's introduction thoroughly explores the digital revolution and the ascent of IoT in advanced manufacturing. It covers the genesis and pivotal technologies propelling Industry 4.0, as well as the shift to Industry 5.0 marked by human-machine collaboration. The segment further probes the IoT's evolution and milestones, encompassing enabling technologies and its game-changing influence on industries. Additionally, it underscores IoT's role in manufacturing, spotlighting predictive maintenance, production planning optimization, and quality control. It culminates by analyzing IoT's revolutionary imprint on supply chain management, particularly in real-time tracking, coordination, collaboration, and demand projection. The chapter discusses the essential IoT infrastructure, detailing components like sensors, controllers, data networks, cloud computing, ERP applications, and data analytics tools. Security's pivotal role is emphasized, addressing data transmission, storage, encryption, access control, compliance, and audits. Powered by batteries, sensors enable diverse monitoring while controllers facilitate local computation and network connectivity. IoT networks link devices to the cloud, where data is processed and stored, and user applications offer visualization and interaction. IoT analytics distills insights from the expanding pool of IoT data.

Chapter 2: Embracing IoT in Manufacturing - This chapter examines the transformative impact of IoT on various aspects of the manufacturing process. It talks about real-time monitoring and maintenance, highlighting the role of IoT-enabled sensors in predictive maintenance. The chapter examines production planning and how IoT can improve efficiency through real-time tracking and agile planning. Quality control is discussed, emphasizing automation, precision, and data analysis using IoT. The chapter also into the integration of robotics and IoT, discussing innovation, safety, and maintenance. The real-world case studies demonstrate the application of IoT in manufacturing. This chapter demonstrates how the IoT transforms manufacturing processes, from monitoring to production planning, quality control, and robotics.

Chapter 3: The Power of IoT in Supply Chain - IoT wields immense power in supply chain management. By connecting devices and sensors throughout the supply chain network, IoT provides real-time visibility into the movement and condition of goods. This enhanced visibility enables businesses to optimize inventory levels, reduce waste, and improve efficiency. IoT also empowers businesses to make data-driven decisions about their supply chains. By analyzing data collected from IoT devices, businesses can gain insights into customer demand, identify potential disruptions, and optimize transportation routes. This data-driven approach to supply chain management can lead to significant improvements in profitability and customer satisfaction.

Chapter 4: IoT: Use Cases in Smart Factories - The manufacturing world is evolving rapidly due to IoT adoption. With IoT, products, machines, and factories are becoming more connected through sensors and computers, opening up exciting new possibilities. This chapter explores how IoT is transforming manufacturing across the board. We will see how real-time data and insights can boost innovation, productivity, and responsiveness in factories. Through real-world examples, we will show how IoT benefits areas like predictive maintenance, production planning, quality control, robotics, and supply chain management. We will also discuss the technical aspects and strategies for successful IoT adoption, discussing challenges and solutions. This chapter aims to empower readers to harness IoT's potential in the manufacturing world, where optimization, agility, and automation are on the horizon.

Chapter 5: Business Factors and Optimization for IoT Implementation - In this chapter, we will walk through change management within IoT adoption. As the IoT revolution continues to reshape industries and business landscapes, the successful integration of IoT technologies extends beyond mere technical prowess; it hinges on mastering the human dynamics that accompany innovation. Here, we will discuss the strategies essential for facilitating a seamless transition into the IoT era. From understanding IoT's profound impact on organizational culture to fostering an environment where innovation and inclusivity thrive, you will gain the knowledge and tools required to inspire your team's embrace of IoT. Navigate the path to overcoming resistance to change and nurturing a culture where IoT innovation becomes second nature, propelling your organization into a future of boundless possibilities. The outcome of IoT projects frequently proves unpredictable, primarily attributed to the absence of clearly outlined Key Performance Indicators (KPIs) during the planning stage and the formidable challenges in monitoring the generation of value throughout implementation for manufacturing and supply chain. This chapter also offers insights and strategies to enhance the success rates of IoT projects by addressing the critical elements often overlooked in their planning and execution phases.

Chapter 6: Challenges and Solutions - This chapter will cover numerous difficulties while implementing the IoT. Due to the possibility of breaches and illegal access, security and privacy are essential. Interoperability and standards must be established to facilitate seamless communication across various devices. A strong infrastructure is needed to scale IoT implementations to handle increasingly connected devices. The enormous amount of created data must be handled with effective data management and analytics. Optimizing power and energy efficiency is necessary, especially for devices with limited resources. A stable network architecture should support increased traffic. It can be challenging to integrate IoT with existing systems. It is necessary to address ethical and legal issues relating to data ownership, permission, and privacy. For frameworks and best practices to be developed, stakeholders must work together to prioritize security, interoperability, scalability, and privacy while guaranteeing the responsible implementation of the IoT.

Chapter 7: Artificial Intelligence in Manufacturing - Driven by the integration of artificial intelligence (AI) and IoT, the manufacturing industry is in the midst of a digital revolution. AI and advanced analytics translate this data into valuable insights, enabling smart, self-optimizing production environments known as Industry 4.0. This chapter explores AI's diverse applications in manufacturing, from shop floor operations to supply chain coordination, encompassing predictive maintenance, dynamic scheduling, defect detection, demand forecasting, and sustainability. Industrial IoT platforms, computer vision, natural language processing, and edge computing underpin this intelligent, interconnected manufacturing ecosystem. Successful adoption requires infrastructure upgrades, workforce reskilling, and change management, offering manufacturers the potential for increased throughput, cost reduction, improved quality control, and real-time market responsiveness. These technologies pave the way for factories that continuously self-optimize through data-driven learning and decision-making.

Chapter 8: The Future of IoT - The Internet of Things (IoT) is transforming the manufacturing industry by connecting physical devices and assets to the Internet and each other. This convergence of operations technology with information technology unlocks valuable insights, automation, and communication capabilities. IoT represents the next phase in digital manufacturing, building on earlier developments like automation and data analytics. This chapter explores how IoT impacts key manufacturing processes like equipment maintenance, production planning, quality control, logistics, and supply chain coordination. It covers enabling technologies like sensors, connectivity, data analytics, and security that collectively realize the promise of smart, interconnected manufacturing powered by IoT.

Chapter 9: Key Takeaways - This chapter discusses IoT for manufacturing, infrastructure, and business aspects in a summarized way. This will also cover an overview of future trends of IoT, the IoT revolution in manufacturing and supply chain, and the role of emerging technologies in IoT.

Code Bundle and Coloured Images

Please follow the link to download the
Code Bundle and the ***Coloured Images*** of the book:

https://rebrand.ly/p199ivx

The code bundle for the book is also hosted on GitHub at **https://github.com/bpbpublications/Certified-Kubernetes-Application-Developer-CKAD-Exam-Success-Guide**. In case there's an update to the code, it will be updated on the existing GitHub repository.

We have code bundles from our rich catalogue of books and videos available at **https://github.com/bpbpublications**. Check them out!

Errata

We take immense pride in our work at BPB Publications and follow best practices to ensure the accuracy of our content to provide with an indulging reading experience to our subscribers. Our readers are our mirrors, and we use their inputs to reflect and improve upon human errors, if any, that may have occurred during the publishing processes involved. To let us maintain the quality and help us reach out to any readers who might be having difficulties due to any unforeseen errors, please write to us at :

errata@bpbonline.com

Your support, suggestions and feedbacks are highly appreciated by the BPB Publications' Family.

Piracy

If you come across any illegal copies of our works in any form on the internet, we would be grateful if you would provide us with the location address or website name. Please contact us at **business@bpbonline.com** with a link to the material.

If you are interested in becoming an author

If there is a topic that you have expertise in, and you are interested in either writing or contributing to a book, please visit **www.bpbonline.com**. We have worked with thousands of developers and tech professionals, just like you, to help them share their insights with the global tech community. You can make a general application, apply for a specific hot topic that we are recruiting an author for, or submit your own idea.

Reviews

Please leave a review. Once you have read and used this book, why not leave a review on the site that you purchased it from? Potential readers can then see and use your unbiased opinion to make purchase decisions. We at BPB can understand what you think about our products, and our authors can see your feedback on their book. Thank you!

For more information about BPB, please visit **www.bpbonline.com**.

Join our book's Discord space

Join the book's Discord Workspace for Latest updates, Offers, Tech happenings around the world, New Release and Sessions with the Authors:

https://discord.bpbonline.com

Table of Contents

CHAPTER 1

IoT Fundamentals, Architecture, and Protocols

Introduction

The book's introduction thoroughly explores the digital revolution and the ascent of **Internet of Things (IoT)** in advanced manufacturing. It covers the genesis and pivotal technologies propelling Industry 4.0, as well as the shift to Industry 5.0 marked by human-machine collaboration. The segment further probes the IoT's evolution and milestones, encompassing enabling technologies and its game-changing influence on industries. Additionally, it underscores IoT's role in manufacturing, spotlighting predictive maintenance, production planning optimization, and quality control. It culminates by analyzing IoT's revolutionary imprint on supply chain management, particularly in real-time tracking, coordination, collaboration, and demand projection. This chapter covers the essential IoT infrastructure, detailing sensors, controllers, data networks, cloud computing, ERP applications, and data analytics tools. Security's pivotal role is emphasized, addressing data transmission, storage, encryption, access control, compliance, and audits. Powered by batteries, sensors enable diverse monitoring while controllers facilitate local computation and network connectivity. IoT networks link devices to the cloud, where data is processed and stored, and user applications offer visualization and interaction. IoT analytics distills insights from the expanding pool of IoT data.

Structure

The chapter covers the following topics:

- Overview
- The digital revolution: From Industry 4.0 to 5.0
  - Dawn of Industry 4.0
  - Key technologies driving Industry 4.0
  - Industry 5.0: The human-machine interaction
  - Difference between Industry 4.0 and 5.0
- Role of IoT in manufacturing
  - Enabling predictive maintenance
  - Optimizing production planning
  - Enabling quality control
- Role of IoT in supply chain
  - Real-time tracking and tracing
  - Enhancing coordination and collaboration
  - Demand forecasting and inventory management

Objectives

By the end of this chapter, you will learn how to harness different types of IoT technologies for manufacturing. You will gain practical skills to work with IoT components, analyze their data, and appreciate their impact on predictive maintenance, production planning, quality control, and supply chain management. Through hands-on learning, you will explore key IoT concepts, sensor technologies, data networks, cloud computing, and security considerations. This will empower you to comprehend how IoT is transforming the manufacturing landscape.

Overview

The Fourth Industrial Revolution, known as **Industry 4.0**, is causing a transformation in industries across the globe. This revolution builds upon the advancements of the revolution and brings about a new era of interconnectedness automation, machine learning, and real-time data in various industries.

Experts predict that the global Industry 4.0 market is set for growth. By 2026, it is expected to reach a market size of USD 165.5 billion, with a growth rate of 20.6% during the forecast period.[1] Recent data also reveals that the Industry 4.0 market was valued at USD 114.55 billion in 2021 and is projected to reach USD 377.30 billion by 2029 with a growth rate of 16.3%.[2]

Industry 4.0 is driven by manufacturing techniques, intelligent products, and IoT. This transformative innovation aims to provide real-time data on production, equipment, and component flow; allowing companies to enhance their processes, increase productivity, and gain an edge. At its core, Industry 4.0 leverages the power of IoT to create interconnected networks of devices, sensors, and machines that form systems. These advanced technologies enable data exchange and communication, creating opportunities for decision-making, accurate prediction analysis, and flexible industrial operations. Businesses can increase efficiency, boost product quality, and spark creativity using the IoT's many features.

Industry 4.0 centers around the IoT, the backbone for integrating and connecting components in the manufacturing ecosystem. The IoT enables communication between machines, sensors, and systems by creating a network of interconnected devices that share data and collaborate to make decisions and automate processes.

The impact of Industry 4.0 goes beyond sectors, with significant transformations occurring in supply chain management and manufacturing industries. Traditional practices are challenged as enabled solutions provide end-to-end visibility, traceability, and seamless coordination. By integrating physical systems, smart factories are created where machines interact, optimize themselves, and adapt to changing conditions in time. This results in levels of flexibility and agility.

As we transition from Industry 4.0 to the emerging era of Industry 5.0, a new paradigm is introduced emphasizing collaboration between humans and machines. Industry 5.0 aims to combine the efficiency and precision of automation with creativity and problem-solving abilities. This collaboration is expected to bring solutions that drive advancements in manufacturing, agile production methods, and customer-centric approaches.

It is crucial for organizations that want to remain competitive in the changing landscape of manufacturing to understand the digital revolution and the role of IoT in this evolution. By embracing technologies and utilizing real-time data, businesses can achieve efficiencies, improve product quality, enhance supply chain visibility, and drive innovation.

As we move forward into the phase of supply chain and manufacturing, it becomes apparent that opportunities are waiting to be discovered. However, it is important to acknowledge and tackle the challenges that come with adopting Industry 4.0. Concerns regarding security and privacy complexities surrounding data governance, the readiness of the workforce to adapt to advancements, and the need for infrastructure, all require careful attention.

---

[1] Industry 4.0 Market Size, Share, Industry Trends & Growth Drivers 2030 (marketsandmarkets.com).

[2] Industry 4.0 Market Size, Share | Growth Analysis [2022-2029] (fortunebusinessinsights.com).

The digital revolution: From Industry 4.0 to 5.0

We are entering a new era of Industry 4.0, where digital tech and physical systems come together. This change means that automation, the IoT, and **artificial intelligence** (**AI**) are now part of how we make things. Companies are using data and smart analysis to make their work better and make decisions smarter. This move to Industry 4.0 makes businesses work more efficiently, spend less money, and create better products.

Dawn of Industry 4.0

The onset of the revolution, commonly referred to as the Dawn of Industry 4.0, marked a significant turning point in the manufacturing sector. It brought about an era characterized by transformation and technological advancements. This phase completely revolutionized how factories operate, optimize their processes, and interact with their surroundings.

Industry 4.0 stands out because of its features, such as the wide use of sensors, devices, and systems that are all linked and can collect and analyze data in real time. The **Industrial Internet of Things** (**IIoT**), which makes manufacturing processes smarter and more automated, is built on this foundation of connectivity and data sharing. The fourth industrial revolution, also known as Industry 4.0 transforms conventional factories into smart factories.

To better grasp the concept behind Industry 4.0, let us consider an example from the manufacturing industry. Imagine a factory that produces goods. In manufacturing settings, production processes typically follow a path and involve human intervention at various stages, throughout the manufacturing cycle. However, as we enter the era of Industry 4.0, this factory will transform.

The factory's assembly line is equipped with sensors integrated into machinery, equipment, and finished products. These sensors collect real-time data on temperature, pressure, vibration, and quality indicators. The data is continuously transmitted to a system for processing, analysis, and generating insights. By leveraging data analytics and AI, the smart factory can enhance its manufacturing processes. **Machine learning** (**ML**) algorithms help find trends and outliers in the data so that maintenance can fix machines faster and keep them from breaking down as often. For example, if a sensor detects a temperature increase in a piece of machinery, the AI system can promptly generate a repair request to prevent any potential breakdowns.

Industry 4.0 fosters supply chain collaboration, connecting smart factories with consumers and suppliers digitally for real-time data exchange and demand-driven production. For instance, when demand surges, the system adjusts production and orders materials automatically, ensuring order fulfillment. This transformative technology capitalizes on networked devices, data analytics, AI, and automation, enabling efficient, flexible, and high-quality factory operations, enhancing a company's competitiveness in the market.

Key technologies driving Industry 4.0

The rapid advancement of technology has brought about an era in manufacturing called Industry 4.0. This revolutionary wave is fueled by a range of technologies that are spearheading the transformation in the manufacturing sector. In this chapter, we will explore the technologies that form the foundation of Industry 4.0 and how they are revolutionizing operations and manufacturing processes. These technologies are at the forefront of reshaping the manufacturing industry, including the IoT, cyber-physical systems, big data analytics, artificial intelligence, robotics, cloud computing, and additive manufacturing. By understanding these technologies and their capabilities, businesses can optimize efficiency, productivity, flexibility, and innovation. This journey will delve into the power and impact of these technologies driving Industry 4.0.

Several vital technologies facilitate the transformation and integration of processes within the production environment to drive Industry 4.0 forward. These technologies are crucial in merging digital systems to enable real-time data collection, analysis, and decision-making. Let us explore some of these technologies that are propelling Industry 4.0.

Internet of Things

The IoT refers to a type of technology that is revolutionizing businesses worldwide. The term *Internet of Things* refers to a network of devices and sensors that are connected to one another and work together to collect, share, and analyze data in real time. These devices can include items like household appliances and wearable gadgets, as well as more complex machinery used in industries and infrastructure.

The main idea behind IoT is to facilitate communication and collaboration between objects and digital systems. By equipping objects with sensors, actuators, and networking capabilities, they become *smart* and capable of generating and transmitting data. This data is then analyzed to gain insights, optimize operations, and make decisions. IoT devices talk to one another and centralized servers by means of wireless and wired connectivity protocols like Wi-Fi and Bluetooth. Because of their connectivity, systems may be monitored, controlled, and automated in real-time, leading to greater effectiveness, output, and adaptability. The IoT encompasses a network where physical objects connected to the Internet can share information through sensors and software for purposes ranging from household products to advanced industrial equipment. Take a look at the following *Figure 1.1*:

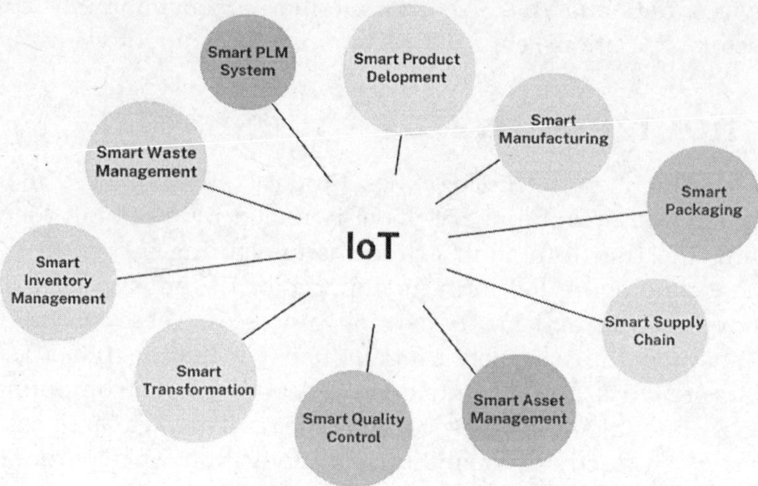

Figure 1.1: Applications of the IoT

Here are some important characteristics of IoT:

- **Devices and objects:** The *Things* in IoT refer to objects that would not normally be anticipated to have an internet connection but may communicate with the network without human intervention. Wearable fitness devices, smart home appliances, connected autos, and sensors monitoring farm crops or industrial machines are some examples.
- **Connectivity:** It refers to the network connection that exists between the devices and the internet, which may include Wi-Fi, Bluetooth, 5G, or other wireless communication technologies. It is the internet component of IoT.
- **Data processing:** After the devices collect data, it is frequently transferred to the next hop capable of processing. This could range from simple tasks such as determining whether the temperature of a building is within a certain range to more advanced ML algorithms capable of detecting trends and making predictions. The analyzed data is then used to execute a function, such as generating an alert or automatically altering the devices without human intervention.
- **Sensors and actuators:** Sensors and actuators are commonly found in IoT devices. Sensors collect data from their surroundings (such as temperature, light, motion, and so on), whereas actuators carry out actions based on the data (such as turning on a light or altering the temperature).
- **Interoperability and security:** For IoT systems to function properly, devices and systems must be able to communicate and collaborate, which is referred to as **interoperability**. At the same time, because IoT involves data gathering and transmission, security is a top priority. IoT devices frequently collect sensitive data, and there are concerns about illegal access or alteration of this data.

IoT can be used in many fields. The IoT makes possible the idea of a *smart factory*, in which interconnected machines, tools, and systems work together to streamline production, keep an eye on how things are going, and do preventative maintenance. IoT can be used in agriculture to monitor soil conditions, manage irrigation systems, and check livestock health. IoT devices in healthcare can capture patient data and transfer it in real-time to healthcare experts, enabling remote monitoring and individualized therapy.

Cyber-physical system

The integration of physical components to build interconnected systems is referred to as **cyber-physical systems** (**CPS**). By combining real-world elements with computing, communication, and control systems, CPS aims to enhance operations' functionality, efficiency, and reliability. At the core of CPS are actuators and sensors. Actuators enable interaction with the world while sensors collect data from the environment. These components are interconnected through embedded systems and network infrastructure forming a cyber network that enables real-time monitoring, analysis, and control.

The manufacturing sector greatly benefits from CPS implementation. In a manufacturing environment, CPS optimizes production processes, improves quality control measures, and enables maintenance. Throughout the manufacturing plant, sensors are strategically placed to collect data on parameters such as temperature, pressure, and vibration. This data is then sent to systems for real-time examination and processing while it is being received.

The CPS has the capability to automatically adjust production parameters, like machine settings and material flow, based on processed data. Its goal is to maximize productivity and maintain high-quality output. For example, if a sensor detects a temperature change that could affect product quality, the CPS can quickly modify cooling or heating systems to ensure proper conditions are maintained. This ensures that the product consistently meets customer expectations. By providing real-time feedback and control, this technique enables adaptable manufacturing processes. Take a look at *Figure 1.2*:

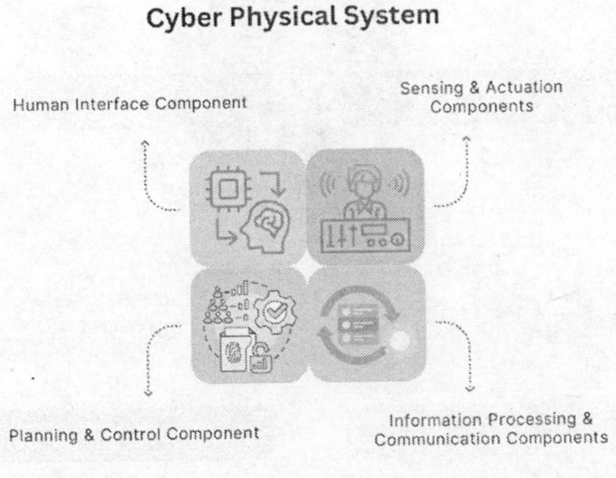

Cyber Physical System

Human Interface Component

Sensing & Actuation Components

Planning & Control Component

Information Processing & Communication Components

Figure 1.2: *The cyber-physical systems*

Moreover, CPS offers maintenance to minimize equipment failures and costly downtime. This is achieved through monitoring and analysis of data. CPS can identify signs of machine faults by monitoring performance using sensors. These signs may include vibrations or increased energy consumption. As a result, the system can proactively schedule maintenance actions for resource utilization and minimal disruptions to production.

The integration of physical systems in CPS offers possibilities for streamlining processes, enhancing control, and making better decisions across various areas of application. CPS empowers businesses to achieve levels of automation, precision, and responsiveness by utilizing real-time data and intelligent algorithms.

Big data analytics

Big data analytics refers to the process of examining diverse information, commonly known as **data**, to discover hidden patterns, correlations, market trends, customer preferences, and other valuable insights that can assist organizations in making well-informed business decisions. With the increasing amount of data generated by IoT devices, the significance of data analytics has become more evident. It falls under data science and focuses on handling and analyzing amounts of data to extract relevant knowledge and insights. The proliferation of devices and digital systems has led to an influx of data from various sources, such as sensors, social media platforms, and online transactions. Although managing this amount of data poses challenges. Big data analytics equips us with the tools and methodologies to effectively analyze it and uncover important information amidst this flood of data. Take a look at *Figure 1.3*:

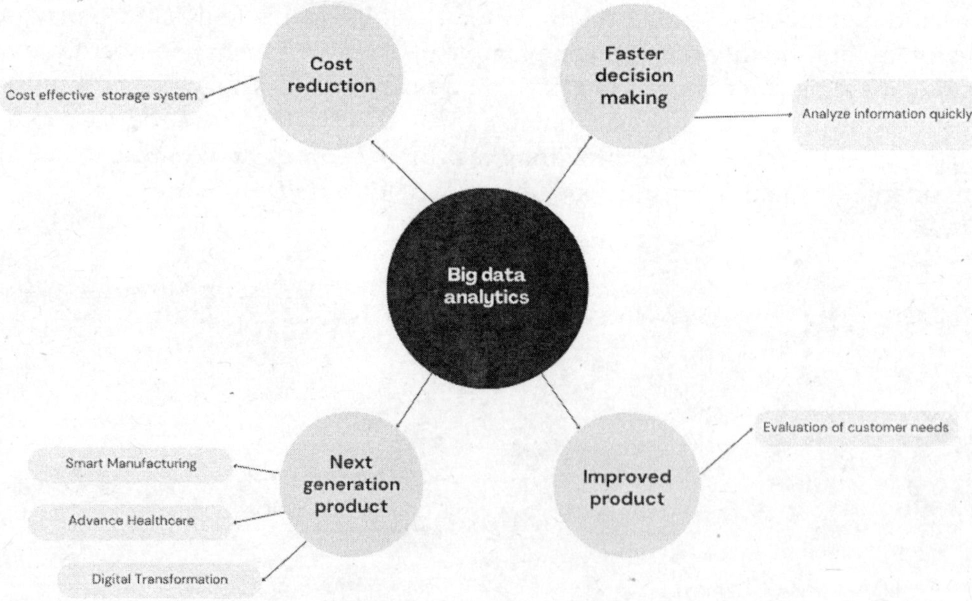

Figure 1.3: *Big data analytics*

The following are some aspects related to big data analytics:

- **Big data and IoT:** IoT devices generate ample amounts of data. Ranging from sensors to industrial machines, this data is referred to as *big data* due to its size and complexity surpassing the capabilities of traditional application software for processing purposes.
- **Techniques for big data analytics:** The analytics information gathered from IoT devices can encompass user behavior, environmental conditions, and device performance. These techniques involve algorithms for machine learning, data mining, predictive analytics, and other methods to analyze data and identify patterns and trends.
- **Predictive and prescriptive analytics techniques:** Predictive analytics employs algorithms and machine learning techniques to assess data and determine the likelihood of future outcomes. By evaluating performance data, it can predict events like equipment malfunctions. This form of analysis not only offers insights into why future events will occur but also refrains from predicting them.
- **Decision-making and process optimization:** Big data analysis helps make better decisions by providing helpful insights. For instance, it can predict machine problems, so maintenance can be planned to avoid downtime. It can also find places where too much energy is being used, helping to reduce cost.
- **Identifying opportunities for improvement:** Using data analytics, businesses can pinpoint opportunities to improve their operations and make strategic decisions. For example, data analysis might reveal inefficiencies in a production process and suggest ways to enhance customer satisfaction.

Big data analytics provides an understanding of patterns within the amount of data generated by IoT devices. This capability leads to decision-making, improved operational efficiency, cost savings, and the development of new products and services.

Robotics and automation

Robotics and automation play a role in Industry 4.0 which is revolutionizing the manufacturing sector. Robotics involves using robots that can perform tasks with precision, speed, and efficiency. Equipped with sensors, actuators, and sophisticated programming, these robots can interact with their environment to carry out tasks. By handling labor repetitive work, they free up resources to focus on more intricate and creative endeavors.

Automation technologies are another aspect of Industry 4.0. Automation involves the application of technology and systems to streamline business processes and minimize the need for intervention. Through automation, tasks previously performed by humans can now be executed by machines resulting in improved efficiency, accuracy, and consistency. Automation facilitates the integration of devices, systems, and processes into a network that operates seamlessly for optimized production outcomes. Take a look at *Figure 1.4*:

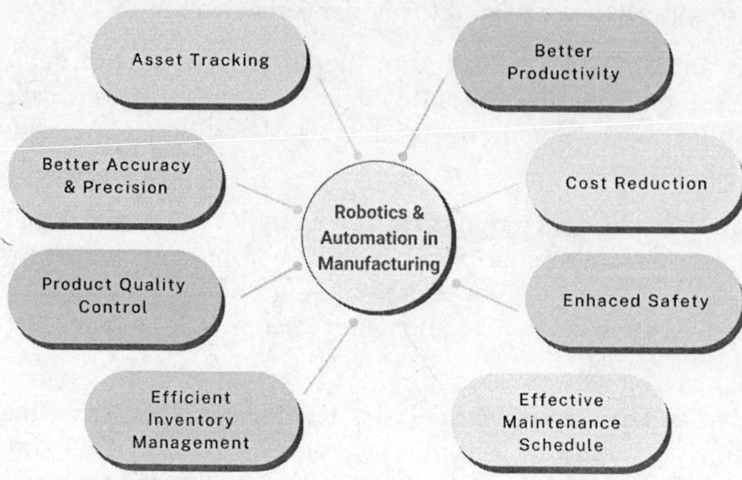

Figure 1.4: *Benefits of robotics and automation in manufacturing*

Robotics and automation used in the manufacturing are:

- **Role of robotics in Industry 4.0:** Industry 4.0 organizes and improves the industrial value chain. Robotics is a key part of this change, with robots becoming more precise, productive, and efficient. They can learn, make decisions, and do complex tasks previously done by humans.
- **Advanced robots:** The next generation of robots possess capabilities like autonomy, adaptability, and interaction with both humans and other robots. They can be programmed to efficiently and accurately carry out tasks that humans often perform.
- **Automation technologies:** Implementing automation technologies in Industry 4.0 utilizes intelligence and machine learning to control and monitor processes, make decisions, and solve problems. These technologies streamline operations by minimizing the need for intervention and reducing errors while boosting productivity.
- **Integration of machines and systems:** Industry 4.0 integrates machines, systems, and processes using IoT for data exchange and cloud computing for data storage and analysis. This seamless integration makes production processes adaptable.
- **Robotic process automation: Robotic process automation** (**RPA**) uses software bots to mimic human interactions with digital systems, automating repetitive tasks across departments. It reduces errors, boosts efficiency, and seamlessly integrates with existing systems, optimizing business processes.

Overall, these advancements in robotics result in increased productivity levels along with improved precision and consistency compared to human-executed tasks. Automation allows for the seamless integration of devices, systems, and processes to create a network that functions together to achieve the possible production results. The manufacturing sector is progressing significantly, largely attributed to the integration of robotics and automation. They enhance productivity, efficiency, and safety while reducing costs and improving product quality. As Industry 4.0 progresses, robotics and automation will have a role in transforming the manufacturing process and revolutionizing the industrial sector.

Additive manufacturing

Additive manufacturing, also called **3D printing**, has become more common in the age of Industry 4.0. It changes the way things are made by making it possible to make parts and goods that are customized on demand. Unlike subtractive manufacturing methods that involve cutting or shaping materials to create the product, additive manufacturing builds products layer by layer using digital designs.

Additive manufacturing enables intricate designs, fostering customization and innovation. Due to layer-by-layer creation, it can reduce material waste which enhances sustainability and lowers costs. Companies can meet customer demands effectively, boosting their market competitiveness.

Take a look at *Figure 1.5*:

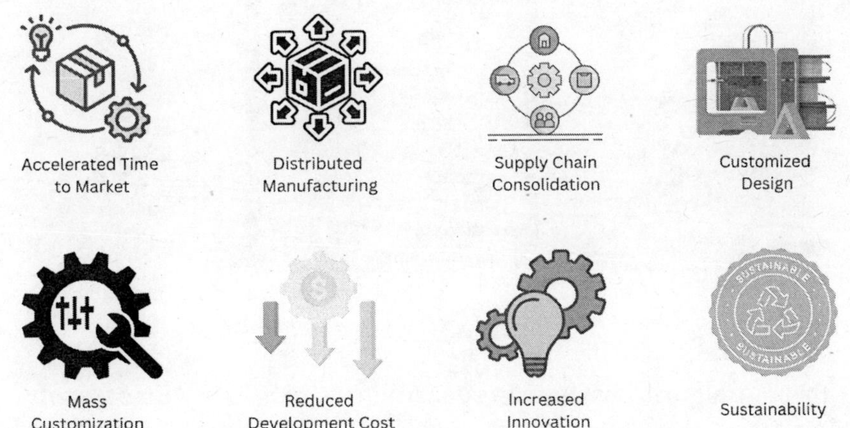

***Figure 1.5:** Additive manufacturing (3D printing)*

Additive manufacturing, like 3D printing, speeds up product development. It lets businesses make prototypes and designs quickly, saving time and money. This means they can get products to market faster. Traditional manufacturing frequently entails complex supply chains with various suppliers, shipping, and inventory control. Companies can use 3D printing to make items on-demand, eliminating the need for huge inventory and shortening lead times. This can result in significant cost reductions and greater operational efficiency.

Artificial intelligence, machine learning, and **deep learning** (DL) are rapidly reshaping industries and society. AI involves equipping machines or computer systems with human intelligence, while ML focuses on creating algorithms that enable machines to learn from data and improve their performance over time. DL, a subset of ML, mimics the brain's functioning through neural networks allowing computers to process complex data patterns. These technologies empower machines to interpret information, identify patterns, make predictions, and adapt to changing circumstances without programming. The advent of Industry 4.0 has witnessed advancements in automation, optimization, and decision-making capabilities through leveraging the power of AI and ML. These capabilities are transforming processes unlocking unprecedented levels of efficiency and productivity.

The term *artificial intelligence* pertains to developing computer programs for performing tasks that would typically require intelligence. These activities may involve understanding language, identifying patterns, solving problems, and making decisions. The industry is being transformed by AI in ways such as automation, predictive maintenance, and quality control. It enhances efficiency leading to process optimization and the ability to make real-time decisions. This ultimately results in increased productivity and cost savings. Take a look at *Figure 1.6*:

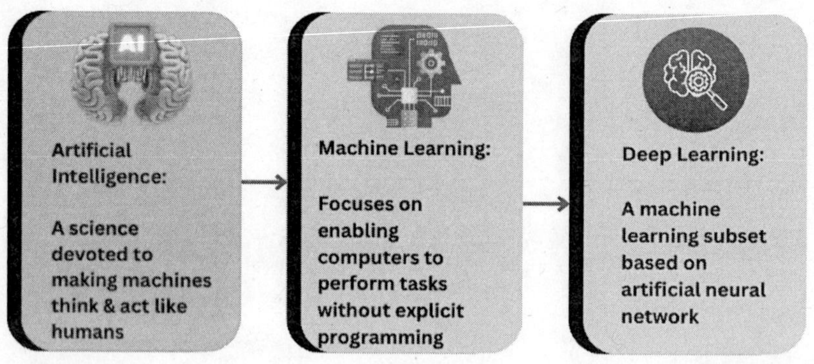

Figure 1.6: *Overview of AI, ML, and DL*

AI operates through algorithms that can be seen as rules or instructions for solving problems or completing tasks. These algorithms enable machines to understand and respond to input patterns, adapt to changing environments, and improve their performance through learning over time. ML is a subset of AI that focuses on creating computer systems of learning from data without human assistance. In ML, algorithms are used to analyze datasets, identify patterns within the data, and generate predictions or judgments without programming for each task. DL techniques enable computers to acquire the capability of learning representations of data, discovering correlations, and extracting valuable insights, from large and diverse datasets.

AI, ML, and DL are widespread in Industry 4.0, especially in manufacturing. AI detects anomalies in sensor data, predicting equipment failures for better maintenance. ML enhances production by identifying trends, boosting efficiency, and reducing waste. DL-based computer vision enables machines to analyze data, and perform tasks like object recognition and quality checks.

Industry 5.0: The human-machine interaction

The term *human-machine interaction* refers to the integration and teamwork between humans and machines in jobs or work processes. Humans and machines collaborate to accomplish these tasks or processes. The aim of this collaboration is to enhance productivity, decision-making, and problem-solving abilities by leveraging the strengths and capabilities of both humans and machines. The cognitive abilities of individuals, such as creativity, intuition, and empathy, are combined with the power and efficiency of machines through a process called human-machine interaction. This partnership enables the automation of labor time-consuming processes allowing human workers to focus on mental activities that require the application of their specialized knowledge. Moreover, human-machine interaction facilitates individuals in improving their work processes and skills by harnessing the capabilities of intelligence systems utilized in this collaboration.

In Industry 5.0, the primary objective is to create an environment where interaction with machines feels natural and seamlessly integrated into the work environment. This means that machines are not seen as separate entities but valuable collaborators, making the workplace more intuitive and user-friendly. Additionally, Industry 5.0 emphasizes the concept of hyper-personalization, where the interaction between humans and machines becomes highly tailored to individual needs and preferences. This level of personalization ensures that each worker can maximize their potential and contribute effectively to the overall productivity and success of the organization.

The interaction between humans and machines can take forms. Let us discuss it in detail.

Human-machine coexistence

The concept of *human-machine coexistence* refers to the integration of machines into the workplace, allowing them to collaborate with humans. This can include using robots, also known as **cobots**, that work closely with humans and assist them in demanding risky or repetitive tasks.

In the manufacturing industry, cobots are becoming increasingly common on assembly lines working alongside employees. These cobots can perform tasks like quality inspections and pick and place operations while ensuring the safety of workers. This partnership boosts productivity, reduces errors, and allows humans to focus on responsibilities.

Human-machine cooperation

When we talk about human-machine cooperation, it means coordinating activities between humans and machines to achieve a goal. This requires developing technologies that facilitate communication and collaboration between humans and machines. For example, in the healthcare industry, human-machine cooperation may involve utilizing devices that monitor patient health in time and provide healthcare professionals with valuable data. In industries like manufacturing, humans and robots work together on tasks such as assembly line work. The assembly line is designed to facilitate collaboration between employees and robotic arms. Humans oversee the process, conduct quality checks, and make decisions based on experience, while robots handle lifting and precise welding.

Human-machine collaboration

The collaboration between humans and machines represents the level of interaction between the two. In this type of partnership, humans and machines join forces to achieve a shared objective. It requires the development of systems that enable the exchange of knowledge, skills, and expertise between humans and machines. For example, in manufacturing industries, human-machine collaboration can involve leveraging reality systems that allow workers to interact with machines in time.

Augmented reality (AR) systems are increasingly used in settings to enhance communication and coordination between workers and automated systems. Workers wearing AR headsets can see overlays on real-world objects enabling them to receive instructions and assistance in time. This enables workers to effectively communicate with machines resulting in improved accuracy and productivity.

To establish human-machine interaction, it is essential to integrate technologies, like AI, ML and IoT. These cutting-edge technologies enable the development of systems that analyze data, learn from experience, and adapt to changing circumstances. Furthermore, they facilitate the creation of user technologies that can effortlessly communicate and cooperate with humans. Human-machine interaction plays a role in Industry 5.0 aiming to optimize manufacturing processes by leveraging the strengths of both humans and machines. This necessitates the implementation of systems that promote productivity, flexibility, and sustainability, across industries, including manufacturing.

Difference between Industry 4.0 and 5.0

There have been two phases in the development of industrialization and advancements known as Industry 4.0 and Industry 5.0, respectively. Although both involve digitization and automation, there are differences between them.

Here are the main contrasts between Industry 4.0 and Industry 5.0:

- **Focus:** Industry 4.0 integrates tech and automation for smart factories and production efficiency. Industry 5.0 shifts to human-machine collaboration, emphasizing creativity and skill development for efficient task completion.
- **Role of humans:** In Industry 4.0, humans oversee automated equipment, which is vital for success despite tech enhancements. Industry 5.0 shifts focus, placing humans at the center. Collaboration with robots harnesses their combined

strengths, turning humans from overseers to active participants, marking a significant change.

- **Interaction between humans and machines:** In Industry 4.0, human-robot interaction is important but not emphasized. Automation improves efficiency by replacing some human tasks. However, collaboration is limited to specific tasks and remote communication. Industry 5.0, in contrast, prioritizes human-machine interaction, encouraging them to work together closely, enabling tasks like assembly, shared decision-making, and skill exchange.
- **Customization and personalized items:** Industry 4.0 uses technology for product innovation and customization. Meeting individual customer needs is crucial. Industry 5.0 aims for even more personalized and customized products, combining human creativity and machine capabilities. This level of personalization was previously impossible.
- **Considerations regarding society and the environment:** Industry 4.0 mainly aims to improve productivity, efficiency, and cost-effectiveness in production. While sustainability gains attention, it is not the primary focus. Industry 5.0 prioritizes social responsibility and environmental sustainability. Organizations aim to balance economic goals with environmental contributions and address concerns.

The main objective of the Industry 5.0 initiative is to create prosperity beyond job creation and economic growth. It aims to do so while considering the resources of our world. The focus of Industry 5.0 is on making manufacturing more personalized and environmentally conscious, in line with goals alongside objectives. Two key elements of this initiative are incorporating reality systems and fostering collaboration between humans and robots. By doing so, Industry 5.0 offers a solution to meet future requirements. Ultimately the approach taken by Business 5.0 is centered around humans and robots working together leveraging their strengths for an efficient collaboration that drives innovation and advances the manufacturing industry. Refer to the following *Table 1.1*:

	Industry 4.0	**Industry 5.0**
Approach	Technology-driven	Value-driven
Focus	Integration of digital technologies and automation in manufacturing processes.	Human-machine collaboration and customization through cyber-physical systems.
Role of humans	The supervisory role, overseeing automated systems.	Central role, collaboration with machines.

	Industry 4.0	Industry 5.0
Human-machine Interaction	Exists but is limited to supervisory roles and interaction at a distance.	The central aspect is humans and machines working together in a shared workspace.
Customization and personalization	Industry 4.0 enables some level of customization, typically through advanced technologies, allowing products to be tailored to certain specifications or options. True personalization in Industry 4.0 is somewhat limited. It may involve offering predefined choices to customers.	Enhanced customization and personalization of products. Products and services are highly adaptable and can be configured to meet individual customer needs and preferences in a more dynamic way. It involves tailoring products and services to the unique requirements and preferences of each customer, often in real-time, creating highly individualized experiences.
Social and environmental considerations	Focus primarily on efficiency and productivity.	Emphasis on sustainability, social responsibility, and environmental factors.

Table 1.1: *Comparison of Industry 4.0 vs. Industry 5.0*

Role of IoT in manufacturing

The IoT is a concept that may be further broken down into subcategories, one of which is the IIoT. It plays a role in Industry 4.0, that is, the ongoing industrial revolution. While IoT encompasses consumer-oriented devices like home products and wearable tech, IIoT focuses on how these connected devices are utilized within work settings. It facilitates the interconnection of machines, physical objects, and computing systems enabling communication and information sharing over the Internet.

The industrial sector is projected to witness growth in IIoT adoption with a **Compound Annual Growth Rate** (**CAGR**) of 14.7% expected throughout the forecast period. By 2033, it is estimated that this industry will be valued at US $ 948.6 billion compared to US$ 265.2 billion in 2023.[3]

IIoT marked the start of Industry 4.0, transforming manufacturing by uniting cyber systems, data sharing, and automation. It enhances efficiency, productivity, and adaptability in areas like manufacturing, energy management, and supply chains. Traditional manufacturing

[3] IoT in Manufacturing Market Size, Trends 2033 | FMI (www.futuremarketinsights.com).

relied on expertise and machines. However, *smart manufacturing* increasingly depends on advanced tech like AI, ML, IoT, big data, robotics, and industrial analytics.

Enabling predictive maintenance

Predictive maintenance ensures asset health and performance by real-time monitoring, aiming to prevent breakdowns and align maintenance with production schedules. It relies on real-time data and continuous analysis, facilitated by IIoT. Condition-based IIoT tracking detects issues like bearing speed, lubrication, and temperature, alerting equipment owners in real-time. Unlike fixed schedule-based maintenance, predictive maintenance uses IIoT sensor data to anticipate failures, offering a flexible and adaptive solution.

In addition, it distinguishes itself from **condition-based maintenance** (**CBM**) by its unique ability to detect issues at an earlier stage, enabling the efficient scheduling of maintenance services. To support effective CBM implementation, specific taxonomies can be developed to categorize data, and a domain-specific knowledge base can be established to guide the CBM system in making informed decisions. The advantages of maintenance are evident as it can reduce downtime, enhance worker productivity, decrease field service expenses, improve product design, and promote worker safety. By addressing issues before they lead to equipment breakdowns, predictive maintenance significantly reduces downtime, increases uptime and shortens the time required to resolve problems. This does not save money. It also extends the lifespan of assets, optimizes machine performance, and creates a safer work environment for employees.

Optimizing production planning

IIoT has transformed production planning, connecting equipment and systems to enhance efficiency. It collects data for informed decision-making. Integrating AI and ML into IIoT enables data analysis, uncovering patterns, and aiding in forecasting and resource management. These technologies together process data for advanced manufacturing.

Data analytics further refines insights, informing strategic decisions, optimizing resources, identifying production line inefficiencies, and shaping strategies in the manufacturing industry. This integration empowers manufacturing companies to compete effectively and adapt to changing industrial dynamics by turning data into actionable insights.

Enabling quality control

IIoT revolutionizes quality control by shifting from reactive to proactive methods. It connects devices to monitor production in real-time, enabling early identification and resolution of quality issues, reducing waste, downtime, and improving product quality. IIoT's true value lies in proactive data analysis, identifying patterns and trends for preemptive action. This transforms quality control into a forward-thinking approach, prioritizing prediction and prevention over detection and resolution, ultimately enhancing overall quality and efficiency.

Role of IoT in supply chain

The IIoT is rapidly becoming a part of supply chain management. It offers advantages that enhance efficiency, visibility, and production. By integrating assets with systems, IIoT provides a seamless platform for tracking and monitoring the entire supply chain in real time. This means organizations can have an accurate view of their supply chain operations.

IIoT enhances supply chain transparency and visibility by tracking every aspect, from raw materials to final products, across various locations and stages. This real-time tracking provides insights into inventory levels, order status, and transportation conditions, enabling informed decisions to optimize supply chain performance. Predictive analytics forecasts demand accurately, helping manage inventory efficiently, prevent overstock or stockouts, and proactively address disruptions, reducing risks.

Additionally, IIoT facilitates improved collaboration and communication among supply chain players. Suppliers, manufacturers, distributors, and customers can easily share real-time data, enhancing transparency, cooperation, and decision-making. This synchronization adapts the supply chain to meet consumer expectations efficiently while responding to market changes. Furthermore, IIoT aids in sustainability efforts by identifying waste and environmental impact, allowing businesses to take proactive measures, aligning with corporate social responsibility goals.

Real-time tracking and tracing

Real-time monitoring is a cornerstone of effective supply chain management, employing an interconnected network of sensors, GPS technology, and **radio frequency identification (RFID)** tags attached to products in transit. Data collected from these sources is transmitted to a centralized platform, providing organizations with valuable insights. Firstly, it offers an up-to-date view of inventory, reducing storage costs, and ensuring product availability to meet customer demands. Secondly, real-time monitoring optimizes the supply chain by improving logistics management, route optimization, and delivery speed.

In contrast, tracing involves meticulously recording the history, origin, and location of items or activities throughout the supply chain. This practice is especially critical in industries like food, pharmaceuticals, and automobiles, where product safety and compliance are paramount. Tracing offers multiple advantages, including enhanced quality management through the rapid identification and resolution of quality issues. It plays a crucial role in risk management, enabling timely product recalls in case of defects and demonstrating compliance with industry regulations, ultimately fostering customer trust and regulatory compliance while safeguarding a company's reputation.

Enhancing coordination and collaboration

The supply chain is a complex network involving the movement of goods, services, and information from suppliers to customers. Effective supply chain management is crucial for meeting consumer demands and gaining a competitive advantage.

IoT technology is transforming supply chains by improving coordination and communication among stakeholders. Enabled devices facilitate real-time data sharing between suppliers, manufacturers, distributors, and customers. These devices, equipped with sensors, exchange data on inventory, production progress, transportation, and customer preferences, promoting transparency and informed decision-making. Furthermore, IoT simplifies system integration, breaking down information silos and fostering collaboration. This streamlined approach aims to reduce lead times, optimize inventory, and enhance customer satisfaction.

Demand forecasting and inventory management

One crucial area where IoT technology makes a significant impact is demand forecasting and inventory management. These are components of supply chain management that directly affect efficiency and customer happiness. By providing real-time data along with capabilities, IoT technology revolutionizes these domains.

IoT devices, including sensors and RFID tags, are seamlessly integrated into products, shelves, and warehouses, enhancing operational efficiency. While RFID tags serve as identifiers, IoT technology enables data collection for analysis. Machine learning and predictive analytics help businesses examine data, identify patterns, and make precise demand forecasts. This knowledge optimizes inventory levels, reduces stockouts, and enhances customer satisfaction.

Real-time data from IoT devices allows businesses to monitor supply chain performance actively. By tracking transportation conditions, order fulfillment processes, and delivery procedures, companies can proactively address bottlenecks, delays, and quality issues. This visibility streamlines operations, increases order fulfillment speed, and improves supply chain efficiency.

IoT technology facilitates the integration of demand data with systems such as **enterprise resource planning** (ERP) or **customer relationship management** (CRM). This integration allows for the interchange of data between systems, which in turn improves the accuracy of demand forecasting activities as well as inventory planning and order management operations.

Conclusion

The IoT has brought a big change to how things are made and moved in manufacturing and supply chains. By linking sensors, gadgets, and systems, IoT gathers and studies data in a completely new way. This flood of real-time data gives super helpful ideas that help make production better, raise quality control, predict when machines need fixing, and organize supply chain tasks. Important IoT parts like smart sensors, edge and cloud computing, and smart computer programs are adding smartness and quick thinking like never before. As more and more people use IoT, it is making really big changes to how things are made. To make the most of IoT's benefits, businesses must take care of important things like safety, getting the right setup, and teaching employees. Ultimately, IoT is making production more flexible, exact, and eco-friendly, setting up how things will be made in the future.

Points to remember

- The IoT refers to a network of connected physical objects and devices that can collect and share data through embedded sensors and software. IoT enables connectivity and automation in manufacturing operations.
- The key components that make up an IoT system include sensors, controllers, edge and cloud computing capabilities, data analytics tools, and security measures. Sensors gather data, controllers process and transmit it, while edge and cloud computing provide storage and analysis capabilities.
- The IoT architecture has multiple layers including a perception layer with physical devices, a network layer to enable communication, an application layer for data visualization and analytics, and a services layer to manage processes and business logic.
- In manufacturing, IoT allows for real-time monitoring of assets, predictive maintenance, optimized production scheduling, and enhanced quality control through advanced data analytics.
- IoT improves supply chain visibility and tracking by connecting assets, inventory, and shipments. It also enables better coordination through information sharing and accurate demand forecasting.
- The data insights provided by IoT systems can help identify process inefficiencies, reduce costs, predict issues, and drive innovations in manufacturing.
- Adopting IoT requires focusing on key aspects like security, infrastructure readiness, network bandwidth, and training workers on using and interpreting IoT data.
- IoT delivers increased automation, flexibility, speed, precision, and responsiveness to manufacturing operations in an interconnected way. It is transforming production and supply chains.

Multiple choice questions

1. **Which of the following is *not* a key component of an IoT system?**
    a. Sensors
    b. Servers
    c. Edge computing capabilities
    d. Actuators

2. **What does the *Perception Layer* in an IoT architecture consist of?**
   a. Physical devices like sensors and actuators
   b. Communication protocols
   c. Cloud platforms
   d. Data analytics software
3. **How does IoT enable predictive maintenance in manufacturing?**
   a. By collecting and analyzing real-time data to forecast equipment failures
   b. By using predetermined maintenance schedules
   c. By performing regular equipment inspections
   d. By reacting to equipment breakdowns
4. **IoT allows supply chain partners to improve coordination through:**
   a. Automated production scheduling
   b. Real-time item tracking
   c. Robotics
   d. 3D printing
5. **What security measures are critical for an IoT system?**
   a. Data encryption
   b. Access controls
   c. Security audits
   d. All of the above
6. **Which of the following is an advantage of adopting IoT solutions?**
   a. Improved workforce communication
   b. Enhanced operational responsiveness
   c. Seamless integration with legacy systems
   d. Guaranteed long-term cost savings
7. **What does the *Network Layer* in an IoT architecture provide?**
   a. Physical devices like sensors
   b. Communication between devices
   c. Cloud data storage
   d. Data analysis

8. **How can IoT improve quality control in manufacturing?**
    a. By randomly inspecting products
    b. By reducing the number of inspectors
    c. By collecting real-time data to identify defects
    d. By increasing the time between inspections
9. **Which of the following best describes the role of IoT in supply chain management?**
    a. Automating all logistic operations
    b. Eliminating the need for inventory management
    c. Enhancing visibility, coordination, and optimization
    d. Utilizing drones for delivery

Answer key

1. b.
2. a.
3. a.
4. b.
5. d.
6. b.
7. b.
8. c.
9. c.

Questions

1. What is IoT, and how is it transforming manufacturing operations?
2. What are the key components of an IoT system architecture? Describe each component.
3. Explain the difference between IoT sensors and actuators. Provide examples of each.
4. What communication protocols are commonly used in IoT systems? Compare their features and applications.

5. What is edge computing, and why is it important in IoT architectures?
6. How does cloud computing enable IoT solutions to be scalable and cost-effective?
7. Describe the various layers in a typical IoT architecture. What is the function of each layer?
8. How can IoT enable predictive maintenance and reduce equipment downtime in manufacturing?
9. How does IoT improve production planning, scheduling, and quality control in manufacturing?
10. How does IoT enhance visibility, tracking, and coordination in supply chain operations?
11. How can IoT data analytics provide valuable insights to optimize manufacturing performance? Give examples.
12. What are some key challenges in adopting IoT solutions? How can they be addressed?
13. What security considerations are critical when implementing IoT systems?
14. What skills are required to effectively implement and manage IoT solutions?
15. What are the potential long-term impacts of adopting IoT across manufacturing?

Key terms

- **Internet of Things:** A network of connected physical objects and devices that can collect and share data through sensors and software.
- **Sensors:** Devices that detect events or changes in the physical environment and provide corresponding outputs.
- **Actuators:** Devices that convert electrical signals into physical actions.
- **Edge computing:** Processing and analyzing data locally on distributed devices rather than in a centralized system.
- **Cloud computing:** Providing services like data storage, servers, databases, software, etc. over the internet.
- **Predictive maintenance:** Maintenance performed based on actual equipment condition and real-time data.
- **Supply chain visibility:** The ability to track the current location and status of inventory, shipments, and assets in real-time.
- **Big data analytics:** Techniques and software used to analyze and extract insights from large, diverse data sets.

Join our book's Discord space

Join the book's Discord Workspace for Latest updates, Offers, Tech happenings around the world, New Release and Sessions with the Authors:

https://discord.bpbonline.com

CHAPTER 2
Embracing IoT in Manufacturing

Introduction

This chapter examines the transformative impact of the **Internet of Things** (**IoT**) on various aspects of the manufacturing process. It delves into real-time monitoring and maintenance, highlighting the role of IoT-enabled sensors in predictive maintenance. The chapter examines production planning and how IoT can improve efficiency through real-time tracking and agile planning. Quality control is discussed, emphasizing automation, precision, and data analysis using IoT. The chapter also delves into integrating robotics and IoT, discussing innovation, safety, and maintenance. Real-world case studies demonstrate the application of IoT in manufacturing. This chapter demonstrates how the **IoT** transforms manufacturing processes, from monitoring to production planning, quality control, and robotics.

Structure

The chapter covers the following topics:

- Real-time monitoring and maintenance
    - o Need for real-time monitoring
    - o Real-time monitoring system architecture

  - IoT and predictive maintenance
  - Case study: Smart predictive maintenance
- IoT-driven production planning
  - IoT for real-time production tracking
  - Case study: IoT in manufacturing
- Ensuring quality control with IoT
  - Traditional quality control methods
  - IoT-enabled approach
  - IoT for automated inspection and testing
  - Data analysis for quality assurance: IoT's role
  - Case study: Use of IoT in quality control
- Robotics in manufacturing
  - Innovation and automation with robotics
  - IoT-robotics synergy: Ensuring precision and safety
  - IoT for robot maintenance and troubleshooting
  - Case study: Robotic solutions powered by IoT

Objectives

By the end of this chapter, you will learn how to harness different types of IoT technologies for manufacturing. You will gain practical skills to work with IoT components, analyze their data, and appreciate their impact on predictive maintenance, production planning, quality control, and supply chain management. Through hands-on learning, you will explore key IoT concepts, sensor technologies, data networks, cloud computing, and security considerations. This will empower you to comprehend how IoT is transforming the manufacturing landscape.

Real-time monitoring and maintenance

Real-time monitoring and maintenance represent the cutting edge of industrial efficiency. We will explore how IoT sensors and data analytics have revolutionized the way machines and equipment are managed, offering proactive insights, predictive maintenance, and reduced downtime. With a focus on practical applications and tangible benefits, we will uncover how this dynamic approach is reshaping industries, ensuring smoother operations, and enhancing the bottom line for businesses.

Need for real-time monitoring

Real-time monitoring has become increasingly crucial in industries like manufacturing, healthcare, transportation, and energy due to the growing complexity and broadness of these fields. **Real-time monitoring** refers to the practice of receiving up-to-date data on systems, processes, or events with no delay between data collection and analysis. By utilizing this type of monitoring, industry experts can quickly access information enabling them to detect any issues, performance challenges, or significant events.

The ability of real-time monitoring to instantly transmit data without delay is an aspect of this practice. This empowers manufacturers to respond swiftly to emerging issues or deviations from desired performance levels, ensuring uninterrupted manufacturing processes. Conducting monitoring is essential for enhancing network security and safeguarding production data. Observing network behavior and security system status allows potential threats to be identified and promptly neutralized.

Real-time monitoring significantly improves the end-user experience by ensuring operations and delivering high-quality products. The IT team plays a role in identifying and addressing issues that could impact product quality or cause production delays. This is achieved by analyzing real-time data resulting in customer satisfaction and loyalty.

Today, software interfaces are commonly used to simplify real-time monitoring. These interfaces present data in formats that allow IT staff and operators to make well-informed decisions promptly. Automation further facilitates the dissemination of signals, reduces response times, and minimizes disruptions.

One major advantage of real-time monitoring is its ability to monitor equipment performance. Manufacturing equipment naturally undergoes wear and tear. With real-time monitoring, problems can be detected as they arise, enabling swift repairs and minimizing downtime. By observing the data from real-time monitoring, we gain insights into performance trends over time. These insights empower us to make decisions based on data analysis, ultimately optimizing overall performance and reducing risks. Take a look at the following *Figure 2.1*:

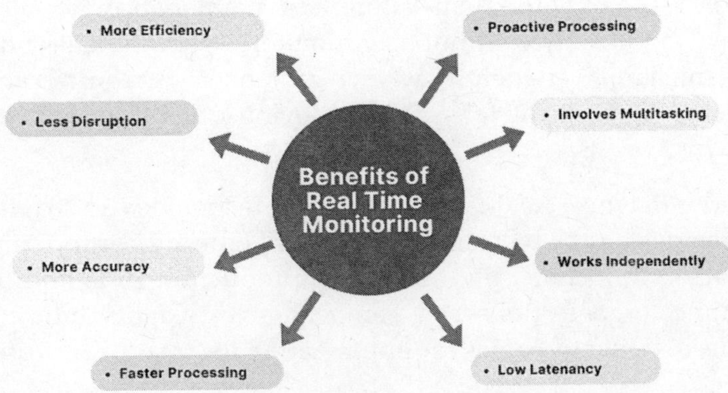

Figure 2.1: *Benefits of real-time monitoring*

In order to successfully implement real-time monitoring, thorough planning and seamless connection with current IT infrastructures are required. Manufacturers must make investments in advanced sensor technologies, data-collecting systems, and powerful data-processing capabilities. Transmission of data between sensors, monitoring systems, and user interfaces must occur without interruption, making the usage of reliable network topologies absolutely necessary.

In the manufacturing industry, real-time monitoring will continue to be an indispensable tool, particularly in light of the growing complexity of processes and the rising bar set by customers for product quality. Real-time data analysis can help industries enhance their productivity, acquire a competitive advantage, and continuously provide superior products if it is embraced and its potential is harnessed.

Real-time monitoring addresses several critical needs and challenges in industrial manufacturing and other sectors. It aims to resolve various issues and current gaps, such as:

- **Prompt intervention:** Real-time monitoring technology aims to address the problem of delayed intervention when anomalies arise. These anomalies can lead to reduced production line yield, unexpected downtime, and deterioration of production **Key Performance Indicators** (**KPIs**). By monitoring the system in real-time, it is possible to promptly intervene in the event of anomalies and take corrective action to optimize performance.

- **Efficient resource use:** Real-time monitoring technology aims to resolve the issue of inefficient resource use by intelligently allocating production according to the optimal energy profile and optimizing resource consumption on a per-product basis. By monitoring the system in real-time, organizations can maximize the yield of energy consumption and make resource use more efficient, reducing waste and associated costs.

- **Predictive maintenance:** Real-time monitoring technology endeavors to resolve the issue of equipment failure and maintenance by predicting imminent equipment failures. By continuously monitoring equipment and systems in real-time, organizations can identify when maintenance is required and take corrective action before equipment fails, thus reducing downtime and preventing costly breakdowns.

- **Improved efficiency:** Real-time monitoring technology is striving to resolve the issue of inefficiency by increasing operational efficiency, improving accountability, and reducing downtime. By monitoring production KPIs and downtime events in real time, organizations can gain valuable insights into current operating conditions and identify areas for optimization to streamline processes.

- **Real-time quality control:** Real-time quality control employs sensors, data analytics, and predictive maintenance to monitor production processes in real time. It enhances product traceability, reduces defects, and ensures compliance, leading to cost savings and improved customer satisfaction in manufacturing.

- **Rapid anomaly detection:** Real-time monitoring allows swift identification of anomalies and deviations from expected behavior. In the industry, machines, and processes may encounter unexpected issues, security events, and incidents, and the ability to detect and address these problems immediately is crucial to prevent production disruptions or equipment failures, ensuring consistent and high-quality output.
- **Improved decision-making:** It provides timely and accurate data, enabling informed decision-making. By having access to up-to-date information about the performance of systems and processes, managers and operators can make better decisions to optimize efficiency, resource allocation, and overall operational performance.
- **Enhanced safety:** Real-time monitoring is crucial in industries where safety is paramount, such as oil and gas, chemical manufacturing, or healthcare. It helps identify hazardous conditions or abnormal situations promptly, allowing for timely intervention to prevent accidents and protect personnel and the environment.
- **Minimizing downtime:** Manufacturing downtime might result in considerable financial losses. Real-time monitoring enables proactive maintenance and predictive analytics, lowering the risk of unanticipated equipment failures and limiting downtime, assuring continuous production and effective resource usage.
- **Customer experience and satisfaction:** In service-oriented industries like telecommunications and e-commerce, real-time monitoring ensures that services are delivered seamlessly. It helps maintain optimal network performance, minimal service disruptions, and swift issue resolution, improving customer satisfaction and loyalty.
- **Network security:** With the rise of cyber threats, real-time monitoring has become critical for detecting and mitigating potential security breaches and cyberattacks. By monitoring network activity and identifying suspicious behavior in real-time, organizations can respond swiftly to security threats and protect sensitive data, safeguarding their operations and reputation.
- **Compliance and regulatory requirements:** Many industries are subject to strict regulations and compliance standards. Real-time monitoring helps companies comply by continuously monitoring critical parameters and ensuring operations adhere to established standards, avoiding potential penalties and legal issues.
- **Resource optimization:** Real-time monitoring enables better utilization of resources, such as energy, raw materials, and manpower. By closely monitoring consumption and performance in real-time, organizations can identify areas for optimization and cost savings, promoting sustainability and reducing operational expenses.

Real-time monitoring technology is essential in closing the current gaps in industrial manufacturing and other sectors. Organizations may maximize performance, efficiency, and safety by keeping tabs on systems and procedures in real-time, leading to greater gains in output, savings, and patron satisfaction.

Real-time monitoring system architecture

In the context of industrial manufacturing, real-time monitoring is accomplished by utilizing a confluence of cutting-edge technologies, data collection systems, and analytical instruments. Take a look at the following *Figure 2.2*:

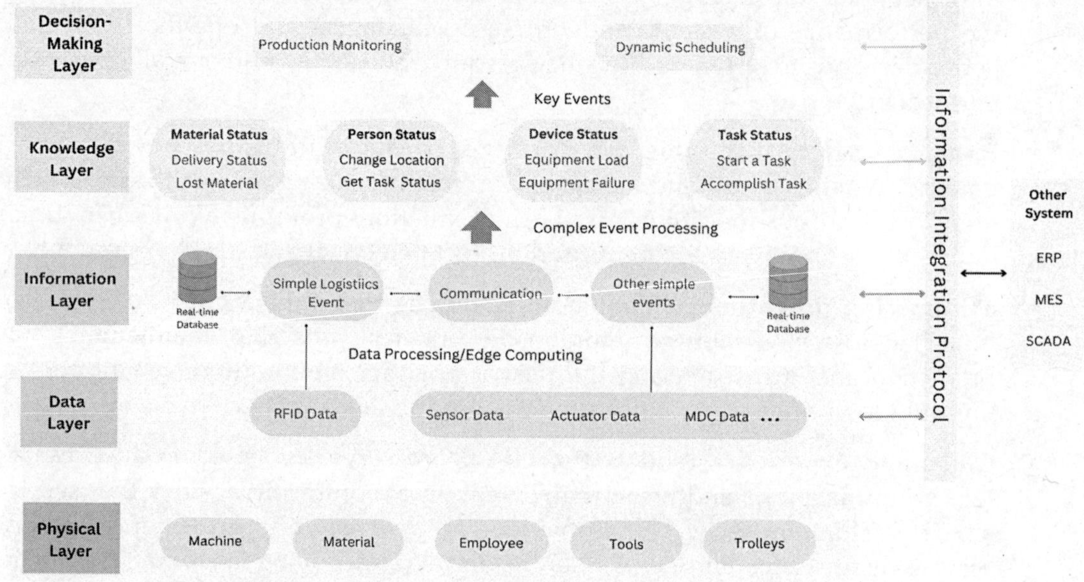

Figure 2.2: Real-time monitoring system architecture

The procedure consists of the following important stages:

- **Data collection:** Data collection for real-time monitoring involves gathering information from various manufacturing-related sources. These sources include connected sensors, actuators, machine control systems, **human-machine interfaces** (HMIs), and other devices. These devices transmit data as it becomes available or periodically, providing insights into output, environmental conditions (like temperature, pressure, vibration, and humidity), energy consumption, and other pertinent metrics.

Sensors and actuators

Real-time monitoring consists of components, including sensors and actuators. These components are commonly used in production environments. Sensors can detect and measure qualities like temperature, pressure, vibration, and humidity. By converting these measurements into impulses, they provide insights into various production processes. These sensors are strategically placed throughout the plant to record data and offer a view of manufacturing operations continuously. Monitoring systems utilize a range of sensors such as temperature, pressure, flow, air quality, chemical level, smoke level and position sensors to capture real-time data. The combination of these sensors helps in obtaining an understanding of the processes at hand. This enables problem identification and system performance improvement. Actuators do not directly contribute to sensor functionality; instead, they play a crucial role in closed-loop control systems by executing actions guided by feedback obtained from sensors. They initiate responses to ensure that the system operates within its intended boundaries. Take a look at the following *Figure* 2.3:

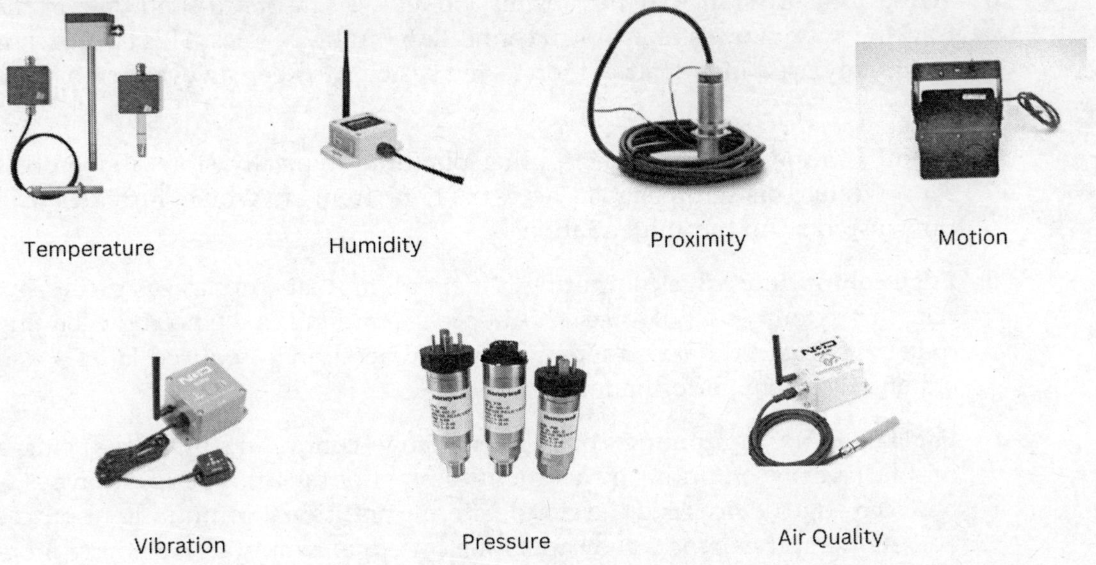

***Figure* 2.3:** *Various sensors*

Actuators are commonly employed in operations to ensure stability, safety, and precision. They operate through mechanisms such as electrical, hydraulic, pneumatic, and mechanical. By doing so, they guarantee product quality while also enhancing operational efficiency.

The following *Figure* 2.4 shows hydraulics and electrical actuators:

***Figure* 2.4:** *Hydraulics and electrical actuators*

There are several ways that sensors usually send information to the tracking system:

- **Gateways:** Gateways serve as the connection between sensors and the monitoring system. They facilitate the transfer of information from sensors to the monitoring system. In building systems, gateways are commonly used to gather data from monitors throughout the building.
- **Wireless transmission:** Wireless transmission enables sensors to transmit data to the monitoring device without the need for wires. This method is frequently employed in sensor networks to monitor assets using multiple devices within the same network.
- **Wired transmission:** Wired transmission allows sensors to send data to the tracking system by establishing a connection through cables. This approach is commonly used in industrial monitoring systems to keep an eye on tools and systems.
- **Cloud computing:** Cloud computing platforms typically store and process sensor data. This setup enables access to data, from anywhere. Provides real-time insights and recommendations.
- **Edge computing:** Edge computing is a paradigm that emphasizes processing data in proximity to its source. This approach minimizes the need for sending data to centralized data centers or the cloud, leading to reduced latency and enhanced system performance.
- **Fog layer:** Fog computing complements edge computing by introducing a middle layer of computing infrastructure known as the **fog layer**. This layer sits between edge devices and the cloud, offering additional computing resources and services. It enhances the capabilities of edge computing, enabling more complex data processing and analysis closer to the data source.

Once the data gets to the monitoring system, it is processed and analyzed to report the state of equipment and systems in real time. By monitoring this data in real time, organizations can rapidly spot problems and fix them to improve performance and general efficiency.

Human-machine interface

Human-machine interfaces (**HMIs**) are crucial components in modern industrial manufacturing because they are a critical link between human operators and the equipment, control systems, and processes in the production environment. HMIs are graphical or command line user interfaces allowing real-time data viewing, process control, and system monitoring. They are critical in improving operating efficiency, optimizing output, and assuring the safety of manufacturing facilities. Take a look at the following *Figure 2.5*:

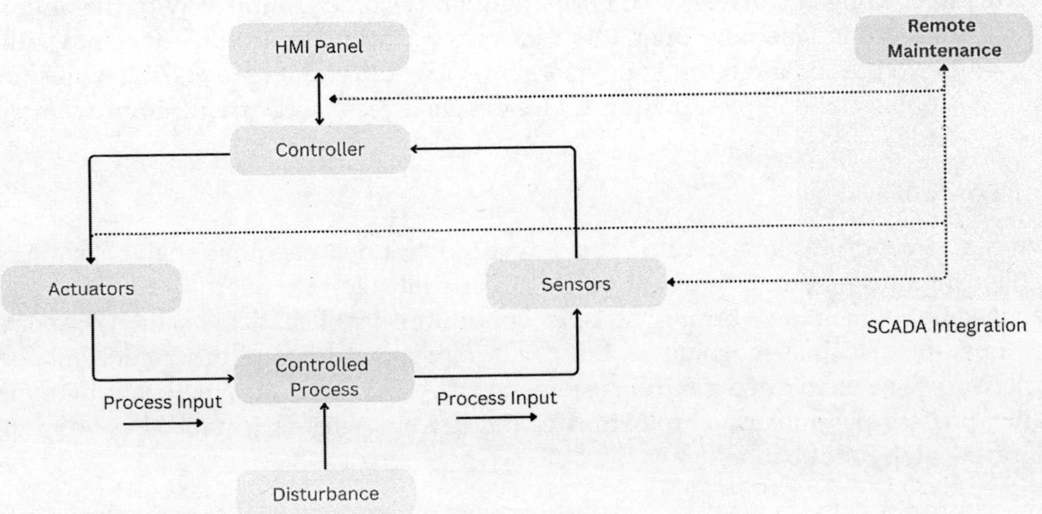

Figure 2.5: Human-machine interface

- **Purpose of HMIs:** The main objective of HMIs is to facilitate interaction between operators and engineers and the manufacturing processes and equipment. HMIs display real-time data received by sensors and control systems to simulate the production environment. Operators may keep tabs on various metrics in real-time, allowing them to spot problems early and act decisively.
- **Graphical user interface:** One essential aspect of HMIs is their **Graphical user interface (GUI)** which utilizes graphics, charts, icons, and other visual elements to represent information. The design of the GUI plays a role in ensuring that the HMI is user-friendly and easy to navigate for operators and engineers without specialized technical training.
- **Real-time data visualization:** HMIs continuously display real-time data visualization, including temperature, pressure, production rates, machine status, and other relevant parameters. This allows operators to quickly identify trends, anomalies, or deviations, from desired values so that immediate corrective actions can be taken.
- **Control and interaction:** Furthermore, HMIs provide capabilities that empower operators to control and adjust processes and parameters in real time. Operators can utilize touchscreens, buttons, and input devices to initiate commands, modify setpoints, or adjust production parameters.
- **Process visualization:** HMIs offer operators a way to understand production processes. With a glance, operators can grasp systems and workflows. This functionality helps them recognize how different process components are interconnected and spot any bottlenecks or inefficiencies.

- **Recording historical data:** HMIs frequently come equipped with the ability to log data enabling operators to access past data and trends for analyzing performance and optimizing operations. Historical data proves invaluable for troubleshooting, conducting root cause analyses, and driving improvement endeavors.

Machine control systems

Machines and control systems, with their advanced technologies that enable seamless data collecting and real-time monitoring, play a critical role in modern manufacturing. These machines, which have built-in sensors, continuously collect data on many aspects of their operation, such as machine health, performance metrics, and production-related characteristics. The embedded control systems in these machines automatically regulate and alter process parameters, employing feedback from sensors to maintain accurate conditions during production.

Machine control systems in manufacturing extend beyond data collection and monitoring. They are instrumental in automating various manufacturing processes, including precision machining, robotic assembly lines, **computer numerical control** (**CNC**) machining centers, and 3D printing. These systems ensure precise control over machinery movements, tool adjustments, and production sequences, resulting in consistent product quality and reduced human intervention. Additionally, they play a pivotal role in safety systems, instantly halting operations in case of anomalies or emergencies and safeguarding equipment and personnel.

CNC machines excel at performing a wide range of machining tasks in metalworking. Some common examples include precision milling, turning, drilling, and grinding operations. In addition to these traditional machining tasks, CNC machines are versatile and adaptable, making them suitable for advanced applications such as laser cutting, **electrical discharge machining** (**EDM**), and even 3D printing using various materials like metals, plastics, and ceramics. Their ability to precisely control tool movements and manipulate workpieces makes CNC machines a cornerstone of modern manufacturing across various industries, including automotive, aerospace, electronics, and beyond.

The sensors integrated into CNC machines work continuously to monitor components such as motors, spindles, bearings, and tool heads. They measure factors like temperature, vibration, and motor current to assess the health of these components. By analyzing this real-time data, the control system can detect signs of wear or irregularities in the machine's systems. For instance, if the vibration sensor detects vibrations in the spindle, it alerts the operator through the control system. This serves as a warning sign that there may be issues with the spindle's bearings. Acting based on this alert helps prevent damage and minimizes downtime.

Furthermore, CNC machine control systems gather performance related information during machining processes. Metrics, like cutting speed, feed rate, tool wear and tool life are monitored to optimize efficiency and productivity for example, during a milling operation, if the control system detects a decrease in tool lifespan, it can automatically adjust the feed rate or cutting speed. This adaptive response enhances efficiency and prolongs tool life. This helps prolong the tools life while ensuring high quality machining output Take a look at the following *Figure 2.6*:

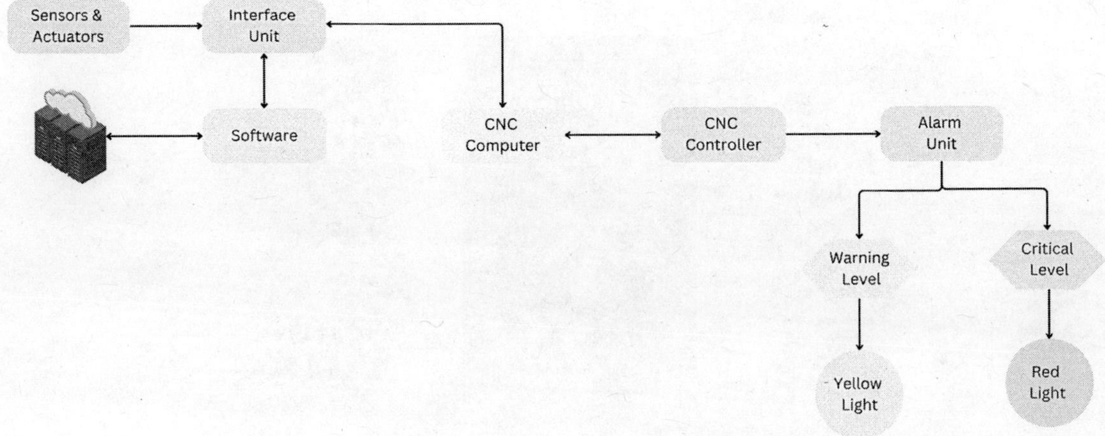

Figure 2.6: *Machine control system*

CNC machines are often connected to **manufacturing execution systems** (**MES**) or **enterprise resource planning** (**ERP**) systems making data transmission easy. Due to the system integration, the control system can now gather production-related information such as cycle times, part counts, and reject rates. To illustrate further, if a CNC machine starts producing rejected parts than usual, the control system can inform the MES. The MES can then initiate an investigation into the causes of this increased rejection rate. This timely action allows manufacturers to take measures promptly and minimize waste while improving product quality.

By collecting data from CNC machines and control systems, valuable insights regarding production efficiency, productivity, and maintenance requirements are gained. Manufacturers can optimize machine settings based on real-time information, identify areas for process improvement, and schedule maintenance tasks according to machine conditions rather than relying on pre-set schedules.

- **Integration of sensors:** Sensor integration in industrial manufacturing is critical for providing real-time data collecting and monitoring. The possibilities for efficient data-intensive applications have risen tremendously since the advent of wireless sensor technology. The requirement for quicker computer processing has boosted the demand for real-time monitoring systems in the context of Industry 4.0.

  IoT-generated sensor data is wirelessly delivered to web servers in wireless sensor technology, allowing engineers to track parameters in real time. Long-distance wireless communication not only improves cost efficiency but also decreases the requirement for a large number of people. The basis of a real-time monitoring system is its capacity to catch changes around the sensor node quickly, which necessitates fast data delivery with low latency. Any delays in getting data to the cloud can undermine the usefulness of a real-time monitoring system. Take a look at the following *Figure 2.7*:

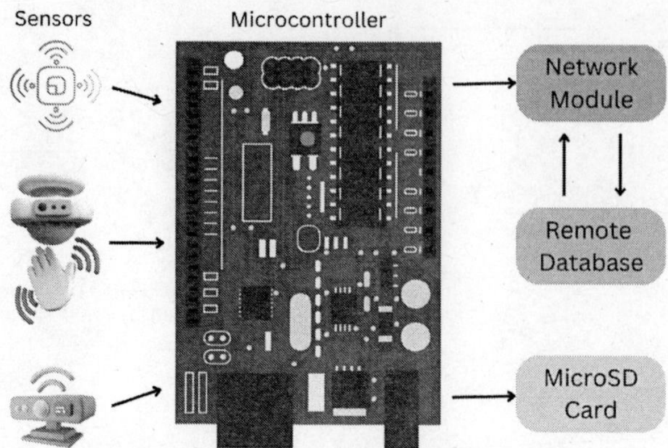

Figure 2.7: *Example of sensor integration*

Wireless sensor networks (**WSN**s) are useful in real-time systems because they consist of numerous independently running sensor nodes that can collect, store, and process environmental data without relying on pre-existing infrastructure. These networks are ideal for remote and low-maintenance settings due to their low cost, small size, low power requirements, diverse sensing capabilities, and dynamic networking. WSNs capture data and send it to a host for management and analysis.

Sensor network technology's architecture consists of sensor nodes, a microcontroller linked to a transceiver, and a remote database. The microcontroller saves sensor data to an external storage disk. It is subsequently uploaded to a remote monitoring database via the transceiver module, providing users with real-time data access. The data is simultaneously registered into the database and stored in the cloud, ensuring data is accessible from any location.

Efficient design flow and network architecture are crucial in maximizing sensor network performance. Using parallel processing rather than serial architecture to reduce internal hardware latency can enhance computational load and overall system efficiency. Data is frequently transferred through the static Sink by multi-hop or point-to-point transmission in densely deployed WSNs.

It is important to discuss an issue known as the **hotspot problem** in WSNs. When nodes near the Sink (the central data collection point) in the network consume more energy than other nodes due to their proximity to the Sink, it can lead to network disconnections and performance degradation. To address this problem, a solution is proposed: Dynamically positioning the Sink closer to the source of the event being monitored. This approach reduces the distance data needs to travel, minimizing end-to-end data-gathering latency and alleviating energy consumption issues. However, implementing this solution effectively requires careful design and planning of the sensor network to ensure optimal performance.

- **Data transmission:** The data acquired by sensors is sent to a central data repository or a cloud-based platform in real-time. In certain situations, edge computing can be employed for local data processing near the data's point of origin. This occurs before sending the relevant information to centralized systems. Data transmission could make use of wired or wireless communication techniques, depending on the particulars of the industrial setting and the necessities.

- **Data processing:** The real-time data goes through processing after it reaches the data repository or cloud platform where it is stored. Data processing involves several key steps to ensure the accuracy and reliability of the information:

  - **Data organization:** The raw data collected from sensors may be unstructured and require organization. During data organization, relevant data elements are sorted and structured to facilitate further analysis.

  - **Data aggregation:** Data aggregation involves combining multiple data points into meaningful summaries or higher-level representations. Data can be aggregated to help minimize the complexity of analysis and to facilitate the identification of patterns and trends.

  - **Data analysis:** In the data analysis stage, the processed data is subjected to various analytical techniques, such as statistical analysis, machine learning algorithms, or predictive modeling. The objective is to derive actionable insights from the data, identifying anomalies, patterns, or potential issues in real time.

  - **Data filtering:** Data filtering is used to remove irrelevant or noisy data points that may have been captured by sensors. By eliminating outliers or irrelevant information, the accuracy of the analysis is enhanced.

  - **Data cleansing:** Data cleansing is the process of identifying and rectifying errors or inconsistencies in the data. This step is crucial in ensuring that the data is accurate and free from discrepancies.

  - **Data normalization:** Data normalization is used to scale the data to a common format, making it comparable and consistent for analysis. Normalization ensures that different data sources and units do not skew the analysis.

Take a look at the following *Figure 2.8:*

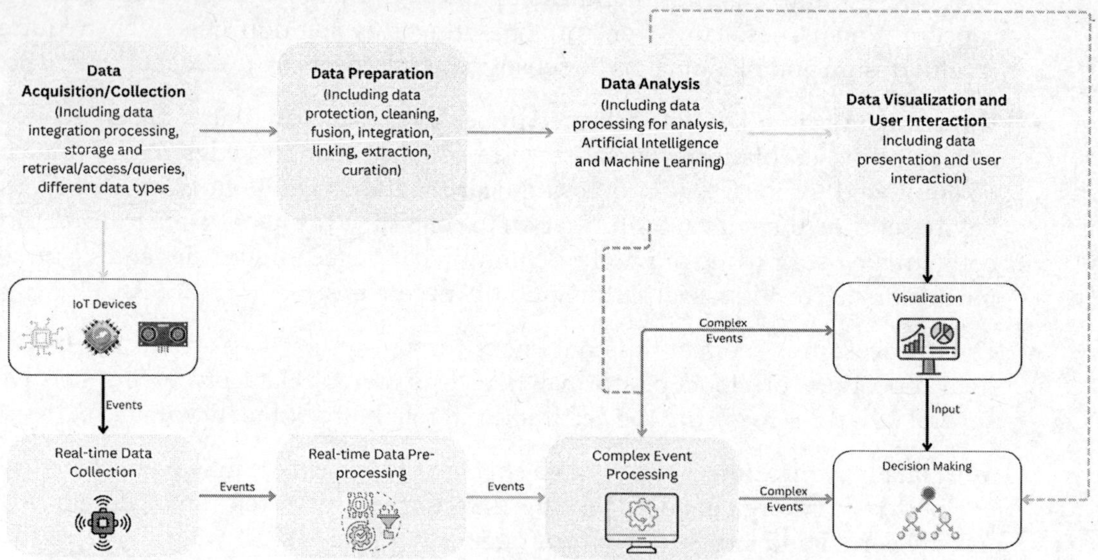

Figure 2.8: Data processing architecture

- **Visualization:** Once data has been analyzed, it is displayed to operators, engineers, and management using representations that are user-friendly and intuitive. To display real-time information in a way that is understandable and succinct, several visual representations such as graphs, charts, and dashboards are utilized. The monitoring and identification of trends, patterns, and anomalies can be made much simpler with the use of visualization tools.

- **Alters and notification:** Real-time monitoring systems can be set up to create alerts and notifications depending on predetermined thresholds or conditions, and this alerting and notification functionality can be adjusted by the system administrator. The system will send messages to the appropriate channels if critical events or deviations from the intended behavior take place. These notifications will allow for immediate action and problem resolution.

- **Integration with automation:** Integration with automation is a common practice in real-time monitoring, and it enables automatic responses to certain events or conditions. For example, if the temperature of a machine rises above a certain safe limit, the system may initiate an automatic shutdown to protect the unit from being harmed.

- **Analytics and predictive maintenance:** Algorithms for advanced analytics and predictive maintenance can be applied to real-time data in order to identify probable problems or demands in equipment repair. Predictive models can be used to anticipate machinery breakdowns. This enables proactive preventive maintenance, preventing costly malfunctions.

- **Continuous improvement:** Real-time monitoring provides actionable insights for implementing continuous improvement projects. It highlights areas of a process that could be optimized and identifies opportunities for improvement. Decision-making in the manufacturing industry informed by data enables the implementation of improvements that boost productivity, quality, and overall performance.
- **Integration with existing systems:** The implementation of real-time monitoring frequently requires integration with pre-existing production systems, such as production Execution Systems, Enterprise Resource Planning systems, and **Supervisory Control and Data Acquisition** (**SCADA**) systems. Integration guarantees that data flows without interruption and provides a holistic perspective of the entire manufacturing process.

IoT and predictive maintenance

IoT predictive maintenance can be used to maintain assets, equipment or machinery. It focuses on keeping them in optimal condition. It harnesses the power of the IoT to collect and analyze data. By using sensors and other devices, this method allows for monitoring of equipment status enabling detection of potential issues before they cause any major disruptions.

In the realm of maintenance, this network primarily consists of strategically placed sensors and monitors on or within equipment. These sensors keep an eye on variables that may indicate problems with the equipment. They collect real-time performance data which is then transmitted to components within the network such as predictive maintenance software, **Computerized Maintenance Management System** (**CMMS**) software, or other intelligent manufacturing systems. Take a look at the following *Figure 2.9*:

***Figure 2.9:** Benefits of IoT-based predictive maintenance*

The IoT predictive maintenance system allows for integration with IoT technologies by continuously gathering and transmitting asset data. Utilizing algorithms, these analytics are able to identify issues that could lead to equipment failure. Organizations have the opportunity to prevent issues and implement maintenance measures by being proactive in identifying and anticipating the possibility of outages or disruptions.

Predictive maintenance in the realm of the IoT allows businesses to stay ahead of their maintenance requirements, minimize downtime, improve equipment performance, and boost operational efficiency. This innovative approach brings a data-driven, efficient, and cost-effective perspective to modernizing maintenance practices. Take a look at the following *Figure 2.10*:

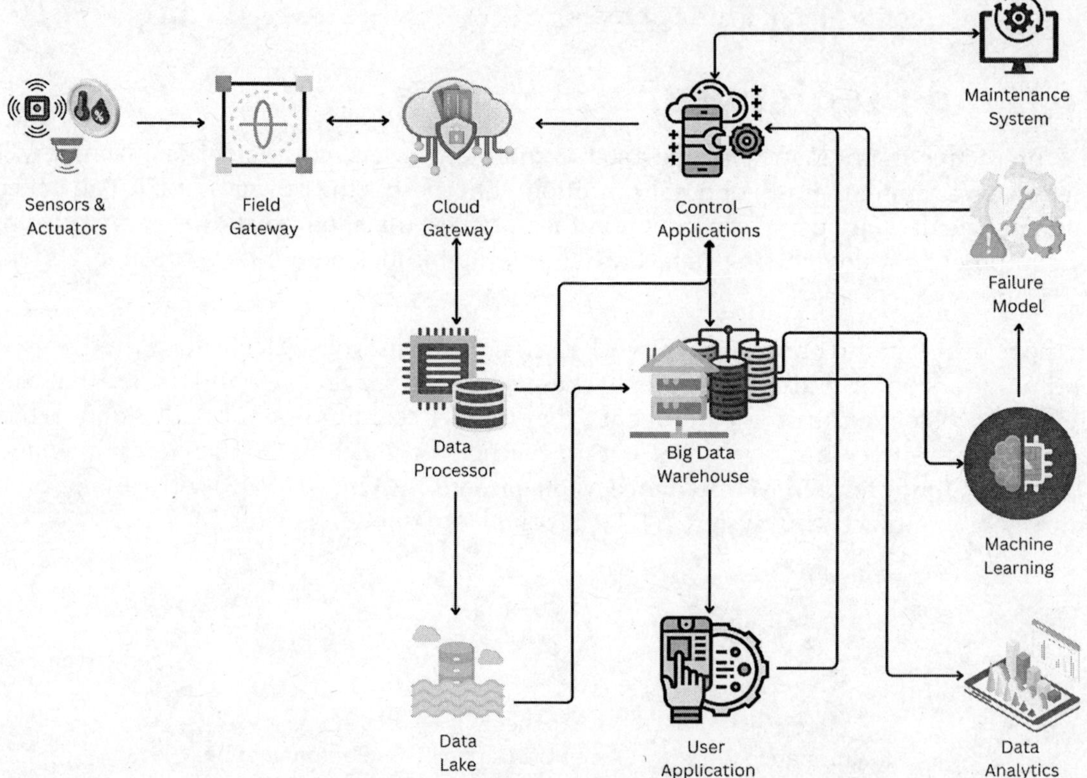

Figure 2.10: *Example of IoT-based predictive maintenance architecture*

Case study: Smart predictive maintenance

In the highly controlled and important field of manufacturing medical devices, making sure that operations are efficient and reliable is still the most important thing. Implementing the IoT in predictive maintenance has become a game-changing way to deal with these problems. It improves **Overall Equipment Effectiveness** (**OEE**) and cuts down on unexpected downtime. This case study looks at how a major medical device manufacturer successfully used IoT predictive maintenance. It shows how this changed the way they maintained their equipment and led to huge improvements in OEE.

The medical device manufacturer encountered significant hurdles in sustaining high OEE levels, primarily stemming from unforeseen equipment breakdowns, production delays, and escalating maintenance expenses. Their reliance on reactive maintenance practices resulted in costly downtime, adversely affecting production schedules and product quality. Furthermore, the lack of real-time insights into equipment health hindered their ability to proactively address potential issues before they become critical.

In response to these challenges, the company embarked on a journey to implement IoT predictive maintenance. By strategically deploying a network of advanced sensors across critical equipment and machinery, they collected real-time data on key performance indicators such as temperature, vibration, humidity, pressure, and energy consumption.

This approach aligns with the concept of **direct numerical control** (**DNC**), a manufacturing term that refers to a system connecting multiple CNC machine tools through a central computer. Similarly, the collected data from various sensors in critical machinery was centralized in the cloud-based platform. Here, sophisticated data analytics tools processed the information. Through powerful predictive algorithms and machine learning models, the platform analyzed historical data to identify early warning signs of equipment deterioration, continuously refining its predictions for greater accuracy. Take a look at the following *Figure 2.11*:

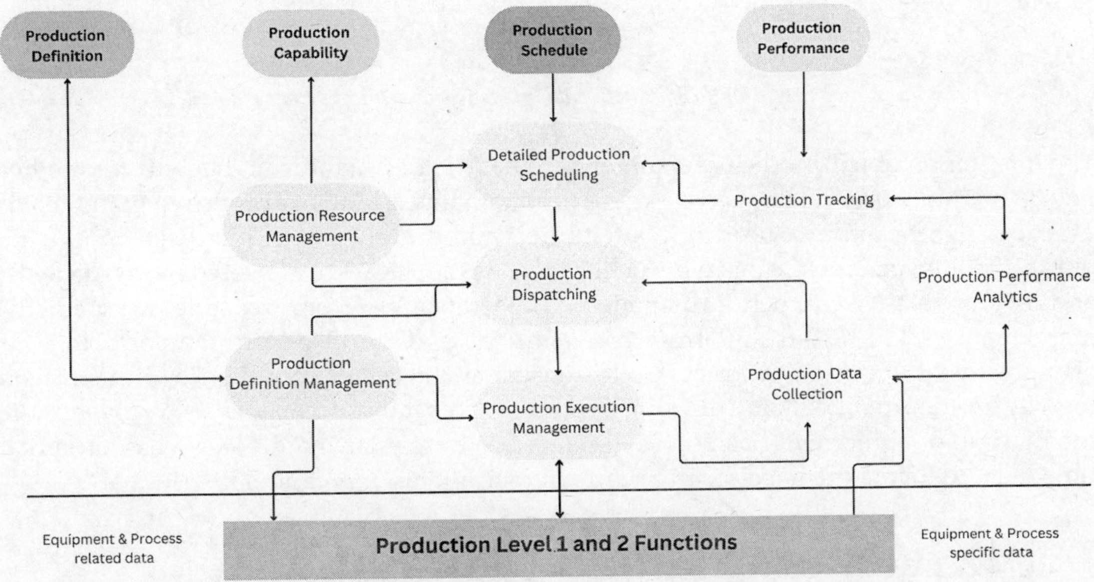

***Figure 2.11:** Data flow in IoT based predictive maintenance*

Much like DNC technology that connects multiple CNC machines to a central computer for coordinated instructions, the IoT system in place allowed the medical device manufacturer to receive proactive alerts whenever potential issues were detected. These alerts prompted the maintenance team to schedule predictive maintenance activities promptly, optimizing downtime and ensuring equipment remained in peak condition. Take a look at the following *Figure 2.12*:

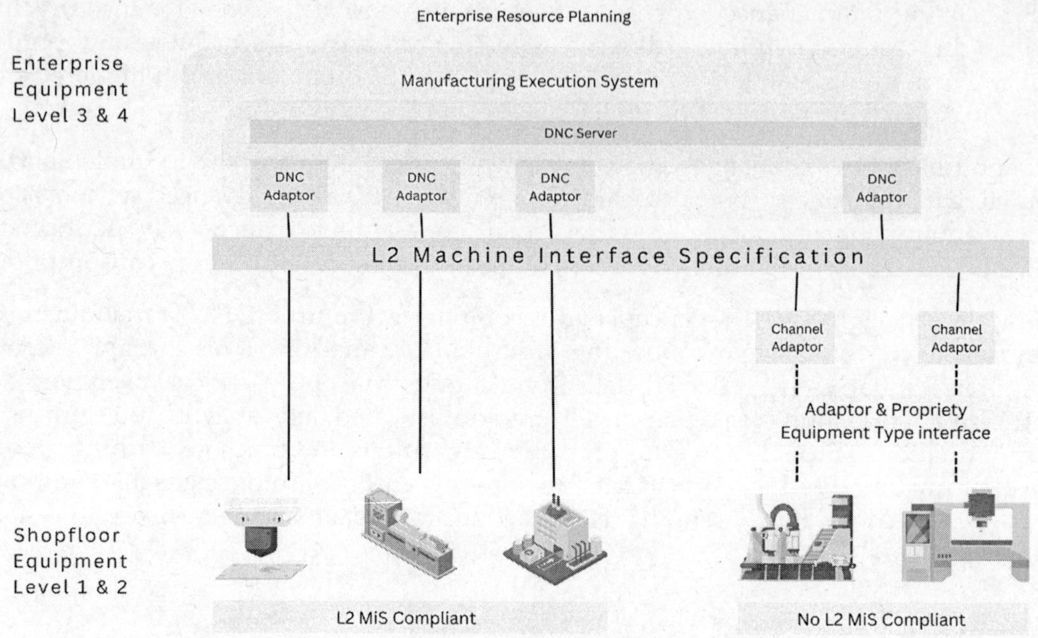

Figure 2.12: *Integrating IoT predictive maintenance for medical device manufacturer*

The integration of IoT predictive maintenance has yielded significant benefits for medical device manufacturers. They have experienced enhanced OEE, as proactive maintenance practices significantly reduced unplanned downtime, resulting in increased production output. Moreover, cost savings were achieved as resources were allocated more efficiently, and spare parts were better managed. The transition from reactive to predictive maintenance, akin to the shift from conventional CNC to DNC in manufacturing, has also positively impacted product quality, ensuring consistent compliance with stringent regulatory requirements and meeting customer expectations consistently. Furthermore, the lifespan of equipment has been extended due to regular maintenance based on real-time data, reducing the need for premature replacements and capital investments.

IoT driven production planning

Production systems are frequently the key factor in establishing a sustainable competitive advantage in the manufacturing industry. This has led many companies to embrace best practices such as lean manufacturing and Six Sigma. Lean manufacturing is a production methodology that focuses on eliminating waste, streamlining processes, and maximizing value for customers. Originally developed by *Toyota* as the **Toyota Production System** (**TPS**), companies worldwide have widely adopted lean principles. On the other hand, Six Sigma is a data-driven methodology aimed at achieving near-perfect process performance by identifying and eliminating defects and variations. Originally developed by *Motorola*, Six Sigma has become a widely adopted approach for process improvement in various industries.

IoT is a powerful enabler for lean manufacturing and Six Sigma methodologies. By providing real-time data insights, improving process visibility, enhancing quality control, and promoting continuous improvement, IoT complements and strengthens the impact of lean and Six Sigma in creating sustainable competitive advantages for manufacturing companies.

One of the fundamental processes where the IoT plays as an effective enabler is production planning and scheduling. This revolves around efficiently managing machines, materials, and labor scheduling to meet customer demand. The primary goal is to strike a balance between maximizing productivity and minimizing costs while ensuring products are delivered on time and in the desired quantities. Traditionally, production planning relied on manual methods, which often led to inefficiencies and challenges in dealing with the market's ever-changing demands.

Manual production planning methods involved complex calculations, relying on historical data and assumptions. However, these methods often fell short of capturing real-time changes in demand, supply chain disruptions, or unforeseen events. As a result, manufacturers faced difficulties in promptly adjusting production schedules and resource allocation. This lack of adaptability could lead to overproduction, excess inventory, or stockouts, ultimately impacting customer satisfaction and the company's bottom line.

It is worth noting that even before the advent of IoT solutions, companies were managing their production planning effectively, especially larger enterprises. However, IoT has introduced significant advancements, enabling companies to enhance their planning processes further and respond more efficiently to dynamic market conditions and unexpected disruptions.

With constantly changing variables, MRP/ERP software has become a basic resource planning tool for keeping everything organized. Resource planning tools are valuable, but they rely on the quality of data input. IoT provides a solution by enabling the capture of previously too complex or expensive data. Organizations can collect vast real-time data from equipment, facilities, supply chains, and more with IoT sensors and devices. This new influx of data provides more input for resource planning tools, allowing them to produce more accurate and dynamic plans. The combination of resource planning tools and IoT data offers the potential for organizations to optimize resource allocation and respond faster to changes. However, fully realizing this potential requires carefully managing the implementation of IoT and integrating it effectively with planning tools. Like any technology, IoT and resource planning tools must work together to maximize value. Production scheduling benefits greatly from increased amount of data utilization, providing tangible and quantifiable improvements. Right amount of data empowers internal managers with actionable insights, enabling real-time operational enhancements.

The technologies enabling smarter production planning in Industry 4.0 are the Internet of Things, which provides real-time data from connected devices and assets; **big data analytics** (**BDA**), which analyzes massive amounts of IoT data for insights; **cyber-manufacturing** (**CMg**), which creates digital twins of the manufacturing environment for simulation and scenario modeling; and cyber-physical systems, which controls equipment to implement optimized plans. These technologies interact in a virtuous cycle: IoT feeds data to BDA for analysis, BDA identifies optimization opportunities, CMg simulates plans, CPS implements plans by controlling equipment, and CPS sends IoT data on process performance back to refine models and planning in an ongoing loop. This integrated system gives unprecedented visibility, analytics, and agility to production planning. Take a look at the following *Figure 2.13*:

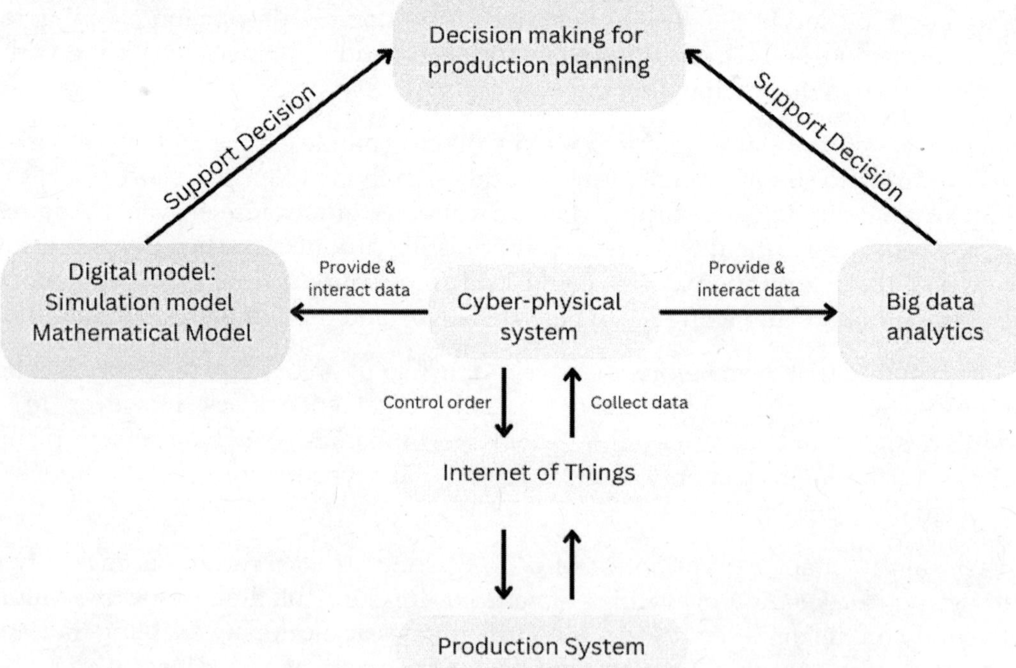

***Figure 2.13:** The overview of the production planning in Industry 4.0*

The key elements for production planning in Industry 4.0 include IoT, Big data analysis, IoT, cloud environment, and cyber-physical systems. The interaction between them is illustrated in *Figure 2.13*, as well as how they collaborate to assist with the decision-making of production planning.

Key aspects of efficient production planning

Production planning is vital for manufacturers to maximize output, profitability, and on-time delivery according to customer demand signals. For optimal planning, managers need to consider several interdependent factors:

- **Production sequencing:** The sequence in which different products or variants are produced is crucial to minimize changeover times between batches. Optimal sequencing enables longer production runs with fewer changeovers, which improves asset utilization and output.
- **Batch sizing:** Determining the right batch size is dependent on inventory levels, material availability, shelf-life constraints, and demand. Larger batch sizes improve efficiency, but smaller batches allow greater responsiveness. This trade-off needs balancing based on product characteristics.
- **Equipment allocation:** Production planning involves allocating shared equipment capacity on the manufacturing floor. The plan must optimize asset utilization and output while avoiding bottlenecks. This requires coordination between lines producing intermediate and final products.
- **Staff scheduling:** Scheduling staff across shifts and work cells is interlinked with production plans. Labor requirements vary by product. Efficient operator allocation and skills mapping are key to achieving plant output targets.
- **Sourcing and inventory:** Planners need to source materials and components aligning with production schedules. Inventory levels across the plant need to be managed through just-in-time supply and movement to avoid shortages while minimizing excess stock.

By holistically addressing these constraints, manufacturers can create feasible production plans that maximize plant efficiency, quality, and on-time order delivery despite volatility in supply, production variability, and changing customer demand. Efficient planning ensures on-time delivery despite supply, production, and demand variability.

IoT for real-time production tracking

Shop floors are highly dynamic with frequent changes. Materials get delayed, machines break down, defects occur, orders change, and so on. Production planners need real-time visibility rather than relying on daily or hourly ERP snapshots.

IoT allows real-time production tracking in smart factories through interconnected devices and sensors. Sensors attached to production equipment, assets, and materials can continuously monitor status, condition, and environment. Data from these sensors is communicated in real-time over wired and wireless networks to IoT platforms that aggregate and analyze the data streams. The real-time insights allow managers to identify issues, make quick data-driven decisions, and dynamically adapt production planning. Real-time tracking through IoT transforms production monitoring, control, and optimization. However, it requires integrating various sensor systems, networking infrastructure, IoT platforms, and data analytics capabilities. IoT-enabled real-time production tracking provides unprecedented visibility and manufacturing agility when implemented well. These IoT devices are strategically placed across the production line, machines, inventory, and other relevant points, creating a network of smart objects that continuously communicate and share information. The data collected from these devices is then analyzed and used to optimize production processes, improve efficiency, and enable timely decision-making.

IoT devices and sensors

The foundation of IoT-enabled real-time production tracking lies in deploying various IoT devices and sensors. These devices can include:

- **Machine sensors:** Installed on manufacturing equipment, these sensors collect data on machine performance, such as operating temperature, speed, vibrations, and energy consumption.
- **Inventory sensors:** Placed on storage units and products, inventory sensors monitor stock levels and item movements and identify the need for reordering.
- **Environmental sensors:** These sensors measure factors like temperature, humidity, and air quality, which can impact the manufacturing process and product quality.
- **RFID tags:** Used for item-level tracking, RFID tags provide unique identification for each product or component, facilitating precise tracking throughout the production process.

Here is a detailed explanation of how IoT-enabled real-time production tracking works:

- **Data collection and transmission:** IoT devices continuously gather data from their respective sources and transmit it in real-time to a centralized data repository or cloud-based platform. This data transmission can occur via wired or wireless connections, such as Wi-Fi, Bluetooth, or cellular networks.
- **Data integration and analysis:** The collected data is aggregated and integrated into a central database or cloud platform. Advanced analytics tools and algorithms process this data to extract meaningful insights, identify patterns, and detect anomalies. Real-time analytics help monitor the production process and promptly respond to any deviations or potential issues.
- **Visualization and reporting:** The processed data is then visualized through intuitive dashboards and reports, which provide a comprehensive view of the production process. Real-time production metrics, such as machine uptime, downtime, and production rates, are presented user-friendly for easy monitoring by production managers and other stakeholders.

- **Automation and alerts:** IoT-driven production tracking systems can be configured to automate certain actions based on data insights. For example, if an inventory sensor detects low stock levels, the system can automatically trigger a supplier reorder request. Additionally, the system can generate real-time alerts and notifications to production managers and relevant teams when critical thresholds are breached or deviations occur.

- **Integrating with other systems:** To achieve a seamless production flow, IoT-enabled real-time production tracking systems can be integrated with other enterprise systems, such as **enterprise resource planning** (**ERP**) and **manufacturing execution systems** (**MES**). Integrations enable data exchange between systems, streamlining information flow across departments and optimizing overall production processes.

- **Continuous improvement:** Continuous improvement is a key aspect of IoT-enabled real-time production tracking. The data collected over time allows manufacturers to identify bottlenecks, optimize workflows, and make data-driven decisions for process optimization. Historical data analysis also aids in identifying long-term trends and performance patterns, enabling informed strategic planning for the future.

  In addition to real-time visibility, IoT analytics help improve planning agility. In today's rapidly changing manufacturing landscape, adaptability and agility in production planning have become crucial for companies to remain competitive. IoT technology is pivotal in enabling agile production planning by providing real-time visibility and advanced analytics capabilities.

  This section explores how IoT enhances planning agility through data fusion, scenario simulation, cognitive algorithms, ERP and MES integration, and automation, facilitating near real-time re-planning to address variability and drive significant efficiency in plant scheduling:

- **Data fusion:** IoT leverages a network of interconnected sensors and devices to collect real-time operating data from machines, production lines, and other critical points in the manufacturing process. This data is fused with historical trends, demand forecasts, and constraints, creating a comprehensive and dynamic data pool. By integrating diverse data sources, manufacturers gain a holistic view of their production environment, enabling better-informed planning decisions.

- **Scenario simulation:** IoT-driven analytics enable the simulation of multiple scheduling scenarios based on the fused data. Manufacturers can explore various what-if scenarios to identify optimal production sequences and resource allocations. Scenario simulation helps assess the impact of different production plans on key performance indicators, such as lead times, throughput, and resource utilization, aiding in effective decision-making.

- **Cognitive algorithms:** Cognitive algorithms learn from historical data patterns and production performance powered by the data generated by IoT. These algorithms analyze vast amounts of data to identify trends, patterns, and correlations. Cognitive algorithms can continuously learn from real-time data to suggest improvements and recommendations for more efficient and effective production planning strategies.

- **ERP and MES integration:** IoT-enabled production planning systems seamlessly integrate with ERP and MES. This integration facilitates rapid plan updates and ensures production planning aligns with overall business objectives. Real-time data sharing between systems allows for dynamic adjustments in response to changing demand, inventory levels, or resource availability.
- **Automation:** IoT-driven automation replaces repetitive manual work involved in rescheduling production plans. The system can automatically trigger plan adjustments based on pre-defined rules or predictive algorithms when unexpected events or variations occur. Automation expedites the re-planning process, reducing manual intervention and human error.

The culmination of these IoT capabilities enables near real-time re-planning to address production volatility and adapt to changing circumstances. Production plans must be flexible and responsive in a volatile environment, and IoT-driven agility empowers manufacturers to achieve this objective. By leveraging IoT for agile production planning, manufacturers can optimize production schedules, minimize downtime, reduce lead times, and maximize resource utilization, leading to significant efficiency gains in plant scheduling.

IoT's integration with production planning provides manufacturers with the tools to adapt to volatility effectively. Through data fusion, scenario simulation, cognitive algorithms, ERP and MES integration, and automation, IoT empowers manufacturers to create agile and responsive production plans. With near real-time re-planning capabilities, manufacturers can adjust to variability and make data-driven decisions that drive efficiency and competitiveness in their production processes. Embracing IoT for agile production planning is essential for manufacturers seeking to thrive in an ever-changing and challenging manufacturing landscape.

Case study: IoT in manufacturing

A medical devices contract manufacturer was facing challenges with volatile demand and production delays impacting delivery performance. Complex, manual production planning processes took hours to adapt plans.

The company implemented an IoT system to track work-in-progress dynamically on the shop floor using RFID and barcodes. Machine sensors monitored equipment status. The IoT platform analyzed the real-time data to update production plans automatically, far faster than their old method.

Operational responsiveness increased markedly. The planning cycle time was reduced from 3 hours to 20 minutes. Overall equipment effectiveness increased by 6% in the first year and on-time delivery improved by 8%.

This led to higher customer satisfaction and increased business. The agile, data-driven production planning approach enabled by IoT delivered significant benefits.

Ensuring quality control with IoT

Quality control is vital for manufacturing companies to deliver products that meet specifications and satisfy customers. Statistical sampling and manual inspection have been the mainstay of quality control for decades. However, traditional methods are proving inadequate for modern production environments' complexity, speed, and precision needs. IoT technologies enable a revolutionary new, smart, proactive, and integrated approach to quality management.

Traditional quality control methods

In statistical sampling method, a small sample of units is taken off the production line and inspected for defects. The defect rate in the sample is used to judge the overall quality of the full population of products. However, sampling comes with inherent risks and limitations:

- Samples may not represent the total batch accurately if randomness is not maintained.
- Low defect samples can miss problems occurring at low frequencies across the full lot.
- High-impact defects can escape into field products even with low sample defect rates.
- Tightening sampling rates substantially increase inspection time and cost.
- Sampling delays defect detection until end-of-line rather than during production.

Manual inspection by technicians suffers from subjectivity, variability, and human errors. Visual checks and testing involve specialized skills and meticulousness to be reliable. Maintaining consistency across changing inspectors, shifts, and sites remains challenging. The rise of ultra-precision manufacturing also demands zero-defect verification, exceeding human capabilities.

IoT-enabled approach

An IoT approach provides complete inline inspection by instrumenting the production line with sensors and imaging systems. Data analytics and machine learning algorithms convert the wealth of IoT data into actionable intelligence. Closed loop automation enables real-time corrections before defects multiply.

IoT allows continuous assessment of each product rather than statistical sampling. It enables unmanned automated quality checks around the clock, minimizing inconsistencies. The focus shifts from reactive identification of issues to proactive and predictive prevention driven by data analytics. This transforms legacy reactive quality control to intelligent quality assurance across the entire value chain from components to post-sale.

Key capabilities of an IoT quality management approach

An IoT-powered smart quality management system provides several key advantages over traditional approaches to enable proactive, data-driven quality control. The key capabilities of an IoT quality management approach include:

- **Inline monitoring:** Sensors and vision systems provide continuous measurements and imaging for in-process inspection along the production line.
- **Centralized data:** IoT connectivity consolidates dispersed data from different stations, systems, and facilities onto unified analytics platforms.
- **Advanced analytics:** Big data analytics, machine learning, and AI are applied to identify trends, correlations, patterns, and anomalies that indicate quality issues.
- **Predictive maintenance:** Analytics models predict potential failures and degradation, allowing proactive maintenance to avoid unplanned downtime and scraps.
- **Closed-loop automation:** Integration between sensors, controllers, and analytics models allows real-time adjustments to keep parameters within quality limits.
- **Traceability:** The interconnected data empowers end-to-end traceability across the value chain from components to final customer.

Benefits of the IoT approach

Adopting an IoT strategy for quality management brings powerful benefits, such as:

- Reduce defects through continuous inline monitoring rather than post-production inspection.
- Cut quality management costs with fewer manual inspections.
- Speed up **root cause analysis (RCA)** using integrated sensor data insights.
- Improve consistency and minimize human subjectivity errors through automated analytics.
- Enable traceability for compliance, recalls, and warranty management.
- Uncover hidden factory optimizations with equipment effectiveness analytics.
- Enhance customer satisfaction through zero-defect quality targets.

The IoT advantage comes from real-time data, pervasive connectivity, advanced analytics, and closed-loop automation. IoT provides the end-to-end visibility, intelligence, and control needed to evolve quality management from reactive to predictive.

IoT for automated inspection and testing

Inspection and testing are integral to quality control to detect defects and confirm specification compliance. Traditional manual approaches cannot provide the automation, consistency, and micro-precision needed for quality assurance today. The IOT enables precise inline inspection with reliability, efficiency, and scale.

Automated in-line inspection

IoT-enabled sensors and vision systems provide monitoring and measurements at critical points along the production line and assembly stations. Sensors continuously track parameters like temperature, vibration, pressure, flow rate, torque, and so on. High-resolution cameras capture detailed images to detect minute surface and component defects.

Issues can be flagged immediately in real-time rather than waiting for end-of-line checks when many defective units may have already been produced. Automated inline inspection comprehensively assesses each product coming off the line rather than relying on sampling statistics.

Benefits of automated inline inspection

Automated inline inspection powered by sensors and vision systems brings major improvements in quality control by enabling continuous, comprehensive testing. The benefits of automated inline inspection include:

- Early detection reduces defects escaping to customers
- Real-time corrections minimize wastage and rework
- Continuous tracking rather than sampling or periodic inspection
- Consistent objective evaluation preventing human oversight
- Detailed dimensional, performance, and functional testing

Unmanned inspection and hazardous environments

IoT allows automated quality checks in hazardous environments like paint shops with toxic fumes, confined spaces like chemical tanks, loud/hot/dirty industrial facilities, and production lines dealing with chemicals and hazardous materials and heavy machinery operations without endangering human inspectors. Automated drones empower unmanned inspections in difficult-to-reach areas within factories.

Computer vision algorithms continuously analyze video streams to detect surface defects rather than relying on infrequent and partial manual inspections. This prevents safety risks while improving quality.

Micro and nano-precision testing

High-precision IoT-connected instrumentation performs a non-destructive evaluation to identify micro defects and early degradation that are difficult to detect otherwise. For example, micro-vibrations in turbine blades measured by IoT sensors reveal developing cracks before catastrophic failures.

In microelectronics, nanoscale sensors and imaging methods detect minute contaminants and structural flaws to avoid escapes. IoT connectivity provides centralized monitoring and diagnostics of such precision test data for accurate traceability.

Consistency and objectivity

Automated systems apply consistent standards without human inspector subjectivity and variability. IoT analytics minimizes the natural variations arising from different inspectors, shifts, sites, and subjective assessments of visual defects. Machine learning algorithms trained on empirical sensor data improve consistency for reliable quality benchmarks across the enterprise.

Proactive testing and predictive maintenance

IoT-enabled sensors facilitate continuous monitoring for proactive rather than periodic inspection. This enables identifying issues as early as possible instead of fixed schedule checks. Advanced analytics predict potential failures before they occur based on sensor data correlations and patterns.

This predictive maintenance approach avoids unplanned machinery downtime, which causes unfinished work and quality issues. The focus becomes preventing problems before they arise rather than detecting them after actual failure events.

Inspection integration across facilities

IoT networking and cloud analytics combine test data from diverse equipment, lines, and facilities onto centralized platforms. This aggregated view enables unified insights into overall equipment effectiveness, benchmarks, and emerging quality issues across the manufacturing network.

IoT transforms testing and inspection from a manual sampling activity into an automated, consistent, and predictive process by enabling unattended precision at a massive scale. This drives significantly higher quality, reliability, and efficiency.

Data analysis for quality assurance: IoT's role

Effective quality assurance requires extracting actionable intelligence from the vast inspection data collected on the manufacturing floor and supply chain. IoT is crucial in managing, contextualizing, analyzing, and interpreting quality data to provide meaningful insights that drive improvements.

Data management challenges

Equipment and systems on the production floor generate massive amounts of data across the manufacturing process. However, this data is often trapped in silos that hinder a unified view of quality due to following reasons:

- Proprietary data formats and communication protocols used by different sensor systems, testing machines, and equipment.
- Factory data fragmented across fragmented data silos, reporting tools, and data repositories.
- Operational data isolated from the business context in ERP, MES, and SCM systems.
- Limited coordination between management, engineering, and shop-floor perspectives on quality.

IoT enables unified data

IoT technologies break down these data silos to create a unified view for quality assurance:

- Standards like **Open Platform Communications Unified Architecture** (**OPC UA**) enable connectivity between diverse systems regardless of underlying protocols. It is an industry-standard communications protocol that enables connectivity and data exchange between diverse industrial and automation equipment, devices, controllers, sensors, and so on. The ease of connectivity can really help enable deeper IIoT and smart manufacturing use cases by allowing more systems to share data.
- Edge gateways aggregate and preprocess data from disparate sources.
- Cloud IoT platforms integrate fragmented data into unified big data lakes.
- IT/OT convergence bridges plant floor data with business context.
- Digital twin models provide a virtual representation connecting all data.

With quality data integrated, contextualized, and interconnected via IoT, meaningful insights can be extracted using advanced analytics.

Advanced analytics for intelligence

IoT enables advanced analytical techniques on the unified quality data set to gain intelligence:

- Real-time analytics
  - o Dashboards displaying live feeds of critical quality metrics from production lines and enterprise systems.

- Anomaly detection algorithms on sensor streams to identify deviations.
- Notification of emerging issues enabling immediate corrective actions.

- **Predictive modelling**
  - Machine learning on historical data to predict potential defects and failures.
  - Identifying correlations leading to quality issues.
  - Simulation of production scenarios to quantify the impact of changes.
- **Diagnostic analytics**
  - Root cause analysis of issues using integrated supply chain data.
  - Traceability mechanisms to track origins of raw materials and process conditions.
  - Benchmarking to compare performance across facilities.

IoT transforms disconnected data into live, actionable insights that drive smart quality assurance.

Case study: Use of IoT in quality control

The following case studies illustrate how leading companies leverage IoT and analytics to transform quality management. These real-world examples showcase uses of IoT data for:

- In-process quality monitoring during production.
- Centralizing and analyzing dispersed data at scale.
- Applying machine learning to derive insights.
- Enabling predictive maintenance of equipment.
- Creating closed-loop quality control systems.
- Providing end-to-end supply chain visibility.
- Building digital twins of products using field data.
- Incorporating emerging data sources such as wearable devices like smart helmets.
- Implementing flexible IoT platforms to integrate new data easily.

The key takeaways include:

- IoT creates a digital thread connecting data across the product lifecycle.
- Analytics extract value from IoT data to improve quality and yield.

- Combining IoT with advanced analytics enables predictive, preventative, and proactive quality management.
- Agile IoT architectures allow easy integration of new data sources and use cases.
- Quality management is a major business application driving IoT adoption for manufacturers.

Case study 1

Ford[1] uses IoT data for in-process quality checks to quickly detect issues during manufacturing. *Ford* has implemented an IoT architecture across its manufacturing facilities to collect real-time data from production equipment and vehicles through the assembly line[2]. Sensors installed at critical points along the assembly line monitor key parameters like:

- Torque levels applied to bolts and lug nuts
- Vehicle dimensions
- Paint thickness and coverage
- Engine performance and emissions
- Integrity of welds
- Component alignment

This real-time IoT sensor data is collected and analyzed using statistical process control and machine learning algorithms to detect anomalies and minute defects during production without waiting for end-of-line testing.

For example, if torque gun sensors show that lug nuts on a wheel assembly are below the specified torque levels, an automated alert is triggered. The wheel can then be reworked immediately, rather than allowing the issue to persist, which would produce many defective vehicles in the meantime.

Similarly, gaps in paint coverage captured by optical sensors can adjust the painting process in real time to prevent quality issues down the line. By leveraging in-process quality data, Ford aims to build quality into the manufacturing process rather than just inspecting quality at the end. This IoT-enabled analytics approach allows *Ford* to detect and rectify quality issues rapidly during production rather than after many defective units have been built.

[1]Ford and Vodafone Harness Private 5G Networks to Continually Optimise Vehicle Manufacturing | Internet of Things. (2021). Internet of Things. https://www.gsma.com/iot/resources/5g-iot-manufacturing-ford-vodafone/

[2]Vodafone Business. (2022, Apr 22). Ford MPN [Video]. Vodafone Business. https://www.vodafone.com/business/news-and-insights/case-studies/5g-enabled-ev-manufacturing-ford-and-vodafone-create-the-car-factory-of-the-future

Case study 2

Hitachi[3] for quality data analysis. It provides IoT solutions to manufacturers that allow aggregating and analyzing vast amounts of sensor data from production equipment and processes. For example, in auto manufacturing plants, *Hitachi*'s IoT platform ingests terabytes of data daily from sensors tracking variables like equipment vibration, temperature, pressure, torque, etc.

This huge volume of **operational technology** (**OT**) data is converged with IT systems like ERP and CRM using *Hitachi*'s Edge Intelligence. The data is stored in a scalable cloud-based data lake using big data technologies like *Hadoop*. Machine learning algorithms are applied to this sensor data for quality analysis to identify trends, predict failures, and enable predictive equipment maintenance. This prevents production issues that impact quality and yield. The platform utilizes advanced analytics and quick data caching to support real-time quality monitoring. The manufacturing execution system is connected to adjust production in real-time based on quality analysis.

Hitachi designs the architecture using microservices and containers to enable agile changes to the system as new analytics use cases emerge. The fault-tolerant and distributed architecture provides the volume, variety, and velocity capabilities crucial for industrial big data platforms handling IoT data at scale. By providing robust, flexible, and scalable data management with integrated analytics, *Hitachi* enables manufacturers to maximize the value of IoT data for boosting quality and minimizing defects.

Case study 3

Philips applies AI to quality control sensor data to optimize semiconductor fabrication processes. *Philips* has deployed IoT and AI solutions [4]to improve quality control and yield for semiconductor manufacturers. In fabrication plants sensor data is captured from hundreds of production tools and metrology equipment to monitor parameters like temperature, pressure, vibration, flow rate, and so on.

This vast sensor data provides critical insights into equipment health and performance. However, detecting issues requires analyzing complex interactions between the many equipment sensors.

Philips applies machine learning algorithms to identify patterns and correlations between sensor data streams. By analyzing historical data, models can detect signatures indicative of process deviations. For example, a slight change in chamber pressure and gas flow rate, combined with increased vibrations, may indicate a pending valve failure. Finding these

---

[3] Hitachi, Ltd. (2018). IoT Platform Solution for Manufacturing that Connect the Manufacturing Site and Management through Data : Hitachi Review. Hitachi Review. https://www.hitachi.com/rev/archive/2018/r2018_02/12a06/index.html

[4] Manufacturing Quality Control | Philips Engineering Solutions. (2023, June 30). Philips Engineering Solutions. https://www.engineeringsolutions.philips.com/looking-expertise/design-for-reliability-solutions/manufacturing-quality-control/

interactions requires AI as they are not obvious to human analysts. These AI models run on the sensor data in real time to detect anomalies and predict potential process disruptions before they occur. This allows proactive maintenance and tuning before quality is impacted.

By leveraging AI for preventative actions, semiconductor fabs can improve yield by 6-10% while reducing scrap costs. This showcases how AI applied to quality control IoT data can optimize complex manufacturing environments.

Case study 4

Lockheed Martin uses sensors[5] on its F-35 fighter jets to stream real-time performance and health data [6]back to ground systems during flights. This includes data on:

- Engine/airframe temperatures
- Vibration
- Oil pressure
- Energy usage
- Structural integrity

This real-time IoT sensor data is critical for identifying maintenance needs and any anomalies impacting flight safety or availability.

Advanced machine learning algorithms analyze the data to detect patterns, trends, and outliers indicative of potential issues. This allows proactive identification and resolution of problems before any major failure or quality incident occurs.

Lockheed Marin highlights the role of:

- Real-time streaming of IoT sensor data from products in use
- Advanced analytics applied to the data to enable predictive maintenance and prevent quality problems
- Closing the feedback loop from products to drive ongoing product improvements and higher quality

This showcases how an IoT architecture can utilize analytics on real-time product sensor data to improve overall product quality and performance.

---

[5] F-35 – Fighter jet maintenance in the age of Data - Technology and Operations Management. (2016, November 17). Technology and Operations Management. https://d3.harvard.edu/platform-rctom/submission/f-35-fighter-jet-maintenance-in-the-age-of-data/

[6] Hebden, I., Crowley, A., & Black, W. (2018). Overview of the F-35 Structural Prognostics and Health Management system. 9th European Workshop on Structural Health Monitoring (EWSHM 2018), July 10-13, 2018 in Manchester, UK. e-Journal of Nondestructive Testing Vol. 23(11). https://www.ndt.net/?id=23392

Case study 5

The *Johnson & Johnson* example highlights the use of IoT and analytics [7]across the supply chain for proactive quality management.

J&J implements IoT sensors for temperature, humidity, and vibration monitoring across its upstream component suppliers, manufacturing plants, warehouses, and distribution. This allows capturing real-time data at each stage of production and distribution to identify potential anomalies that may impact product quality. Big data analytics examine the supply chain data [8]for trends, patterns, and early warning signs of issues that could occur downstream if not addressed early. If anomalies are detected, the root cause can be quickly identified through the sensor data trail, and corrective actions can be initiated to prevent larger quality problems in finished products.

This example illustrates the role of an IoT architecture in:

- Enabling end-to-end supply chain visibility through IoT sensor data integration.
- Applying advanced analytics across the aggregated supply chain data for predictive insights.
- Proactively identifying and addressing potential quality risks before product completion through data-driven insights.

Overall, it showcases how IoT architecture can connect the entire production ecosystem to drive preventative and proactive quality management across the value chain.

Case study 6

The *Bosch* example highlights the role of IoT and analytics for predictive maintenance that helps avoid quality issues.

Bosch equips its manufacturing equipment[9], like CNC machines and stamping presses, with sensors that monitor parameters like vibration, temperature, pressure, torque, and so on. This time-series IoT sensor data feeds into machine-learning models that detect patterns indicative of potential equipment failures or degradation. Identifying these issues proactively allows *Bosch* to schedule preventative maintenance and avoid unplanned

---

[7] Shapiro, M. (2021, November 18). How Johnson & Johnson's innovative supply chain technology is helping transform how we work—and live. https://www.jnj.com/innovation/how-johnson-johnsons-innovative-supply-chain-technology-is-helping-transform-how-we-work-and-live. https://www.jnj.com/innovation/how-johnson-johnsons-innovative-supply-chain-technology-is-helping-transform-how-we-work-and-live

[8] Bradbury, D. (2018, March 13). 3 ways Johnson & Johnson is harnessing digital innovation to better deliver medicine to you. https://www.jnj.com/innovation/3-digital-supply-chain-innovations-johnson-johnson-is-harnessing

[9] Kuever, N. (2023, February 28). Industry 4.0: Predictive maintenance use cases in detail. Bosch Digital Blog. https://blog.bosch-digital.com/industry-4-0-predictive-maintenance-use-cases-in-detail/

downtime of production assets. This ensures manufacturing processes continue uninterrupted, avoiding scraps and rework that hurt quality and throughput.

This example illustrates how an IoT architecture enables:

- Real-time streaming of sensor data from production equipment to provide insights into equipment health.
- Analytics and machine learning applied to the data to predict failures before they occur.
- Taking proactive actions through predictive maintenance recommendations.
- Maintaining production quality by preventing disruptions to processes and equipment downtime.

This showcases the role of IoT analytics for predictive maintenance and avoiding process disruptions that cause quality issues.

Case study 7

The example of *Honda* highlights how IoT data [10]and analytics can enable digital twin capabilities to optimize product design and quality.

Honda equips its cars with sensors that monitor performance parameters like engine emissions, fuel efficiency, ride handling, and so on. IoT connectivity streams this vehicle usage data back to *Honda*'s product development teams. *Honda* integrates this field data with design and simulation models to create a digital twin of each vehicle model. Engineers analyze the digital twin using data analytics and simulations to identify opportunities for improving quality, performance, and safety. Insights from the field data are used to refine and enhance the vehicle design for the next model year.

This example demonstrates how an IoT architecture:

- Facilitates collection of sensor data from products in the field.
- Enables integration of field data with design models to create living digital twins.
- Leverages analytics on the digital twin to optimize future product designs and enhance quality.
- Closes the loop from products back to R&D and manufacturing.

This allows companies to continuously improve product quality and performance by leveraging data from the field.

[10] Honda, M., & Honda, M. (2021, May 24). How IoT technology promises to boost success for Honda. IBM Blog. https://www.ibm.com/blog/iot-boosts-success-for-honda/

Case study 8

The example of *Schlumberger* highlights how IoT [11]analytics can improve quality in oil drilling operations.

Schlumberger instruments oil drilling equipment like rigs pumps with sensors that monitor parameters like vibration, pressure, torque, and temperature. IoT connectivity enables the streaming of this equipment data to central analytics systems. Advanced analytics on the time-series data identifies anomalies indicative of potential failures or suboptimal drilling performance. This allows preventative actions like shutting down or adjusting equipment to avoid major disruptions. Averting equipment issues results in higher-quality drilling operations by minimizing non-productive rig time and optimizing drilling precision.

This example shows how an IoT architecture:

- Connects instruments on drilling sites to provide rich data on equipment health.
- Applies analytics algorithms to detect issues proactively.
- Recommends actions to avoid disruptions, rework, and delays.
- Improves overall drilling quality through timely interventions enabled by data.

Thus, IoT analytics has a major role in driving quality in complex industrial environments like oil drilling.

Case study 9

The *Intel* example demonstrates how IoT[12] data and analytics can optimize semiconductor manufacturing quality:

Intel instruments its chip fabrication plants with sensors that monitor temperature, humidity, vibration, and air purity at different production stages. IoT connectivity streams this sensor data to analytics systems for real-time and historical analysis. Advanced analytics identifies correlations between production line variables and chip defect rates. Machine learning models help predict potential yield issues based on sensor data signatures. These insights are used to fine-tune manufacturing processes in real time to maintain quality and maximize yield.

This example highlights how an IoT architecture:

- Collects vast production line sensor data at scale.
- Applies analytics techniques like correlation analysis and machine learning prediction models to the data.

[11] Edge AI. (n.d.). https://www.software.slb.com/ai/edge-ai

[12] Joining IoT with Advanced Data Analytics to Improve Manufacturing Results. (2015, October). https://www.intel.com/content/dam/www/public/us/en/documents/white-papers/joining-iot-with-advanced-data-analytics-to-improve-manufacturing-results-paper.pdf

- Provides real-time and predictive visibility into process-quality interdependencies.
- Enables corrective actions to optimize processes and prevent quality issues proactively.

Thus, IoT analytics is key in boosting quality, reducing defects and variability for semiconductor manufacturers like *Intel*.

Case study 10

Siemens leverages IoT and analytics to create a closed-loop system [13]that automatically adjusts manufacturing equipment to maintain quality standards.

Sensors are added to machinery like stamping presses, CNC machines, plastic injection molding equipment, etc., to monitor critical variables like temperature, pressure, vibration, and energy use. This time-series sensor data is fed into analytical models defining the optimized operating thresholds and ranges for each machine based on the manufactured product. The analytics models detect deviations, trends, and anomalies indicating potential quality issues. For example, pressure exceeding a threshold could indicate a worn-out part. These analytical insights are automatically fed in real-time to the machine controllers to take corrective actions like adjusting pressure, speed, heat, and so on, to stay within quality limits. *Siemens MindSphere* IoT platform enables connectivity between sensors, controllers, and analytics models to complete this closed control loop from data to action.

By automatically adjusting operating parameters, *Siemens* prevents minor issues from escalating into larger quality problems. The closed-loop architecture continually maintains quality standards. This increases OEE while reducing scrap and rework.

Case study 11

PTC designed its IoT platform to integrate with new quality data sources and analytics easily.

PTC's ThingWorx platform[14] provides an agile IoT architecture that enables manufacturers to rapidly incorporate new data sources and analytics use cases as their quality management needs evolve. Some key capabilities that support this include:

- Drag-and-drop connectivity links new IoT sensors, devices, and sources to the platform through pre-built connectors.
- Allows quickly capturing emerging data like vibration, acoustics, etc.

---

13 IoT and Lifecycle Analytics for Heavy Equipment I Siemens Software. (n.d.). Siemens Digital Industries Software. **https://www.plm.automation.siemens.com/global/en/industries/heavy-equipment/iot-lifecycle-analytics.html**

14 ThingWorx from PTC is an Enterprise-ready IIoT Platform. (n.d.). **https://www.designtechproducts-ptc-iiot.com/thingworx-platform**

- Scalable data storage and management since new data sources exponentially increase volume.
- The platform allows storing this data efficiently on-premises or in the cloud.
- App composer to build role-specific dashboards to visualize new data and quality KPIs.
- Analytics Builder to bring own data science models. Data scientists can quickly deploy new ML algorithms to uncover insights from new data sets as needs arise.
- Out-of-the-box quality management capabilities like predictive maintenance, traceability, and rapid root cause analysis.
- Published APIs to connect with third-party quality systems. Can integrate legacy data sources and proprietary analytics modules into the architecture.

With these capabilities, manufacturers can dynamically adapt to changing quality data and analytical needs through reusable modules rather than custom coding. This agility and flexibility help maximize value from IoT for quality.

Case study 12

The *Steelcase* example illustrates how unstructured data analytics like computer vision and NLP can be integrated into an IoT architecture for quality management[15].

Steelcase deployed cameras on the manufacturing line to collect image data of finished products. This previously untapped data source provides valuable visual insights. NLP analytics are applied to unstructured text data from customer call logs and social media to identify reported quality issues. AI techniques like deep learning and natural language processing enable these new image and text data sources. The unstructured data is analyzed alongside IoT sensor data from production equipment to get a holistic quality view. Issues identified from images or customer feedback are fed back to control systems to adjust processes and improve quality in a closed loop.

The *Steelcase* example showcases how integrating computer vision and NLP expands the capability of a quality focused IoT architecture to leverage new data sources. This provides a more complete picture to drive decisions and actions.

The architecture must enable easy integration of AI models on emerging data streams for continuous improvement. This highlights the importance of flexibility as a key requirement.

[15] Steelcase. (2018, June 11). Choice is the new Black. Steelcase. **https://www.steelcase.com/research/articles/topics/design/choice-new-black/**

Robotics in manufacturing

Robotics in manufacturing refers to the integration of autonomous machines and computer systems into industrial processes, enhancing efficiency, precision, and flexibility. These robots can perform a wide range of tasks, from assembly and welding to quality control and material handling. By automating repetitive and labor-intensive operations, robotics minimizes errors, reduces production time, and optimizes resource utilization. This technology revolutionizes modern manufacturing by improving productivity and product quality, reducing costs, and enabling manufacturers to adapt quickly to changing market demands.

Innovation and automation with robotics

Robotic technology has become a part of the manufacturing industry significantly enhancing productivity, efficiency, and overall processes. With the advent of innovation and automation, manufacturing companies are swiftly embracing technologies to elevate industry standards and revolutionize production methods. The incorporation of robots enables businesses to accelerate their manufacturing capabilities, granting them an advantage in today's market.

There are reasons why robots have found their place in the business world. Firstly, robots exhibit productivity and efficiency due to their ability to work tirelessly without breaks. Consequently, production remains uninterrupted while output increases significantly. This contributes to cost reduction and shorter work cycles enabling businesses to meet market demands. Robots excel in tasks that require precision and efficiency beyond capability, such as welding, and assembly operations.

Moreover, robots perform a role in ensuring safety, particularly in hazardous environments where individuals may be exposed to dangerous substances or machinery. By assigning hazardous tasks to robots, manufacturers can free up their workforce to concentrate on more complex and creative aspects of production. This not only fuels motivation, among individuals but also reduces the likelihood of errors. Moreover, incorporating robotics into business operations provides an advantage by allowing processes cost-cutting measures and offering competitive pricing for goods. This aids in maintaining a market position.

Figure 2.14 illustrates the integration of robotics, IoT, and cloud computing in manufacturing, showcasing the synergy among these technologies in modern industrial processes:

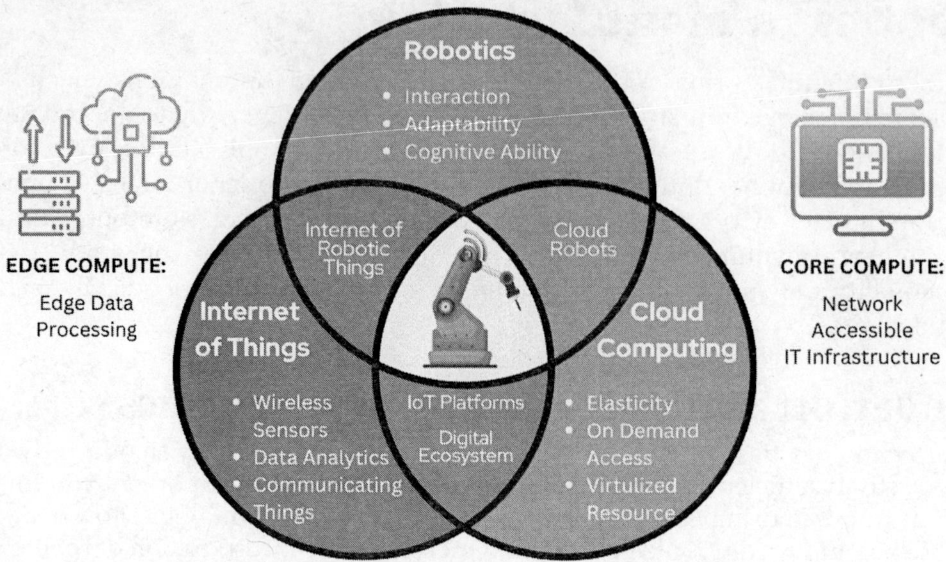

Figure 2.14: *Integration of robotics, IoT, and cloud computing in manufacturing*

The increasing complexity of products necessitates the utilization of robotics in manufacturing. As consumer demands evolve, industries are compelled to produce products with assembly requirements. Robots are well suited to handle tasks ensuring consistent quality and precision. They are crucial for meeting customer expectations and complying with regulations. Furthermore, integrating robots enables manufacturing companies to operate round the clock. Unlike humans who are limited by working hours and fatigue, robots can work tirelessly without compromising productivity or quality. This capability proves valuable in meeting deadlines and fulfilling customer orders promptly.

Robots have become indispensable in the manufacturing industry due to their ability to enhance productivity, accuracy, and workplace safety. They excel at performing repetitive tasks enabling workers to focus on more intricate and innovative aspects of production. Robots offer manufacturers a way to gain an edge, enhance the quality of their products, and streamline their operations, leading to cost savings and increased productivity. With advancements in technology, it is undeniable that robots will play a significant role in manufacturing, bringing about revolutionary changes in various industries, and shaping the future of this sector.

History and evolution of robotics in manufacturing

Robotics in manufacturing has its roots in the 20th century, yet the concept of task automation is older. One notable example is *Joseph Marie Jacquard*'s automated loom, developed in the 1800s. However, it was not until the middle of the century that we started witnessing advancements in robotics:

- **1950s 1960s:** The birth of robotics can be attributed to *George Devol* and *Joseph Engelberger*'s creation of *Unimate*, the digitally operated and programmable robot in the early 1960s. Unimate revolutionized automation within the automotive sector marking a new era for industrial robotics.
- **1970s 1980s:** This period witnessed growth and diversification within the robotics industry. Robots became more sophisticated, capable of handling loads and performing tasks with greater precision. Various industries like electronics, food processing, and pharmaceuticals embraced automation.
- **1990s 2000s:** Further enhancements in capabilities were driven by sensors, computer vision technology, and AI. Robots became more adaptable by working alongside operators in settings known as **cobots**.
- **Present day:** In today's world, manufacturing has embraced cutting-edge systems with AI, machine learning, and natural language processing.

These advancements empower robots to carry out tasks, learn from their experiences, and adjust to changing environments.

Increased robotics integration in manufacturing

The integration of robotics in manufacturing has been driven by several key factors:

- **Labor costs and availability:** In many developed countries, labor costs have been rising, making automated solutions more attractive for cost-effective production. Additionally, industries often face challenges finding skilled labor for specific manufacturing tasks, making robots a viable alternative.
- **Competitive advantage:** Companies that embrace robotics can gain a competitive edge by achieving higher productivity and quality standards. Automation allows businesses to meet market demands more efficiently and deliver products at a competitive price point.
- **Consistency and quality:** Robots can carry out jobs with a level of consistency and precision that leads to an increase in product quality and a decrease in defects. This is of utmost significance in fields where even minute differences can have a significant effect on the functionality or security of the finished product.
- **Occupational health and safety:** Manufacturing processes often involve hazardous tasks that pose risks to human workers. By automating these tasks with robots, companies can protect their employees' well-being and minimize workplace accidents.
- **Increasing complexity of products:** Modern manufacturing demands intricate assembly processes for complex products. Robots are well-suited for handling such precision tasks that may be challenging for human workers to execute consistently.

- **24/7 operations**: Robots can operate continuously without the need for breaks, allowing for round-the-clock production to meet tight deadlines and customer demands.

The role of robotics in modern manufacturing processes has evolved significantly over the years, from early robotic arms to sophisticated autonomous systems. The increasing integration of robotics in manufacturing is driven by a desire for increased productivity, efficiency, precision, and safety, providing numerous benefits to companies and workers alike. As technology continues to advance, the role of robotics in manufacturing is likely to expand further, revolutionizing industries and paving the way for a more automated and efficient future.

IoT-robotics synergy: Ensuring precision and safety

IoT-robotics synergy refers to the collaboration between IoT and robotics in a factory environment. The IoT involves the interconnectedness and communication among computing devices, sensors, and equipment. When applied to robotics in manufacturing, it enables improvements in accuracy, efficiency, and security. In the manufacturing sector, the combination of IoT and robotics plays a role in ensuring production processes. Real-time monitoring by distributed sensors allows for the observation of essential parameters. This information is then related to robots which can take actions accordingly. In areas like microelectronics, medical devices, and aerospace components where precision is vital this integration guarantees assembly while minimizing errors.

Moreover, the integration of IoT and robotics also enhances safety in factories where both humans and machines operate. By placing sensors within the IoT network, temperature variations, gas leaks or equipment malfunctions can be detected immediately. When combined with systems, this data triggers prompt solutions to address safety concerns. Robots equipped with such capabilities can identify risks like chemical leaks and promptly respond by halting their operations and facilitating evacuation of the area (if necessary) while alerting human workers. Overall, leveraging the synergy between IoT and robotics brings benefits to manufacturing settings, From accuracy in production processes to enhanced workplace security for all employees involved.

Some successful applications of robotics include:

- **Collaborative robotics:** Cobots, also known as **collaborative robots**, have brought a big change to manufacturing. They work alongside humans to help them with tasks. Due to this innovation, companies can put robots near workers without safety concerns, making their processes more flexible and agile. Cobots complement human abilities and streamline processes by aiding in activities like assembly, pick-and-place, and quality inspection.

- **Artificial intelligence and machine learning:** A new era of intelligent automation has begun in the manufacturing sector with the combination of AI and ML with robotics. Robots with AI and ML skills can change their behavior in response to new information, improve their efficiency as they work, and learn from their mistakes. This breakthrough paves the way for robots to accurately perform difficult jobs, adapt to novel settings, and optimize their performance over time. Predictive maintenance is another AI-driven robotics feature that helps minimize downtime and maximize production availability.

- **Autonomous mobile robots (AMR):** Another revolutionary development in manufacturing automation is the use of AMRs. Without fixed conveyors or tracks, these self-navigating robots can move freely over the factory floor, bringing supplies to and from various stations. As manufacturing needs shift, AMRs can be rapidly reorganized to meet them. This new method streamlines logistics and material processing, which increases productivity and decreases the need for human labor.

- **Robotic vision and sensing:** Improved robot vision and sensing technology have allowed them to take on more complex tasks in the factory. Robots with vision systems have the ability to detect and localize objects, inspect products for defects, and carry out other sophisticated activities that benefit from visual feedback. In addition, sophisticated sensing technologies enable robots to monitor their surroundings for anomalies and adjust accordingly, leading to risk-free and productive operations. The use of vision-guided robotics has allowed for error-free, more consistent product assembly, packing, and inspection.

- **Digital twin and simulation:** The use of digital twins and simulation software has significantly impacted the development and deployment of robotic automation in the manufacturing sector. Manufacturers can model and optimize robot operations in advance of real deployment with the help of digital twin technology, which generates a digital counterpart of the physical production environment. This advancement reduces the potential for mistakes and boosts the effectiveness of robotic systems. In a virtual setting, manufacturers can try various robotic setups, workflows, and scenarios with little to no risk, resulting in a more efficient and timelier rollout.

- **Cloud robots:** In manufacturing, cloud robotics is a game-changing development since it makes use of cloud computing to expand the capabilities of robots. Manufacturers can have access to a plethora of computational resources, real-time data analytics, and AI algorithms by linking their robots to cloud-based platforms. Through the use of cloud robotics, several robots and factories may be remotely monitored, their data shared, and they can learn together. This breakthrough improves the efficiency of software upgrades, strengthens the safety of data, and allows robots to be seamlessly integrated into the IIoT network.

IoT for robot maintenance and troubleshooting

Robots can help with machine maintenance and fixing problems when they have smart design and automation. By using IoT and AI, robots can keep an eye on industrial equipment, find problems, and fix them before they happen. This means uptime is better, downtime is shorter, and maintenance methods are better. Here is how robots can fix problems and keep machines running:

- **Architecture for robot-led machine maintenance and troubleshooting**

  Refer to the following figure:

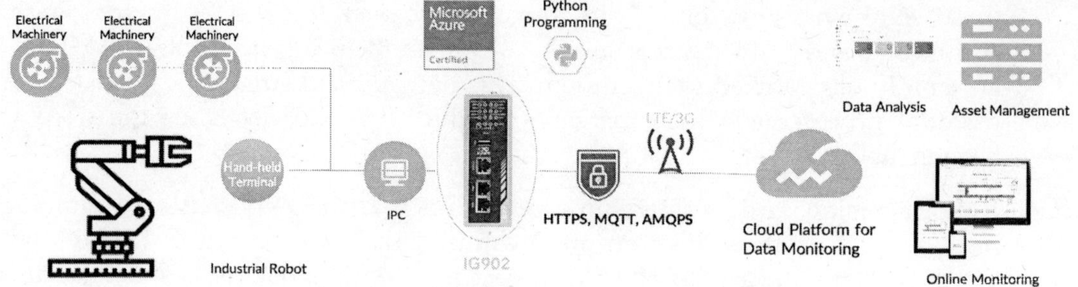

Figure 2.15: Example of industrial robot-led maintenance

  - **IoT sensors and connectivity:** Manufacturing equipment is equipped with IoT sensors that continuously monitor various parameters such as temperature, vibration, pressure, and performance metrics. These sensors collect real-time data and transmit it to a central system or the cloud for analysis.
  - **Data analytics and AI:** The collected data is processed using AI algorithms. AI systems can identify patterns, trends, and anomalies in the data to detect potential issues or deviations from normal operation.
  - **Predictive maintenance models:** With the help of AI and ML powered predictive maintenance models, robots can forecast when machine components might require maintenance or replacement. This allows for proactive planning and scheduling of maintenance tasks, minimizing the risk of unexpected breakdowns.
  - **Robot-embedded maintenance systems:** Some robots are specifically designed with maintenance capabilities, equipped with tools and sensors that enable them to access and service machine components. These maintenance robots can perform tasks like lubrication, cleaning, and minor repairs.
  - **Remote access and control:** Robots can be remotely controlled by maintenance personnel or AI systems, allowing them to access hard-to-reach areas within machines for inspections and repairs. This eliminates the need for human technicians to intervene in hazardous or complex maintenance scenarios physically.

- **Manufacturing use case: Robot-led conveyor belt maintenance**

  To keep production running smoothly and prevent unscheduled downtime in a factory that relies largely on conveyor belts for material handling, regular machine maintenance is essential. Maintenance and troubleshooting of conveyor belts can be handled by robots in the following ways:

  - **Continuous monitoring:** IoT sensors are installed along the conveyor belt to monitor various parameters, such as belt tension, temperature, and speed. The sensors constantly transmit data to a centralized monitoring system.
  - **AI-based anomaly detection:** The AI system analyzes the sensor data to establish patterns of normal conveyor belt operation. When deviations or anomalies are detected, the AI system can raise alerts, signaling the need for maintenance.
  - **Predictive maintenance planning:** Using the data gathered over time, the AI system can develop predictive maintenance models that forecast potential failures or component wear. Maintenance schedules are then optimized to address issues before they escalate.
  - **Robot-embedded maintenance:** Maintenance robots, equipped with tools and sensors, are deployed for regular inspections and routine tasks. These robots can check for belt alignment, adjust tension, and identify signs of wear and tear.
  - **Remote troubleshooting:** In the event of a conveyor belt malfunction, maintenance personnel can remotely control robots to access the affected areas. The robots can provide real-time visuals and data to aid in troubleshooting and decision-making.
  - **Data-driven maintenance decisions:** The data collected from robot-led maintenance activities is continuously fed back into the AI system. Over time, the AI system learns from the data, improving its predictive capabilities and refining maintenance strategies.

  In this manufacturing use case, robots equipped with IoT, AI, and maintenance capabilities offer a proactive approach to machine maintenance and troubleshooting. They ensure the smooth functioning of critical machinery, reduce costly downtime, and optimize the maintenance process, ultimately leading to increased operational efficiency and productivity in the manufacturing facility.

Case study: Robotic solutions powered by IoT

To ensure patient safety and successful medical treatments, surgical sutures must be manufactured with precision, accuracy, and the utmost attention to quality. A medical device manufacturer intended to adopt collaborative robotic workstations is enabled by the IoT to overcome these difficulties and improve the efficiency of suture manufacturing. This case study describes the company's dilemma, the solution developed using collaborative robotics and IoT integration, and the transformative benefits obtained.

Problem

During the traditional suture manufacturing process, the medical device manufacturer encountered various obstacles. Human employees performed delicate jobs that required precision stitching on the manual production line, which was labor-intensive. This could lead to discrepancies in quality, higher production time, and a significant risk of repetitive strain injuries for the trained personnel. To satisfy the increased demand for sutures while maintaining the highest quality standards, the company saw the need for a more efficient and safe manufacturing process.

Solution

To revamp its suture manufacturing process, the company opted to adopt collaborative robotic workstations driven by the IoT. The collaborative robots, or cobots, were chosen for their ability to work safely and seamlessly alongside human operators, complimenting their talents and increasing total efficiency. *Figure 2.16* provides a visual comparison between **Manual Assembly** and **Human-Robot Collaborative Assembly**, illustrating the advantages and features of the robotic solution.[16]

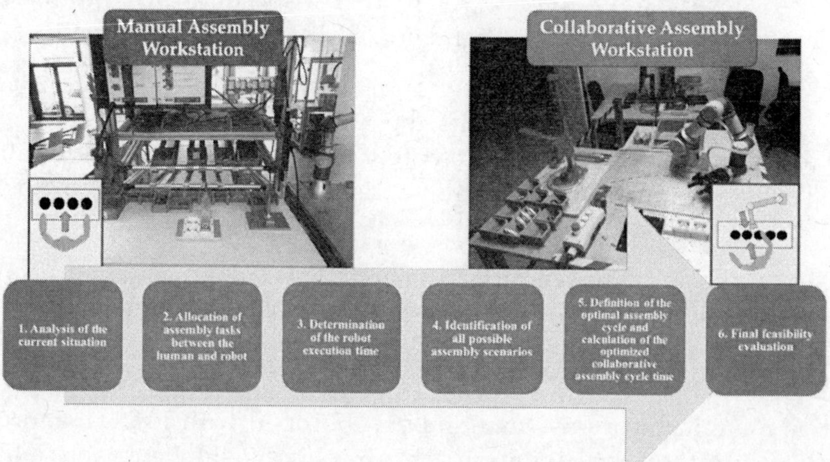

***Figure 2.16:** Manual assembly versus collaborative assembly robotic solution*

The key implementation strategies for the robotic manufacturing systems are as follows:

1. **Integrate IoT sensors:** Each workstation was outfitted with IoT sensors to monitor a variety of important factors such as thread tension, needle alignment, and suture

[16] Gualtieri, Luca & Rauch, Erwin & Vidoni, Renato. (2021). Methodology for the definition of the optimal assembly cycle and calculation of the optimized assembly cycle time in human-robot collaborative assembly. The International Journal of Advanced Manufacturing Technology. 113. 10.1007/s00170-021-06653-y

length. These sensors collected data on the production process in real-time, offering significant insights about stitching quality and spotting any potential deviations or errors.

2. **Virtual simulation and concept validation:** Prior to practical deployment, the company used virtual simulation and proof of concept to optimize the design and programming of the robotic workstations. The simulation made iterative testing feasible. This assurance enabled the cobots to execute highly precise stitching patterns with exceptional accuracy and efficiency.

3. **Collaborative robotic workstations:** The collaborative robotic workstations were carefully placed along the assembly line to ensure seamless integration with human workers. Each cobot was outfitted with superior vision systems and force-sensing technology in order to collaborate without endangering human operators.

4. **Collaboration between humans and robots:** IoT-powered connectivity enabled flawless cobot-human interaction. It facilitated real-time stitching quality monitoring and adjustments. Enhanced collaboration maintained consistent stitching quality in production. IoT data provided real-time stitching quality monitoring and analysis, allowing human operators to make informed judgments and intervene as needed. The cobots were able to respond to changes in thread tension and maintain uniform stitch patterns throughout the manufacturing process.

5. **Constant monitoring and maintenance:** The use of IoT in collaborative robotic workstations enabled continuous monitoring of the system's health and performance. Predictive maintenance models were used to detect possible problems before they caused downtime or quality flaws.

This proactive approach assured continuous production while reducing unanticipated maintenance expenses. The use of collaborative robotic workstations powered by IoT produced dramatic results for the suture manufacturing process:

- **Increased productivity:** The precision and efficiency of the cobots' stitching skills resulted in a considerable increase in suture production output, satisfying expanding market needs without sacrificing quality.

- **Improved quality and consistency:** The use of IoT sensors and real-time data processing provided consistent and high-quality sutures, lowering faults and enhancing patient safety.

- **Worker safety:** By implementing collaborative robots, the organization reduced the danger of repetitive strain injuries while also improving overall worker safety in the production process.

- **Savings:** The simplified production process, fewer defects, and predictive maintenance resulted in cost savings, allowing the company's operational expenses to be optimized.

- **Competitive advantage:** The medical device company achieved a competitive advantage in the industry by implementing cutting-edge technology, promoting itself as an innovative and dependable producer of surgical sutures.

The successful integration of collaborative robotic workstations driven by IoT in suture manufacturing shows the capacity of automation and smart technologies to transform traditional manufacturing processes. The use of collaborative robots in conjunction with IoT sensor integration not only enhanced production and product quality but also prioritized worker safety and overall operational efficiency. This case study demonstrates the transformative influence of advanced robotics and IoT technologies in the medical device industry, paving the path for further improvements in factory automation.

Conclusion

The IoT transforms modern manufacturing through enhanced connectivity, automation, and data-driven insights. By harnessing networks of intelligent, interconnected devices and systems, manufacturers can achieve new levels of speed, precision, and efficiency across their operations. From real-time monitoring to predictive maintenance, optimized production planning, improved quality control, and supply chain coordination, IoT delivers tangible benefits across the manufacturing value chain.

However, to fully leverage the potential of IoT, manufacturers need to focus on critical aspects such as security, infrastructure readiness, data analytics capabilities, and change management. Overall, IoT represents the future of smart, interconnected manufacturing.

By embracing IoT's capabilities for real-time control, visualization, and intelligence across processes, manufacturers can gain substantial competitive advantage through increased productivity, flexibility, and responsiveness to market dynamics. Though adopting IoT necessitates strategic planning and investment, the long-term rewards make the effort worthwhile. With IoT, manufacturers can transform legacy factories into agile, efficient, and truly smart production facilities ready to excel in the 21st-century digital economy.

The next chapter will delve deeper into the transformative potential of IoT in supply chain management. We will continue to explore how IoT sensors, data processing, and blockchain technology are reshaping inventory planning, replenishment, delivery tracking, and asset monitoring, ultimately leading to more efficient and transparent supply chain operations.

Points to remember

- IoT refers to a network of interconnected physical objects and devices that can collect and share data through embedded sensors and software. IoT enables automation, monitoring, and data analytics in manufacturing.
- The key components of an IoT system architecture include sensors, controllers, cloud platforms, data analytics tools, and communication protocols like MQTT

and CoAP. Sensors collect data, controllers process it, while the cloud provides storage and computing capabilities.

- IoT allows real-time monitoring and predictive maintenance in manufacturing plants by analyzing data from sensors on equipment to forecast failures before they occur. This prevents downtime and optimizes maintenance.
- IoT improves production planning and scheduling by providing real-time visibility into inventory, orders, machine performance, and other factors, enabling dynamic adjustments to maximize output.
- IoT enhances quality control by collecting sensor data inline during production to identify defects rapidly using analytics. This facilitates corrective actions before defects multiply.
- IoT gives wide visibility to supply chains by connecting assets, inventory, shipments, and other elements to provide real-time tracking and coordination between partners.
- IoT data analytics, including predictive modeling and machine learning, help identify inefficiencies, trends, and opportunities to optimize manufacturing and supply chain performance.
- Key challenges in adopting IoT include concerns around data security, infrastructure readiness, network bandwidth, system integration, and managing cultural change.
- Critical security measures for IoT include data encryption, access controls, device authentication, network segmentation, security monitoring, and regular audits.
- The long-term benefits of IoT in manufacturing include increased speed, flexibility, accuracy, and responsiveness across integrated, intelligent, and highly automated operations.

Multiple choice questions

1. **Which of the following is *not* a component of an IoT system architecture?**
   a. Sensors
   b. Cloud platforms
   c. Actuators
   d. Blockchain ledgers
2. **What provides short-range wireless communication between IoT devices?**
   a. Wi-Fi
   b. Bluetooth
   c. LTE
   d. LoRaWAN

3. **Which protocol enables lightweight machine-to-machine communication for IoT?**
   a. MQTT
   b. OPC UA
   c. AMQP
   d. HTTP
4. **How does IoT enable predictive maintenance in manufacturing?**
   a. By reacting to equipment failures
   b. By collecting and analyzing sensor data to forecast issues
   c. By using predetermined maintenance schedules
   d. By performing hourly equipment inspections
5. **What does edge computing provide in an IoT architecture?**
   a. Centralized data storage
   b. Cloud computing capabilities
   c. Localized real-time data processing
   d. Long-range connectivity
6. **Which technology enables unique identification and tracking of products in an IoT system?**
   a. GPS
   b. RFID
   c. Robotics
   d. PLCs
7. **Which analytics method can IoT sensor data help support for quality control?**
   a. Descriptive analytics
   b. Prescriptive analytics
   c. Diagnostic analytics
   d. All of the above
8. **How can IoT improve coordination in supply chain operations?**
   a. By automating production lines
   b. By enabling real-time visibility and information sharing

c. By robotizing warehouses

d. By 3D printing spare parts

9. What data security risk can IoT systems be vulnerable to?

a. Data theft

b. Power outages

c. Device malfunction

d. Data encryption

10. What long-term impact will IoT have on manufacturing operations?

a. Increased role of cobots

b. Need for advanced IT skills

c. Lower costs due to automation

d. Highly interconnected and intelligent processes

Answer key

1. d.
2. b.
3. a.
4. b.
5. c.
6. b.
7. d.
8. b.
9. a.
10. d.

Questions

1. What is the IoT, and how is it impacting manufacturing operations?
2. Describe the key components of an IoT architecture. What role does each component play?

3. What are some common IoT communication protocols and what are their applications?
4. How can IoT enable predictive maintenance and reduce equipment downtime in factories?
5. What manufacturing processes can be optimized using IoT data analytics? Give examples.
6. How does IoT improve production planning and scheduling in dynamic environments?
7. How can IoT enhance quality control and bring waste reduction in manufacturing?
8. What are the benefits of IoT for supply chain visibility and coordination?
9. What are some key challenges faced in implementing IoT solutions? How can they be addressed?
10. Why is data security critical for IoT systems? What measures can enhance it?
11. How can manufacturers integrate IoT solutions with existing legacy systems?
12. What impact will robotics and automation have in the future of smart manufacturing powered by IoT?
13. How can digital twin simulation assist in the design and deployment of IoT systems?
14. What skills are required to effectively implement and manage IoT projects?
15. How do you foresee manufacturing operations evolving in the next 5-10 years under the influence of IoT?

Key terms

- **Supervisory control and data acquisition:** Systems used to monitor and control industrial processes remotely.
- **Open Platform Communications Unified Architecture:** An industrial M2M communication protocol for interoperability.
- **Manufacturing execution system:** Software systems used to track and document manufacturing processes.
- **Enterprise resource planning:** Software tools that integrate business processes and data flows.
- **Cyber-physical systems:** Networked monitoring and control systems with integrated physical and computational components.

- **Data mining:** The process of analyzing large data sets to identify patterns for actionable insights.
- **Machine learning:** AI algorithms that can learn from data to make predictions without explicit programming.
- **Computer vision:** Technology that seeks to automate analysis of visual data using AI and deep learning.
- **Digital thread:** The flow of data through product lifecycle stages enabled by connected IT systems.
- **Radio frequency identification:** Technology that uses radio waves for contactless identification and tracking of objects.

Join our book's Discord space

Join the book's Discord Workspace for Latest updates, Offers, Tech happenings around the world, New Release and Sessions with the Authors:

https://discord.bpbonline.com

Chapter 3
The Power of IoT in Supply Chain

Introduction

The **Internet of Things** (**IoT**) wields immense power in supply chain management. By connecting devices and sensors throughout the supply chain network, IoT provides real-time visibility into the movement and condition of goods. This enhanced visibility enables businesses to optimize inventory levels, reduce waste, and improve efficiency.

IoT also empowers businesses to make data-driven decisions about their supply chains. By analyzing data collected from IoT devices, businesses can gain insights into customer demand, identify potential disruptions, and optimize transportation routes. This data-driven approach to supply chain management can lead to significant improvements in profitability and customer satisfaction.

Structure

This chapter will cover the following topics:

- Overview
- Demand forecasting
    - IoT-based demand forecasting
    - Analyzing real-time data for accurate forecasts

  - IoT and AI for predictive demand forecasting
  - Case studies
- Inventory management
  - Challenge of inventory management
  - IoT in real-time inventory management
  - IoT and predictive analysis
  - Case study: IoT for inventory management
- Intelligent logistics: Enhancing delivery with IoT
  - Redefining logistics with IoT
  - Real-time tracking: Role of IoT in transit visibility
  - Enhancing fleet management with IoT
- Smart warehousing with IoT
  - Concept of a smart warehouse
  - IoT devices in warehousing: RFID, sensors, and more
  - Impact of IoT on warehouse operations
  - Case study: IoT-driven warehouse
- Reverse logistics with IoT
  - Current challenges with reverse logistics
  - IoT improvements in reverse logistics
  - Reverse logistics and forward logistics
  - Future of reverse logistics

Objectives

The chapter is intended to demonstrate current challenges in the supply chain without real-time data. It will educate readers about the scale and impact of the problem the industry is facing. In the subsequent sections, the chapter will provide an overview of real-time data benefits in the supply chain. The case studies of some of the successful companies are also discussed further.

Overview

The supply chain is satisfying demand with supply as soon as possible. Any mismatch in demand and supply causes a disruption.

Here are some of the problems that businesses face in the supply chain, including:

- **Uncertainty:** The global supply chain is increasingly complex and interconnected, making it difficult to predict disruptions. This can lead to delays, shortages, and higher costs.
- **Costs:** The cost of shipping and logistics has been rising in recent years. This is due to several factors, including rising fuel prices and increased regulation.
- **Complexity:** The global supply chain is becoming increasingly complex, with more suppliers and partners involved in the process. This can make it difficult to manage and track inventory and shipments.
- **Risk:** The global supply chain is exposed to several risks, including natural disasters, political instability, and cyberattacks. These risks can lead to disruptions and financial losses.

These problems are having a significant impact on businesses. They lead to higher costs, delays, and disruptions, making it difficult for businesses to compete and meet customer demands.

Here are some of the problems that Apple would face if their supply chain is disrupted:

- **Apple**
    - **Shortages of components:** Apple relies on a complex network of suppliers to produce its products. If any of these suppliers are disrupted, it could lead to shortages of components and delays in production.
    - **Increased costs:** Disruptions in the supply chain can lead to increased costs for Apple. This is because Apple may have to pay higher prices for components or delay its production, which would lead to lost revenue.
    - **Damage to brand reputation:** If Apple is unable to meet customer demand due to supply chain disruptions, it could damage its brand reputation. Customers may be disappointed if they cannot access the latest Apple products.

Here are some high-level numbers to show the severity of these problems:

- The average cost of a supply chain disruption is **$600 million**.[1]
- The average company spends **10%** of its revenue on logistics.[2]
- The global supply chain is exposed to over **200 risks**.[3]

[1] Supply Chain Risk and Resilience: **https://www.oliverwyman.com/our-expertise/capabilities/operations/supply-chain/risk-assessment-and-resilience-in-supply-chains.html**

[2] The Logistics and Supply Chain 2025 Report, Capgemini Research Institute, 2020: **https://prod.ucwe.capgemini.com/wp-content/uploads/2022/12/Report-Intelligent-Supply-Chain.pdf**

[3] Supply Chain Risk Management: A Guide to Identifying, Assessing, and Mitigating Risks, BSI Group, 2021: **https://www.bsigroup.com/LocalFiles/en-US/Brochures/Supply%20Chain/Managing%20Risk%20in%20the%20Global%20Supply%20Chain.pdf**

Supply chain disruptions can have a significant impact on businesses of all sizes. By understanding the potential risks and taking steps to mitigate them, businesses can reduce the likelihood of disruptions and protect their bottom line.

The root cause of these problems could be pointing to flaws in any of the following:

- Demand forecasting
- Inventory management
- Intelligent logistics
- Smart warehousing
- Reverse logistics

Let us look at each of them and IoT solutions that can mitigate these challenges in the next sections of this chapter.

Demand forecasting

Demand forecasting is a critical step in supply planning activities. Any inaccuracy may lead to a major impact to the business. The impact could be in excess and obsolescence or in the form of loss of revenue. The next sections provide details about how IoT can transform demand forecasting.

IoT based demand forecasting

Demand forecasting is a signal that drives the entire supply chain. This signal answers two main questions: *How much* and *when*.

For example, an iPhone demand planner might project camera modules required for the next iPhone devices. The planner needs to forecast the quantity of every module (camera, mainboard, display, and so on) and generate weekly or monthly demand for them. This demand signal will drive Apple's internal teams such as operations, manufacturing, logistics, warehousing, reverse logistics (AppleCare). Also, this will drive external teams such as camera supplier(s) and their suppliers, logistics partners, distributors, and so on.

The top challenges in demand forecasting are given as follows:

- **Inaccuracy:** Demand forecasting without real-time data can be inaccurate because it is based on historical data, which may not be representative of current or future demand. This can lead to stockouts, resulting in lost sales and customer dissatisfaction.
- **Waste:** Demand forecasting without real-time data can lead to waste because of overstocking or understocking. Overstocking can lead to inventory costs, while understocking can lead to lost sales.

- **Inflexibility:** Demand forecasting without real-time data can be inflexible because it is difficult to change forecasts once made. This can make it difficult to respond to changes in demand, leading to lost sales and customer dissatisfaction.

IoT can help to solve these challenges by providing real-time data about demand. This data can improve the accuracy of demand forecasts, which can lead to reduced stockouts, waste, and inflexibility.

Here are some specific examples of how IoT can be used to improve demand forecasting:

- **Retail:** IoT sensors can be used to track customer foot traffic to forecast demand for products.
- **Manufacturing:** IoT sensors can be used to track the production process to forecast demand for raw materials.
- **Logistics:** IoT sensors can be used to track the movement of goods to forecast demand for transportation services.

By using IoT to collect real-time data about demand, businesses can improve the accuracy of their demand forecasts and make better decisions about inventory, production, and logistics. This can lead to increased sales, reduced costs, and improved customer satisfaction.

Here are some additional benefits of using IoT for demand forecasting:

- **Improved customer experience:** By using IoT to improve demand forecasting, businesses can ensure that they have the right amount of inventory on hand to meet customer demand. This can lead to a better customer experience and increased customer satisfaction.
- **Reduced costs:** By using IoT to improve demand forecasting, businesses can reduce costs associated with inventory, production, and logistics. This can lead to increased profits.
- **Increased agility:** By using IoT to improve demand forecasting, businesses can be more agile and responsive to changes in demand. This can help companies seize new opportunities and avoid risks.

Overall, IoT is a powerful tool that can be used to improve demand forecasting. By using IoT to collect real-time data about demand, businesses can make better decisions about inventory, production, and logistics. This can lead to increased sales, reduced costs, and improved customer satisfaction.

Analyzing real-time data for accurate forecasts

There are several general demands forecast inputs in industries, including:

- **Historical sales data:** This is the most important input for demand forecasting. It can be used to identify trends and patterns in sales.

- **Seasonal factors: Fast moving consumer goods** (**FMCG**) products are often subject to seasonal demand. For example, ice cream sales are typically higher in summer than in winter.
- **Competitor activity:** FMCG companies need to be aware of their competitors' activities when forecasting demand. This includes new product launches, price changes, and marketing campaigns.
- **Economic factors:** Economic factors can also impact demand for FMCG products. For example, a recession can led to lower demand for non-essential products.
- **Consumer behavior:** FMCG companies need to understand consumer behavior when forecasting demand. This includes factors such as demographics, lifestyle, and preferences.

By taking these factors into account, FMCG companies can develop more accurate demand forecasts. This can help them to ensure that they have the right amount of inventory on hand to meet demand and avoid stockouts.

Here are some additional inputs that can be used for demand forecasting in FMCG industries:

- **Weather data:** Weather data can be used to forecast demand for products that are sensitive to the weather, such as ice cream and snow shovels.
- **Social media data:** Social media data can be used to track customer sentiments and to identify trends in demand.
- **Market research data:** Market research data can be used to gather information about customer behavior, preferences, and demographics.
- **Expert opinions:** Expert opinions can be used to get insights into factors likely to impact demand.

By using a variety of inputs, FMCG companies can develop more accurate demand forecasts. This can help them to make better decisions about production, inventory, and marketing.

Here are some examples from multiple industries where real-time data from IoT can help predict demand, sales, and response to a product:

- **Retail:** Real-time data from IoT sensors in retail stores can be used to track customer behavior, such as how long they spend in a store, what products they view, and what products they purchase. This data can be used to predict demand for products and to optimize inventory levels.
- **Manufacturing:** Real-time data from IoT sensors in manufacturing plants can be used to track the production process, such as the speed of production, quality of products, and efficiency of machines. This data can be used to predict demand for

products, to identify potential problems in the production process, and to improve efficiency.

- **Transportation**: Real-time data from IoT sensors in transportation vehicles can be used to track the location of vehicles, speed of vehicles, and fuel consumption of vehicles. This data can be used to predict demand for transportation services, to optimize routes, and to reduce fuel costs.
- **Healthcare:** Real-time data from IoT sensors in healthcare devices, such as pacemakers and insulin pumps, can be used to track patient health, such as heart rate, blood sugar levels, and body temperature. This data can be used to predict potential health problems, to provide better care for patients, and to reduce costs.
- **Energy:** Real-time data from IoT sensors in energy grids can be used to track energy usage, such as the amount of electricity used and the energy source. This data can be used to predict energy demand, optimize energy usage, and reduce costs.

IoT and AI for predictive demand forecasting

Here are some ways how IoT and AI can be leveraged for predictive demand forecasting:

- IoT sensors can be used to collect real-time data about customer behavior, such as how long they spend in a store, what products they view, and what products they purchase. This data can be used to predict demand for products and to optimize inventory levels.
- AI can be used to analyze this data and to identify patterns and trends. This can help businesses to understand customer behavior better and make more accurate predictions about demand.
- IoT and AI can be used to create predictive models to forecast demand for products. These models can be used to optimize production, inventory, and marketing.
- IoT and AI can be used to create real-time dashboards to track demand and to adjust as needed. This can help businesses avoid stockouts and ensure that they have the right amount of inventory on hand to meet demand.
- IoT and AI can be used to create predictive analytics solutions to forecast demand for products and services. These solutions can be used to optimize operations, improve customer service, and make better business decisions.

By leveraging IoT and AI, businesses can improve their predictive demand forecasting capabilities. This can help them to meet customer demand better, improve efficiency, and reduce costs.

Here are some additional benefits of leveraging IoT and AI for predictive demand forecasting:

- **Improved accuracy:** IoT and AI can help businesses to improve the accuracy of their demand forecasts. This is because IoT sensors can collect real-time data about customer behavior, which can be used to identify patterns and trends. AI can then be used to analyze this data and create predictive models that can be used to forecast demand.
- **Reduced costs:** IoT and AI can help businesses to reduce costs. This is because IoT sensors can help businesses to optimize inventory levels. AI can also help businesses to optimize production and marketing.
- **Improved customer service:** IoT and AI can help businesses to improve customer service. This is because IoT sensors can help businesses to track customer behavior and to identify potential problems. AI can then be used to analyze this data and create predictive models that can be used to improve customer service.
- **Increased profits:** IoT and AI can help businesses to increase profits. This is because IoT sensors can help businesses to optimize inventory levels, reduce costs, and improve customer service. AI can also help businesses to optimize production and marketing.

The next two case studies can help us understand the value of AI in addition to IoT.

Retail

Retailers can use AI to track customer behavior through IoT sensors in stores. This can feed into demand spike or drop. This type of input can further help supply chain teams adjust their forecast.

By analyzing data like the number of people entering and leaving a store each hour, retailers can leverage AI to predict not just store staffing needs but also how many customers are likely to visit and potentially convert into sales. This information can then be used to optimize various aspects of the business, including:

- **Staffing:** AI can predict peak customer hours, allowing for efficient scheduling of employees to ensure optimal service and avoid overstaffing during slower periods.
- **Inventory management:** By understanding the anticipated number of customers and their potential purchase behaviors, AI can help optimize inventory levels, ensuring the right products are on hand to meet demand and minimize stockouts.
- **Marketing and promotions:** AI can help tailor marketing campaigns and promotions based on predicted customer visits, maximizing their effectiveness and generating higher sales.
- **Store layout and design:** Customer traffic data can inform the design and layout of the store, positioning products strategically and creating a more engaging shopping experience. For example, a retailer could use AI to track the number of

times a product is viewed on a shelf. This data could then be used to predict how popular the product is and to place it in a more prominent location in the store. This would make it more likely for the customers to see the product and purchase it.

- **Personalization:** AI can personalize the shopping experience for individual customers based on their past behavior and predicted purchases, leading to higher customer satisfaction and loyalty.

By harnessing the power of AI to analyze customer behavior and predict future trends, retailers can gain valuable insights that improve operational efficiency, drive sales growth, and ultimately enhance the overall customer experience.

Consumer electronics

Consumer electronics companies can use AI to analyze data from IoT sensors (for example, temperature, vibration, humidity, thermal, and so on) in their supply chain to track the location of products, the status of shipments, and the estimated time of arrival. This data can be used to predict demand for products, to optimize shipping routes, and to improve customer service.

For example, a consumer electronics company could use AI to track the location of its products in warehouses and on trucks. This data could then predict when products will arrive at stores. This information could then be used to optimize the placement of products in stores and to ensure that they are always in stock.

AI can also be used to analyze data from IoT sensors to track the performance of suppliers. This data could then be used to identify suppliers that are not meeting expectations and to take corrective action.

For example, a consumer electronics company could use AI to track the delivery time of its suppliers. This data could then identify suppliers not meeting the delivery deadlines. This information could then be used to take corrective action, such as finding a new supplier or working with the supplier to improve its performance.

By using AI to analyze data from IoT sensors, consumer electronics companies can improve their ability to predict demand, optimize shipping routes, improve customer service, and identify and address supplier performance issues. This can lead to increased sales and profits.

Case studies

The industry leaders are already implementing IoT for their supply chains to experience game-changing advantages. A few examples are discussed below:

Company: Walmart

Problem: Walmart was facing the following challenges with demand forecasting:

- Walmart stockouts cost the company an estimated $1 billion per year.[4]
- Walmart's traditional demand forecasting methods were only 60% accurate.[5]

The company was unable to accurately predict product demand, leading to stockouts and lost sales.

Walmart was not able to solve this problem with traditional approaches because traditional approaches rely on historical data and human judgment. This data can be inaccurate and biased, and human judgment can be clouded by emotions and other factors.

Solution: In a pioneering initiative, Walmart implemented a cutting-edge solution that harnessed the synergistic capabilities of the IoT and AI to achieve significant enhancements in demand forecasting accuracy. Strategically deployed IoT sensors throughout retail outlets meticulously gathered granular customer behavioral data, encompassing dwell time in specific aisles, product interactions, and purchase patterns. This vast repository of invaluable data was then meticulously fed into sophisticated AI-powered predictive models, enabling Walmart to gain unparalleled insights into customer demand trends. By leveraging the collective intelligence of IoT and AI, Walmart was able to generate highly accurate forecasts that empowered them to optimize inventory levels, minimize stockouts, and maximize sales opportunities. This innovative approach to demand forecasting not only resulted in enhanced operational efficiency but also translated into a superior customer experience.[6]

Benefits: Walmart benefited from the solution in several ways. The company improved the accuracy of its demand forecasts, which led to reduced stockouts and increased sales. The solution also helped Walmart improve customer service by ensuring its customers could always find their desired products.

Results: According to *Gartner* and *Forrester*, the stock-out reductions and sales could be within the range of 50% and 10% respectively. This claim is made by studying similar organizations implementing the IoT technology.

Conclusion: Walmart's case study shows how IoT and AI can improve demand forecasting and transform supply chains. By using these technologies, businesses can improve the accuracy of their forecasts, reduce costs, improve customer service, and increase profits.

---

4 The True Cost of a Stockout for Your Business: **https://ware2go.co/articles/stockouts/**

5 AI-driven operations forecasting in data-light environments: **https://www.mckinsey.com/capabilities/operations/our-insights/ai-driven-operations-forecasting-in-data-light-environments**.

6 Exclusive: How Walmart is using AI to supercharge its holiday plans: **https://finance.yahoo.com/news/exclusive-how-walmart-is-using-ai-to-supercharge-its-holiday-plans-190849969.html**

Inventory management

One area where IoT has a significant impact is inventory management. IoT can track inventory levels in real time, automate inventory tasks, improve the accuracy of inventory data, and improve the security of inventory data. This can lead to increased profits and improved customer satisfaction.

Here are some specific examples of how IoT is used to improve inventory management:

- **Walmart:** Walmart is using IoT to track the location of its products in its warehouses. This has helped Walmart to reduce the time it takes to find products and to improve the accuracy of its inventory data.
- **Amazon:** Amazon is using IoT to track the movement of its products through its supply chain. This has helped Amazon to reduce the time it takes to get products to customers and to improve the accuracy of its inventory data.
- **John Deere:** John Deere is using IoT to track the performance of its agricultural equipment. This has helped John Deere to improve the efficiency of its equipment and to reduce the risk of breakdowns.

These are just a few examples of how IoT improves inventory management. As IoT technology develops, we expect to see even more innovative ways to use IoT to improve inventory management.

Here are some industry examples of how IoT improves inventory management:

- **Retail:** Retailers are using IoT to track inventory levels in real-time, automate inventory tasks, and improve the accuracy of inventory data. This is helping retailers to reduce stockouts and overstocks, which can save money and improve customer satisfaction.
- **Manufacturing:** Manufacturers are using IoT to track the movement of materials and products through their production lines. This is helping manufacturers to improve efficiency, reduce waste, and improve product quality.
- **Logistics:** Logistics companies are using IoT to track the movement of goods in transit. This is helping logistics companies to improve efficiency, reduce costs, and improve customer service.

Overall, IoT is having a significant impact on inventory management. By using IoT, businesses can improve efficiency, accuracy, and security. This can lead to increased profits and improved customer satisfaction.

Challenges of inventory management

Specific examples of the challenges of inventory management are as follows:

- **Stockouts:** Stockouts occur when a business does not have enough inventory to meet customer demand. This can lead to lost sales and customer dissatisfaction.

- **Overstocks:** Overstocks occur when a business has too much inventory. This can lead to waste, storage costs, and obsolescence.
- **Need for accuracy:** Inventory data must be accurate to make informed decisions about inventory levels, pricing, and production.
- **Need for security:** Inventory data must be secure to prevent theft and fraud.

The traditional approach to inventory management is to manually track inventory levels, order inventory, and manage inventory shipments. This approach can be time-consuming, inefficient, and inaccurate.

IoT in real-time inventory management

IoT is the network of physical devices, vehicles, buildings, and other objects that are embedded with sensors, software, and network connectivity to collect and exchange data. IoT can be used in various settings, including homes, businesses, and cities. It can be used to improve efficiency, productivity, and safety.

One of the areas where IoT is having a significant impact is stock replenishment. IoT can be used to track inventory levels in real time, automate stock replenishment tasks, and improve the accuracy of stock replenishment data. This can lead to increased profits and improved customer satisfaction.

Here are some specific examples of how IoT improves stock replenishment:

- **RFID tags: Radio frequency identification** (**RFID**) tags can be attached to inventory items but it is important to note that the RFID tags themselves are not actively tracking the location and movement. Instead, RFID readers, strategically placed at various locations in the supply chain, enforce scanning when items pass by. This technology can help businesses to identify and correct stock discrepancies, improve the efficiency of picking and packing, and reduce the risk of theft.
- **Sensors:** Sensors can be used to monitor environmental conditions, such as temperature and humidity, to ensure that inventory is stored in optimal conditions. This can help to prevent damage to inventory and extend its shelf life.

IoT is a powerful tool that can be used to improve stock replenishment. By using IoT, businesses can gain a competitive advantage and improve their bottom line.

Here are some benefits of using IoT in stock replenishment:

- **Improved accuracy:** IoT can help businesses improve the accuracy of their stock levels by tracking inventory in real-time. This can help businesses to avoid stockouts and overstocks, which can save money and improve customer satisfaction.
- **Reduced costs:** IoT can help businesses to reduce costs by automating stock replenishment tasks. This can free up employees to focus on other tasks, such as customer service and sales.

- **Improved customer service:** IoT can help businesses improve customer service by providing real-time information about inventory levels. This can help businesses to meet customer demand and avoid disappointment.
- **Increased efficiency:** IoT empowers businesses to automate stock replenishment tasks, leading to a significant boost in operational efficiency. By streamlining this process, employees are freed from manual monitoring and restocking, allowing them to dedicate their time and expertise to more impactful areas like customer service and sales growth. This shift in focus fosters a more productive and customer-centric environment, ultimately contributing to the overall success of the business.
- **Improved security**: IoT can help businesses improve security by tracking inventory in real time. This can help businesses to identify and respond to theft and fraud.

Overall, IoT has the potential to revolutionize stock replenishment. By using IoT, businesses can improve efficiency, accuracy, security, and customer service. This can lead to increased profits and improved customer satisfaction.

Here are some examples of how IoT is being used in stock replenishment:

- **Walmart:** Walmart is using IoT to track the location of its products in its warehouses. This has helped Walmart to reduce the time it takes to find products and to improve the accuracy of its inventory data.
- **Amazon:** Amazon is using IoT to track the movement of its products through its supply chain. This has helped Amazon to reduce the time it takes to get products to customers and to improve the accuracy of its inventory data.
- **John Deere:** John Deere is using IoT to track the performance of its agricultural equipment. This has helped John Deere to improve the efficiency of its equipment and to reduce the risk of breakdowns.

These are just a few examples of how IoT is being used in stock replenishment. As IoT technology develops, we can expect to see even more innovative ways to use IoT to improve stock replenishment.

IoT and predictive analysis

Overstocking in the food industry can lead to several disadvantages, including:

- **Waste:** Overstocked food can spoil or damage, leading to waste. This can be a costly problem, as food waste can account for up to 40% of the cost of food production.
- **Deterioration in product quality:** Overstocked food can deteriorate in quality, making it less appealing to customers. This can lead to lost sales and customer dissatisfaction.

- **Increased storage costs:** Overstocked food requires more storage space, leading to increased storage costs.
- **Increased risk of pests and rodents:** Overstocked food can attract pests and rodents, which can contaminate food and lead to foodborne illness.

IoT can be used to avoid overstocking in the food industry by providing real-time data on inventory levels. This data can be used to track inventory levels and identify when stock levels are getting low. This information can then be used to order new stock before it runs out, preventing overstocking.

In addition, IoT can be used to track the condition of food. This data can be used to identify food that is at risk of spoilage or contamination. This information can then be used to take corrective action, such as moving food to a cooler location or disposing of food that is no longer safe to eat.

By using IoT, food businesses can avoid the disadvantages of overstocking and improve the quality and safety of their food.

Case study: IoT for inventory management

Inventory management in the consumer electronics field is extremely tricky. Mainly because the product life cycles are extremely short. Let us try to understand how IoT can transform the supply chain for companies like Apple.

Problem statement: Apple is estimated to have an annual cost of excess and obsolescence in the range of billions of dollars, similar to the challenge of excess and obsolescence since they are part of the consumer electronics industry.

There are several factors that contribute to Apple's high cost of excess and obsolescence. One factor is the company's rapid product development cycle. Apple introduces new products regularly, and this can lead to excess inventory of older products. Another factor is the company's focus on innovation. Apple often introduces new features and technologies in its products, which can lead to the obsolescence of older products.

Root cause of excess and obsolescence: Here are some of the root causes of Apple's high excess and obsolescence:

- **Rapid product development cycle:** Apple introduces new products regularly, which can lead to excess inventory of older products.
- **Focus on innovation:** Apple often introduces new features and technologies in its products, which can lead to the obsolescence of older products.

High demand for Apple products: Apple products are in high demand, which can lead to customers buying products before they are released. Apple might incorrectly read preorder signals as sustained demand, and this can lead to excess inventory of products that are not yet ready for sale.

- **Short product life cycles:** Apple products have relatively short product life cycles, which means that they become obsolete more quickly than products from other companies.
- **Difficult to predict demand:** It can be difficult for Apple to predict demand for its products, which can lead to excess inventory of some products and shortages of others.
- **Lack of flexibility in production:** Apple's production process is not very flexible, which makes it difficult to adjust production levels in response to changes in demand.
- **High cost of inventory:** Apple's inventory is expensive to store and maintain, which adds to the cost of excess and obsolescence.

Root cause	Fixable by IoT integration?
Rapid product development cycle	No
Focus on innovation	No
High demand for Apple products	Yes
Short product life cycles	Yes
Difficult to predict demand:	Partially
Lack of flexibility in production:	Yes
High cost of inventory	Partially

***Table 3.1:** Supply chain issues versus IoT effectiveness*

IoT implementation to tackle excess and obsolescence:

- **High demand for Apple products**

  Here are some additional details about how IoT can be used to resolve the high demand for Apple products:

  - **Real-time demand tracking:** IoT sensors and devices can be used to track customer demand in real time. This data can be used to ensure that Apple has enough inventory to meet demand, which can help to reduce the risk of excess inventory. For example, Apple could use sensors to track the number of people visiting its stores or the number of times its products are searched for online. This data could then be used to adjust inventory levels in real time.
  - **Demand forecasting:** IoT data can be used to forecast demand for Apple products. This data can be used to plan production levels and inventory levels, which can help to reduce the risk of excess inventory and shortages. For example, Apple could use historical data on customer demand to predict

future demand. This data could then be used to set production levels and inventory levels.

- o **Demand-based pricing:** IoT data can be used to set prices for Apple products based on demand. This can help Apple to maximize revenue and reduce the risk of excess inventory. For example, Apple could use data on customer demand to set different prices for its products in different markets. This could help Apple to maximize revenue in each market.
- o **Demand-based marketing:** IoT data can be used to target marketing campaigns based on demand. This can help Apple to increase sales and reduce the risk of excess inventory. For example, Apple could use data on customer demand to target its marketing campaigns to specific groups of people. This could help Apple to increase sales to these groups of people.

- **Short product life cycles and difficult to predict demand:** All Apple products have shorter product life cycles say few quarters or a couple of years! This is across the industry and all other peers and competitors face the harsh reality of products being obsoleted very soon.
  - o **IoT sensors can be used to track inventory levels**
    - ▪ Apple sells ~30% of lifetime volume within first few weeks. Apple depends on third-party retailers to provide accurate data about sales to drive its supplier base. In case of low sales, Apple might want to reduce production or shut production lines early.
    - ▪ Hence, every serial number scan in Amazon warehouse is a signal to Apple how product sales are performing.
    - ▪ This data can be used to ensure that Apple has enough inventory of popular products to meet demand, while also avoiding excess inventory of unpopular products.
  - o **IoT sensors can be used to track product performance**
    - ▪ This data can be used to identify potential problems with products, so that Apple can take corrective action before they cause customer dissatisfaction or product recalls.
    - ▪ For example, if iOS-based telemetry reports are showing 10% failure while camera captures, then it is potentially pointing at camera hardware failures from the field.
    - ▪ These failures can be corrected for the future generations and warranty costs can be avoided by fixing the hardware issue in the manufacturing plant. Also, service centers can fix camera panels quickly by looking at the serial numbers.

- **Lack of flexibility in production**
- **Turnaround time to react to changing demand**
  - The supply chain takes time to react to the changing demand.
  - This affects delay in responding to production lines
  - A majorly successful marketing campaign can increase iPhone demand overnight, but production lines may not react another few weeks due to the lag in supply chain.
  - This may cause *stockouts* in Apple stores.
  - On the other hand, if production lines operate on the assumption of sustained high demand vs. demand is softened in the market due to a competing product launching. This may result in excess and obsolescence for apple.

- **High cost of inventory**
  - Apple uses top of the line hardware for each component. For example, custom silicon chips, high-end camera hardware, display glass.
  - Apple can keep costs low due to high volume orders.
  - IoT can help react to changing demand quickly and change forecast shared with suppliers, keeping shortages and E&O in check.

Intelligent logistics: Enhancing delivery with IoT

Intelligent logistics utilizes IoT to enhance delivery by providing real-time visibility, traceability, and control over the logistics chain. IoT devices collect data on goods, enabling businesses to track shipments, monitor conditions, and identify disruptions. This data optimizes routes, improves delivery on-time, and reduces costs. Additionally, IoT-enabled logistics systems automate tasks, freeing up personnel for value-added activities. As a result, intelligent logistics enhances delivery performance, improves customer satisfaction, and drives operational efficiency.

Redefining logistics with IoT

Not having real-time logistics data can cause several supply chain challenges, including:

- **Reduced visibility:** Without real-time data, it can be difficult to track the location of goods and materials throughout the supply chain. This can lead to delays, lost shipments, and increased costs.

- **Inaccuracy:** Without real-time data, it can be difficult to track inventory levels accurately. This can lead to stockouts, resulting in lost sales and customer dissatisfaction.
- **Increased risk:** Without real-time data, it can be difficult to identify and respond to risks in the supply chain. This can lead to disruptions, which can have a negative impact on the company's bottom line.
- **Inefficient decision-making:** Without real-time data, it can be difficult to make informed decisions about the supply chain. This can lead to suboptimal decisions, which can impact on the company's profitability.

Overall, not having real-time logistics data can have a significant negative impact on the supply chain. By implementing real-time data collection and analysis, companies can improve visibility, accuracy, risk management, and decision-making, leading to a more efficient and profitable supply chain.

Here are some specific examples of supply chain challenges that can be caused by a lack of real-time logistics data:

- *How an Amazon shipment* is delayed because it is not clear where it is located.
- *The iPhones are out of stock* in a region because the inbound supply ETA was inaccurate.
- A supplier experiences a disruption that causes a delay in production, which leads to a shortage of goods for the company.
- A company is unable to respond to a change in demand because it does not have real-time data on customer behavior.

In the next section, we will see how by implementing IoT based real-time data collection and analysis, companies can improve their supply chains and avoid these challenges.

Real-time tracking: Role of IoT in transit visibility

Here are some specific examples of how IoT is transforming logistics and supply chain management:

- **Real-time tracking:** IoT devices can be used to track the location of goods and materials in real time, providing visibility into the entire supply chain. This information can be used to improve efficiency by optimizing routes and scheduling deliveries. It can also be used to reduce costs by identifying areas where waste can be eliminated.
- **Predictive analytics:** IoT devices can be used to collect data on the performance of goods and materials throughout the supply chain. This data can be used to develop predictive models that can forecast demand, identify potential problems,

and optimize processes. This information can be used to improve customer service by ensuring that goods are available when and where they are needed.

- **Automated decision-making:** IoT devices can be used to automate decision-making processes in logistics and supply chain management. This can free up human resources to focus on more strategic tasks. It can also improve efficiency by reducing the need for manual intervention.

Real-time tracking

- Walmart uses IoT devices to track the location of its products in its warehouses and distribution centers. This information is used to optimize routes and schedules, ensuring that products are delivered to stores as quickly as possible.
- UPS uses IoT devices to track the location of its packages in transit. This information is used to provide customers with real-time updates on the status of their deliveries.
- FedEx uses IoT devices to track the temperature of its packages in transit. This information is used to prevent spoilage of temperature-sensitive goods.

Predictive analytics

- Amazon uses predictive analytics to forecast demand for its products. This information is used to ensure that it has enough inventory to meet demand and to avoid stockouts.
- Target uses predictive analytics to identify customers who are likely to be pregnant. This information is used to send these customers targeted marketing campaigns for baby products.
- John Deere uses predictive analytics to identify potential problems with its agricultural equipment. This information is used to send alerts to farmers so that they can take corrective action before the problems cause a breakdown.

Automated decision-making

- Amazon uses automated decision-making to schedule deliveries. This system takes into account factors such as the location of the customer, the size of the order, and the time of day to determine the best time to deliver the order.
- UPS uses automated decision-making to route its delivery trucks. This system takes into account factors such as traffic conditions, weather, and the location of the packages to determine the most efficient route for each truck.
- FedEx uses automated decision-making to manage its inventory. This system takes into account factors such as demand, lead times, and storage costs to determine the optimal level of inventory for each product.

These technologies are transforming the way goods are moved and delivered, and they are helping companies to improve efficiency, reduce costs, and improve customer service.

Enhancing fleet management with IoT

Electronic data interchange (**EDI**) integration systems can integrate logistical fleet management and maintenance for supply chain companies by automating the exchange of data between different systems. This can help to improve efficiency, reduce costs, and improve customer service.

Here are some examples of how EDI integration systems can be used to integrate logistical fleet management and maintenance:

- **Automating the exchange of data between shippers and carriers:** EDI integration systems can automate the exchange of data between shippers and carriers, such as shipping orders, tracking information, and invoices. This can help to improve the accuracy and timeliness of data, which can lead to improved efficiency and reduced costs.
- **Managing maintenance schedules:** EDI integration systems can be used to manage maintenance schedules for vehicles and equipment. This can help to ensure that vehicles and equipment are properly maintained, which can help to prevent breakdowns and improve safety.
- **Tracking vehicle and equipment performance:** EDI integration systems can be used to track vehicle and equipment performance. This information can be used to identify areas where performance can be improved, which can help to reduce costs and improve efficiency.
- **Optimizing routes:** EDI integration systems can be used to optimize routes for vehicles and equipment. This can help to reduce fuel costs and improve delivery times.
- **Managing inventory:** EDI integration systems can be used to manage inventory levels for parts and supplies. This can help to ensure that there are enough parts and supplies on hand to meet demand, which can help to prevent delays and improve customer service.

Smart warehousing with IoT

A warehouse is a key component of a supply chain. A well-organized smart warehouse can be a game changer in an efficient supply chain.

Concept of a smart warehouse

A smart warehouse is a warehouse that uses technology to improve efficiency, accuracy, and visibility. Smart warehouses use a variety of technologies, including sensors, RFID tags, and **automated guided vehicles** (**AGVs**), to collect data and make decisions in real time. This data can be used to track inventory levels, optimize picking and packing, and improve order fulfillment.

There are many benefits to using a smart warehouse. Smart warehouses can help to improve efficiency by automating tasks, such as picking and packing. This can free up employees to focus on more strategic tasks, such as customer service. Smart warehouses can also help to improve accuracy by reducing the risk of human error. This can lead to fewer damaged goods and fewer lost orders. Smart warehouses can also help to improve visibility by providing real-time data on inventory levels and order status. This can help to improve customer service by giving customers accurate information about when their orders will arrive.

There are a number of challenges to implementing a smart warehouse. One challenge is the cost of the technology. Smart warehouses can be expensive to set up and maintain. Another challenge is the need for skilled workers to operate and maintain the technology. Smart warehouses require employees with knowledge of technology and logistics.

Despite the challenges, smart warehouses offer a number of benefits that can help companies to improve their supply chain. Smart warehouses can help to improve efficiency, accuracy, and visibility. This can lead to reduced costs, improved customer service, and a competitive advantage.

Here are some specific examples of how smart warehouses are being used:

- **Walmart** is using smart warehouses to improve the efficiency of its picking and packing operations. Walmart is using RFID tags to track the location of products in its warehouses. This information is used to create pick paths that optimize the time it takes to pick products. Walmart is also using AGVs to transport products between picking stations and packing stations. This has helped Walmart to reduce the time it takes to pick and pack orders.
- **Amazon** is using smart warehouses to improve the accuracy of its order fulfillment. Amazon is using sensors to track the temperature and humidity of its warehouses. This information is used to prevent damage to products. Amazon is also using RFID tags to track the location of products in its warehouses. This information is used to ensure that products are picked and packed correctly.
- **UPS** is using smart warehouses to improve the visibility of its supply chain. UPS is using sensors to track the location of its packages in transit. This information is used to provide customers with real-time updates on the status of their deliveries. UPS is also using RFID tags to track the location of its packages in its warehouses. This information is used to ensure that packages are delivered to the correct address.

These are just a few examples of how smart warehouses are being used. Smart warehouses are becoming increasingly common as companies look for ways to improve their supply chains.

IoT devices in warehousing: RFID, sensors, and more

Here is a brief overview of how environmental sensors, accelerometers and gyroscopes, RFID tags, AGVs, and WMS are implemented in smart warehouses:

- **Environmental sensors:** These sensors monitor various environmental factors, such as temperature, humidity, and shock, inside shipping containers. This data can be used to ensure optimal storage conditions for sensitive electronics and identify potential issues that could damage products during transport.
- **Accelerometers and gyroscopes:** These sensors measure the movement and tilt of products during shipping, providing insights into potential rough handling or damage. This information can be used to improve packaging and handling procedures, reducing the risk of product damage during transport.
- **Automated guided vehicles (AGVs):** AGVs are typically implemented by installing them in the warehouse. AGVs can be used to transport products around the warehouse. This can help to improve the efficiency of warehouse operations by freeing up employees to focus on other tasks.
- **Warehouse management systems (WMS):** WMS are typically implemented by installing software on a computer server. The WMS software can be used to collect and manage data about warehouse operations. This data can then be used to improve the efficiency of warehouse operations, as well as to provide real-time visibility into the status of inventory and orders.

Here are some additional details about how each of these devices are implemented:

- **Sensors:** Sensors can be implemented in a variety of ways, depending on the specific needs of the warehouse. For instance, temperature sensors can monitor the climate conditions of storage areas, ensuring the preservation of sensitive goods, while motion sensors can detect movement within the warehouse, enhancing security and enabling better tracking of personnel and inventory. Some common methods of implementing sensors include:
    - **Wireless sensors:** Wireless sensors can be used to collect data about the environment in a warehouse without the need for wires. This can make it easier to install and maintain sensors.
    - **Wired sensors:** Wired sensors can be used to collect data about the environment in a warehouse with the use of wires. This can provide more accurate data than wireless sensors, but it can also be more difficult to install and maintain.
- **RFID tags:** RFID tags can be implemented in a variety of ways, depending on the specific needs of the warehouse. Some common methods of implementing RFID tags include:

- **Adhesive tags:** Adhesive tags can be attached to products with adhesive. This is the most common method of implementing RFID tags.
- **Inlay tags:** Inlay tags can be inserted into products. This is a more secure method of implementing RFID tags, but it can also be more expensive.
- **Hard tags:** Hard tags are attached to products with screws or rivets. This is the most secure method of implementing RFID tags, but it can also be the most expensive.

- **Automated guided vehicles: Automated guided vehicles** (**AGV**s) can be implemented in a variety of ways, depending on the specific needs of the warehouse. Some common methods of implementing AGVs include:
    - **Wire guided AGVs:** Wire guided AGVs follow a path that is defined by wires that are embedded in the floor of the warehouse. This is the most common method of implementing AGVs.
    - **Laser guided AGVs:** Laser guided AGVs use lasers to create a map of the warehouse and then follow that map to move around the warehouse. This is a more accurate method of implementing AGVs, but it can also be more expensive.
    - **Vision guided AGVs:** Vision guided AGVs use cameras to create a map of the warehouse and then follow that map to move around the warehouse. This is the most accurate method of implementing AGVs, but it can also be the most expensive.
- **Warehouse management systems (WMS):** WMS can be implemented in a variety of ways, depending on the specific needs of the warehouse. Some common methods of implementing WMS include:
    - **On-premises WMS:** On-premises WMS is installed on a computer server that is located in the warehouse. This is the most common method of implementing WMS.
    - **Cloud-based WMS:** Cloud-based WMS is hosted on a server that is located in the cloud. This can be a more cost-effective method of implementing WMS, but it can also be less secure.

Impact of IoT on warehouse operations

The IoT is having a transformative impact on warehouse operations. By connecting devices, sensors, and machines to the internet, IoT is enabling real-time data collection, monitoring, and control. We will dive into the case study for IoT driven warehouses.

Case study: IoT-driven warehouses

Amazon is one of the world's largest retailers, and it relies on a vast network of warehouses and distribution centers to deliver its products to customers around the globe. In recent years, Amazon has been investing heavily in IoT technology to improve the efficiency and effectiveness of its warehouse operations.

One of the most significant ways that Amazon is using IoT in its warehouses is through the use of sensors. Sensors are being used to track a variety of data points, including the temperature and humidity of products, the location of assets, and the movement of people and equipment. This data is then used to improve a variety of warehouse operations, such as:

- **Product quality:** Sensors are being used to monitor the temperature and humidity of products to ensure that they are stored in the correct conditions. This helps to prevent spoilage and damage.
- **Asset tracking:** Sensors are being used to track the location of assets, such as forklifts and pallets. This helps to prevent lost or misplaced assets.
- **Security:** Sensors are being used to improve security by providing real-time alerts of unauthorized access or tampering. This helps to protect employees and inventory from harm.

In addition to using sensors, Amazon is also using IoT to automate tasks. For example, Amazon is using IoT enabled robots to pick and pack orders. Robots can move quickly and efficiently through warehouses, and they can handle a variety of tasks that would be difficult or dangerous for humans.

Amazon is also using IoT to improve visibility into warehouse operations. By collecting data from sensors and other devices, Amazon is able to create a real-time view of its warehouse operations. This information can be used to make better decisions about how to allocate resources and how to improve efficiency.

Overall, Amazon is using IoT to transform its warehouse operations. By collecting data, automating tasks, and improving visibility, Amazon is able to improve the efficiency, accuracy, and security of its warehouse operations. This helps Amazon to deliver products to customers more quickly and efficiently, and it helps Amazon to reduce costs.

Here are some of the benefits that Amazon has seen from using IoT in its warehouses:

- **Improved efficiency:** Amazon has seen a significant improvement in the efficiency of its warehouse operations. For example, Amazon has been able to reduce the time it takes to pick and pack an order significantly.
- **Reduced costs:** Amazon has also seen a reduction in costs as a result of using IoT in its warehouses. For example, Amazon has been able to reduce the number of accidents in its warehouses by a large extent.

- **Improved customer service:** Amazon has also seen an improvement in customer service as a result of using IoT in its warehouses. For example, Amazon is now able to provide customers with real-time updates on the status of their orders.

Overall, Amazon has seen significant benefits from using IoT in its warehouses. IoT has helped Amazon to improve the efficiency, accuracy, security, and customer service of its warehouse operations.

Reverse logistics with IoT

Reverse logistics is the process of moving returned products back through the supply chain to the point of origin for repair, remanufacturing, or disposal. It is a strategically important part of supply chain management because it can help to improve customer satisfaction, reduce costs, and protect the environment.

Here are some of the ways that reverse logistics can be used to manage returned products:

- **Return:** Returned products can be returned to the manufacturer for repair or replacement. This is the most common way to manage returned products.
- **Repair:** Returned products that are not damaged can be repaired and resold. This can help to reduce costs and to improve customer satisfaction.
- **Recycle:** Returned products that cannot be repaired can be recycled. This can help to reduce waste and to protect the environment.
- **Remanufacturing:** Returned products that are still in good condition can be remanufactured and resold. This can help to reduce costs and to extend the life of products.
- **Disposal:** Returned products that cannot be repaired, recycled, or remanufactured must be disposed of properly. This can be done through incineration, landfilling, or other methods.

The best way to manage returned products will vary depending on the product, the condition of the product, and the company's policies.

Here are some of the reasons why reverse logistics is strategically important:

- **Customer satisfaction:** Reverse logistics can help to improve customer satisfaction by providing a way for customers to return products that are defective, damaged, or no longer needed. This can help to build customer loyalty and reduce the number of returns.
- **Reduced costs:** Reverse logistics can help to reduce costs by recovering the value of returned products. This can be done through repair, remanufacturing, or recycling. Reverse logistics can also help to reduce the costs of disposal.

- **Environmental protection:** Reverse logistics can help to protect the environment by reducing the amount of waste that is sent to landfills. This can be done by recycling returned products or by refurbishing them for reuse.

Here are some of the ways that supply chain can provide an edge in reverse logistics over competitors:

- **Integration:** Supply chain integration is the process of connecting all of the parts of the supply chain, including suppliers, manufacturers, distributors, and retailers. This can help to improve communication and coordination, which can lead to more efficient reverse logistics operations.
- **Technology:** Technology can be used to improve reverse logistics operations in a number of ways. For example, RFID tags can be used to track the location of returned products, and software can be used to manage the reverse logistics process.
- **Sustainability:** Supply chain sustainability is the practice of designing and operating supply chains in a way that minimizes environmental impact. This can be done by using recycled materials, reducing energy consumption, and minimizing waste.

Overall, reverse logistics is a strategically important part of supply chain management. By integrating technology, sustainability, and other best practices, supply chain can provide an edge in this area over competitors.

Current challenges with reverse logistics

Here are some of the top challenges in reverse logistics due to non-real time data and traditional supply chain:

- **Lack of visibility:** One of the biggest challenges in reverse logistics is the lack of visibility into the process. This can make it difficult to track the location of returned products, identify problems, and make necessary decisions.
- **Cost:** Reverse logistics can be expensive. This is due to the cost of transportation, storage, and processing of returned products.
- **Regulations:** Reverse logistics can be complex due to the various regulations that govern the handling and disposal of returned products.
- **Damage:** Returned products can be damaged during transportation or storage. This can increase costs and make it difficult to resell or refurbish the products.
- **Reputational risk:** Reverse logistics can damage a company's reputation if it is not handled properly. This is because customers may be concerned about the safety and security of their returned products.

Here are some examples of the challenges of reverse logistics from diverse industries:

- **Retail:** In the retail industry, reverse logistics is often used to handle returns of defective or unwanted products. The challenges of reverse logistics in the retail industry include the high volume of returns, the cost of transportation and storage, and the need to comply with regulations.
- **Manufacturing:** In the manufacturing industry, reverse logistics is often used to handle returns of products that are recalled or that have been damaged in transit. The challenges of reverse logistics in the manufacturing industry include the need to identify and track returned products, the cost of repairing or replacing the products, and the need to comply with regulations.
- **Healthcare:** In the healthcare industry, reverse logistics is often used to handle returns of medical devices and pharmaceuticals. The challenges of reverse logistics in the healthcare industry include the need to ensure the safety and security of returned products, the cost of disposal, and the need to comply with regulations.

Overall, the challenges of reverse logistics can be significant. However, by using technology and best practices, companies can overcome these challenges and improve the efficiency and effectiveness of their reverse logistics operations.

Here are some of the ways that technology can be used to improve reverse logistics operations:

- **Tracking:** Technology can be used to track the location of returned products. This can help to improve visibility into the process and to identify problems early on.
- **Data analytics:** Technology can be used to analyze data from reverse logistics operations. This can help to identify areas for improvement and to make better decisions.
- **Automation:** Technology can be used to automate tasks in reverse logistics operations. This can help to improve efficiency and reduce costs.

By using technology and best practices, companies can overcome the challenges of reverse logistics and improve the efficiency and effectiveness of their reverse logistics operations.

IoT improvements in reverse logistics

IoT can help understand the condition of returned products by collecting data from sensors embedded in the products. This data can be used to track the temperature, humidity, and location of the products, as well as to monitor their performance. This information can be used to identify problems with the products early on, which can help to prevent further damage and to improve the efficiency of the reverse logistics process.

There are a number of advantages to using IoT to understand the condition of returned products. These advantages include:

- **Improved visibility:** IoT offers real-time visibility into the condition of returned products. For instance, in the pharmaceutical industry, IoT sensors can monitor the temperature and humidity levels of returned medications. If these conditions deviate from acceptable ranges, automated alerts can be triggered, allowing for swift corrective actions to ensure the safety and efficacy of the products. IoT also enables real-time tracking of returned goods in the supply chain, helping companies quickly locate and inspect items, reducing delays, and improving overall visibility into the return process.
- **Reduced costs:** IoT can lead to cost reduction by preventing further damage to returned products. For instance, if a retailer uses IoT-enabled sensors to monitor the condition of returned electronics, any issues like mishandling or exposure to extreme temperatures can be detected promptly. This enables the retailer to take corrective actions, refurbish the product if necessary, and resell it at a higher value, rather than incurring losses due to irreversible damage. Additionally, IoT streamlines the reverse logistics process, reducing transportation costs and improving overall efficiency by optimizing routes and scheduling for returned items.

There are a number of industries that are using IoT to understand the condition of returned products. Some examples of these industries include:

- **Retail:** In the retail industry, IoT is being used to track the condition of returned electronics. This information is used to identify products that have been damaged in transit or that have been tampered with. For example, Walmart is using IoT to track the condition of returned electronics. This information is used to identify products that have been damaged in transit or that have been tampered with. If a product is damaged, Walmart can take action to prevent further damage and to ensure that the product is disposed of properly. This helps to protect Walmart's customers and to comply with environmental regulations.
- **Manufacturing:** In the manufacturing industry, IoT is being used to track the condition of returned jet engines. This information is used to identify problems with the engines early on and to improve the manufacturing process. For example, *General Electric* is using IoT to track the condition of returned jet engines. This information is used to identify problems with the engines early on and to improve the manufacturing process. If a problem is identified, GE can take action to prevent the problem from occurring in future engines. This helps to improve the quality of GE's jet engines and to reduce the number of warranty claims.
- **Healthcare:** In the healthcare industry, IoT is being used to track the condition of returned medical devices. This information is used to identify problems with the devices early on and to improve patient safety. For example, the *Mayo Clinic* is using IoT to track the condition of returned infusion pumps. This information is used to identify problems with the pumps early on and to improve patient safety. If a problem is identified, the Mayo Clinic can take action to prevent the problem

from occurring in future patients. This helps to improve patient safety and to reduce the risk of medical errors.

Overall, IoT is a valuable tool for understanding the condition of returned products. By collecting data from sensors embedded in the products, IoT can help to improve visibility, reduce costs, and improve customer satisfaction.

Reverse logistics and forward logistics

Some of the quality-related feedback that reverse logistics can provide include:

- **Defect data:** Reverse logistics can collect data on defects found in returned products. This data can be used to identify patterns and trends in defects, which can help to improve the quality of products.
- **Customer feedback:** Reverse logistics can collect feedback from customers about their experiences with products. This feedback can be used to identify areas for improvement in the quality of products.
- **Product usage data:** Reverse logistics can collect data on how products are being used. This data can be used to identify areas where products are being used incorrectly, which can help to reduce the number of defects.

By using the feedback that reverse logistics can provide, quality engineering or manufacturing can improve the quality of products, reduce the number of defects, and improve customer satisfaction.

Overall, reverse logistics can be a valuable tool for quality engineering or manufacturing by providing quality-related feedback. By using this feedback, businesses can improve the quality of products, reduce the number of defects, and improve customer satisfaction.

Here are some specific examples of how reverse logistics can be used to improve quality:

- A company that makes shoes can use reverse logistics to collect data on the types of defects that are found in returned shoes. This data can be used to identify patterns and trends in defects, which can help the company to improve the quality of its shoes.
- A company that makes electronics can use reverse logistics to collect feedback from customers about their experiences with its products. This feedback can be used to identify areas where the company can improve the quality of its products.
- A company that makes food can use reverse logistics to collect data on how its products are being used. This data can be used to identify areas where the company can improve the safety of its products.

Overall, reverse logistics can be a valuable tool for improving quality. By collecting data and feedback from customers, businesses can identify areas where they can improve the quality of their products. This can lead to a number of benefits for businesses, including increased profits, reduced costs, improved customer satisfaction, and reduced environmental impact.

Future of reverse logistics

IoT is transforming reverse logistics in multiple ways by reducing waste and also by predicting type of returns and quality failures:

- **Real-time tracking:** IoT sensors can track the location of returned products, which can help businesses to improve efficiency by reducing the time it takes to find and process them.
- **Condition monitoring:** IoT sensors can monitor the condition of returned products, which can help businesses to identify problems early on and prevent further damage.
- **Customer feedback:** IoT can collect feedback from customers about their experiences with the reverse logistics process, which can help businesses to improve customer satisfaction.

Overall, IoT is transforming reverse logistics by providing real-time data and insights that can help businesses improve efficiency, reduce costs, and improve customer satisfaction.

Here are some of the changes that are expected in reverse logistics in the future:

- **Increased use of IoT:** IoT is expected to play a major role in reverse logistics in the future. IoT can provide businesses with real-time data and insights that can help them to improve efficiency, reduce costs, and improve customer satisfaction. For example, IoT sensors can be used to track the location and condition of returned goods, which can help to optimize transportation and reduce waste.
- **Improved customer experience:** The use of IoT can also lead to improved customer experience in reverse logistics. For example, customers can be provided with real-time updates on the status of their returns, which can help to reduce anxiety and improve satisfaction.
- **Reduced environmental impact:** IoT can also help to reduce the environmental impact of reverse logistics. For example, IoT-enabled devices can be used to optimize transportation routes and reduce fuel consumption.
- **Greater visibility and control:** IoT can provide businesses with greater visibility and control over their reverse logistics operations. This can help to identify and address inefficiencies, improve compliance with regulations, and reduce the risk of fraud.
- **More sustainable practices:** IoT can also enable more sustainable practices in reverse logistics. For example, IoT sensors can be used to monitor the condition of returned goods and identify those that can be repaired or refurbished.

- **Capacity planning:** IoT can provide real-time data on the volume and type of returned products, which can help businesses to plan their capacity for reverse logistics operations. This can help to avoid bottlenecks and ensure that returned products are processed in a timely manner.
- **Material planning:** IoT can provide real-time data on the condition of returned products, which can help businesses to plan their material requirements for remanufacturing, repair, and recycling. This can help to ensure that businesses have the necessary materials on hand to process returned products in a timely manner.
- **Remanufacturing:** IoT can be used to monitor the condition of returned products and to identify those that are suitable for remanufacturing. This can help businesses to improve the efficiency of their remanufacturing operations and to reduce the amount of waste that is generated.
- **Repair:** IoT can be used to monitor the condition of returned products and to identify those that are suitable for repair. This can help businesses to improve the efficiency of their repair operations and to reduce the amount of waste that is generated.
- **Recycling:** IoT can be used to monitor the condition of returned products and to identify those that are suitable for recycling. This can help businesses to improve the efficiency of their recycling operations and to reduce the amount of waste that is generated.

Conclusion

In this chapter, we discussed the power of IoT in supply chain management. We began by explaining the challenges businesses face in the supply chain, including uncertainty, costs, complexity, and risk. We then discussed the role of IoT in addressing these challenges. IoT can provide real-time visibility into the movement and condition of goods, which can help businesses optimize inventory levels, reduce waste, and improve efficiency. IoT can also be used to collect and analyze data to improve demand forecasting, inventory management, intelligent logistics, smart warehousing, and reverse logistics.

By using IoT, businesses can make better decisions about their supply chains and improve their overall performance.

In the next chapter, we will dive deep into the manufacturing revolution. We will explore how real-time data and insights can elevate innovation, productivity, and responsiveness within factory environments. Through real-world examples, we will illustrate how IoT delivers benefits across various facets of manufacturing, including predictive maintenance, production planning, quality control, robotics, and supply chain management. We will also discuss the technical nuances and strategies necessary for a successful IoT implementation, all while addressing the challenges that may arise along the way.

Points to remember

- **Demand forecasting**
  - o The IoT can be used to collect real-time data on demand, production, and inventory levels. This data can be used to create predictive models that can forecast future demand. These models can then be used to optimize supply chain and manufacturing operations, resulting in improved efficiency, profitability, and customer satisfaction.
  - o For example, IoT sensors can be used to track the usage of products in the field. This data can be used to predict when products will need to be replaced, which can help to ensure that there are always enough products on hand to meet demand. Additionally, IoT sensors can be used to monitor the performance of machines in a factory. This data can be used to predict when machines will need to be repaired or replaced, which can help to prevent unplanned downtime.
- **Inventory management**
  - o Smart warehousing is a new approach to warehouse management that uses IoT technology to collect and analyze real-time data about inventory levels, location, and movement. This data can be used to improve inventory accuracy, optimize picking and packing operations, and reduce costs.
  - o One of the most important benefits of smart warehousing is real-time inventory visibility. This means that warehouse managers can see exactly what products are in stock, where they are located, and how many are available. This information can be used to make better decisions about order fulfillment, preventing stockouts and overstocks.
- **Smart warehousing**

  IoT smart warehousing is the use of IoT technology to automate and optimize warehouse operations. This can be done by using sensors, actuators, and software to collect and analyze data about inventory levels, location, and movement. This data can then be used to improve inventory accuracy, optimize picking and packing operations, and reduce costs. IoT smart warehousing can provide a number of benefits for supply chain management, including:
  - o **Improved inventory accuracy**: IoT sensors can track the location and movement of inventory in real time, which can help to prevent stockouts and overstocks.
  - o **Optimized picking and packing operations**: IoT sensors can help pickers find the items they need quickly and easily, which can lead to faster order fulfillment.

- **Reduced costs**: IoT smart warehousing can help to reduce costs by improving inventory accuracy and efficiency.

- **Reverse logistics with IoT**
    - Reverse logistics faces several challenges due to the lack of real-time data and traditional supply chain practices. These challenges include lack of visibility, high costs, complex regulations, product damage, and reputational risk. These challenges are present in various industries, such as retail, manufacturing, and healthcare.
    - Technology can be used to improve reverse logistics operations by providing tracking, data analytics, and automation. The IoT can be particularly helpful in understanding the condition of returned products by collecting data from sensors embedded in the products. This data can provide real-time visibility into the condition of returned products, help to prevent further damage, and improve the efficiency of the reverse logistics process. By using technology and best practices, companies can overcome the challenges of reverse logistics and improve the efficiency and effectiveness of their reverse logistics operations.

Multiple choice questions

1. **Which of the following is not a problem in the supply chain?**
    a. Uncertainty
    b. Costs
    c. Complexity
    d. Demand
2. **Which of the following companies would be most affected by a supply chain disruption?**
    a. Apple
    b. Tesla
    c. Saudi Aramco
    d. Emirates Airlines
3. **Which of the following is not a risk in the supply chain?**
    a. Natural disasters
    b. Political instability
    c. Cyberattacks
    d. Customer satisfaction

4. **Which of the following is not a benefit of IoT for demand forecasting?**
    a. Improved customer experience
    b. Reduced costs
    c. Increased agility
    d. Increased profits
5. **Which of the following is not a way to improve demand forecasting with IoT?**
    a. Collect real-time data about demand
    b. Analyze data with AI
    c. Create predictive models
    d. Create real-time dashboards
6. **Which of the following is not a benefit of leveraging IoT and AI for predictive demand forecasting?**
    a. Improved accuracy
    b. Reduced costs
    c. Increased agility
    d. Increased profits
7. **Which of the following is not a use case for IoT in demand forecasting?**
    a. Retail
    b. Manufacturing
    c. Transportation
    d. Healthcare
8. **Which of the following is not a challenge in using IoT for demand forecasting?**
    a. Data collection
    b. Data analysis
    c. Model development
    d. Deployment
9. **Which of the following is not a factor to consider when collecting data for demand forecasting?**
    a. Historical sales data

b. Seasonal factors

c. Competitor activity

d. Customer behavior

10. Which of the following is not a factor to consider when analyzing data for demand forecasting?

a. Trend analysis

b. Pattern recognition

c. Causal analysis

d. Classification

Answer key

1. d.

2. a.

3. d.

4. c.

5. d.

6. d.

7. d.

8. c.

9. d.

10. c.

Questions

1. What are some of the key problems and risks that traditional supply chains face without real-time data?
2. How can IoT provide real-time visibility into the supply chain?
3. What are the benefits of using IoT for demand forecasting?
4. How can IoT data help improve the accuracy of demand forecasts?

5. What are some examples of how IoT is being used for demand forecasting in industries like retail and manufacturing?
6. What are some of the main challenges faced in inventory management?
7. How can IoT help in real-time inventory management and stock replenishment?
8. What are the benefits of using IoT for inventory management?
9. How is Walmart using IoT to improve its inventory management?
10. How is IoT transforming logistics and providing real-time tracking capabilities?
11. How can IoT improve fleet management for supply chain companies?
12. What is a smart warehouse and how does IoT help in smart warehousing?
13. What are some of the IoT devices used in smart warehouses?
14. How can IoT help overcome challenges faced in reverse logistics?
15. What changes can we expect to see in reverse logistics driven by IoT in the future?

Key terms

- **Demand forecasting:** The process of predicting future demand for a product or service.
- **Inventory management:** The process of planning and controlling the levels of inventory in a business.
- **Intelligent logistics:** The use of technology to improve the efficiency of logistics operations.
- **Smart warehousing:** The use of technology to improve the efficiency of warehousing operations.
- **Reverse logistics:** The process of managing the return of products from customers.
- **Internet of Things:** A network of physical objects that are embedded with sensors and software that allow them to collect and exchange data.
- **Artificial intelligence:** Artificial intelligence is a field of computer science that focuses on developing intelligent agents, which are systems that can reason, learn, and act autonomously.
- **Predictive analytics:** The use of data analysis to make predictions about future events.
- **Real-time data:** Data that is collected and processed in real time, as it is generated.

CHAPTER 4

IoT: Use Cases in Smart Factories

Introduction

The manufacturing world is evolving rapidly due to IoT adoption. With IoT, products, machines, and factories are becoming more connected through sensors and computers, opening up exciting new possibilities. This chapter explores how IoT is transforming manufacturing across the board. We will see how real-time data and insights can boost innovation, productivity, and responsiveness in factories. Through real-world examples, we will show how IoT benefits areas like predictive maintenance, production planning, quality control, robotics, and supply chain management. We will also discuss the technical aspects and strategies for successful IoT adoption, discussing challenges and solutions. This chapter aims to empower readers to harness IoT's potential in the manufacturing world, where optimization, agility, and automation are on the horizon.

Structure

This chapter will cover the following topics:

- Case study 1: Smart warehousing insight with IoT
    - Warehouse layout
    - Warehouse operations overview
    - Heatmap
    - Resource indoor positioning

- Case study 2: Smart delivery insights for ordered items
- Case study 3: Smart contracts for supply chain
- Case study 4: Smart packaging and monitoring
  - Smart packaging implementation process
  - Benefits of smart packaging
- Case study 5: Augmented reality in manufacturing
  - AR implementation in manufacturing
  - Use case 1: AR technology for equipment maintenance
  - Use case 2: AR to transform staff training in manufacturing
- Case study 6: Smart data entry
  - Data entry accuracy using CPA
  - Difference between CPA and traditional automation
  - Architecture of CPA IoT-driven manufacturing
- Case study 7: Health and safety compliance monitoring
  - Cloud-based monitoring and analytics
  - Edge computing for real-time response
  - IoT solution strategies for OHS management
- Case study 8: Smart material handling
  - IoT solution strategies for AMRs
- Case study 9: Last-mile delivery optimization
- Case study 10: Smart waste management
  - Inefficient waste collection
  - Illegal dumping
  - Recycling contamination
- Case study 11: Smart Product Lifecycle Management
- Case study 12: Real-Time Production Performance

Objectives

This chapter aims to provide readers with a comprehensive understanding of how IoT technology transforms manufacturing. By the end of this chapter, readers will be able to grasp the power of IoT in enabling real-time equipment monitoring, predictive maintenance, and optimization. They will also comprehend its role in enhancing production planning, quality control, and supply chain coordination through data analytics. Furthermore, readers will gain insights into automation opportunities, the integration of AI, machine learning, and robotics, and the challenges of adopting IoT solutions in manufacturing. This chapter aims to equip readers with practical knowledge and showcase the strategic value of IoT in smart factories through real-world use cases and benefits.

Case study 1: Smart warehousing insight with IoT

The industries can acquire and analyze IoT data sourced from warehouse assets to support geofencing, real-time status monitoring, and visualization of current positions. This data is leveraged to enhance warehouse operations and optimize the utilization of resources. IoT data can be used for the following things:

- To reduce empty trip distances by optimizing task assignment to resources.
- To examine warehouse operation KPIs, such as workload and resource trip lengths.
- To see the layout of the warehouse and the routes taken by the resources.
- To specify and modify the coordinates for storage bins.
- To employ an IoT indoor positioning system to integrate the real-time position of resources on the warehouse layout.

You can track the whereabouts of your resources in real time, observe their travel routes on an interactive warehouse plan, and get a general overview of your warehouse's activities. Take a look at the following *Figure 4.1:*

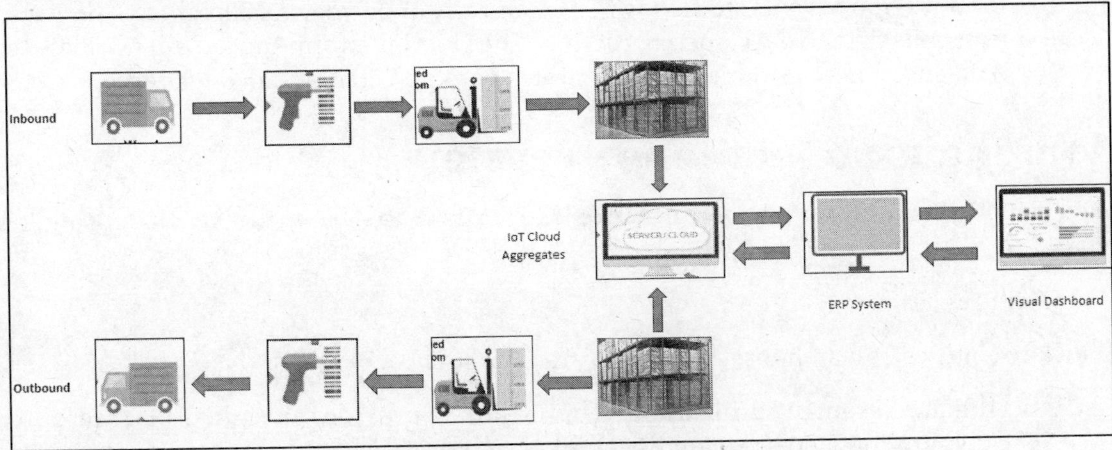

Figure 4.1: *Warehousing insights with IoT*

Warehouse layout

You can see and interact with your warehouse layout using IoT data.

Key features

The key features of the warehouse layout are as follows:

- Visualize and interact with your warehouse's layout graphically. For example, IoT sensors and tags on products and equipment. IoT Gateway collects data from sensors and transmits data to the cloud for processing. The cloud platform processes and analyzes data and generates graphical representations of the warehouse layout. A web-based interface is accessible to warehouse managers and staff.
- Locate a storage container on the warehouse plan, then determine its specifics. For example, RFID tags on storage containers. IoT Gateway collects data from RFID tags and sensors and transmits data to the cloud for processing. The cloud platform processes and analyzes data and generates graphical representations of the warehouse layout.
- Use the start and destination positions to search for resource travel routes. For example, motion sensors and RFID tags on resources like forklifts and automated guided vehicles. IoT Gateway collects data from motion sensors and RFID tags and sensors and transmits data to the cloud for processing. The cloud platform processes and analyzes data and generates optimal travel routes based on start and destination positions.
- Look for resource travel routes for a warehouse order that has been fulfilled. For example, motion sensors and RFID tags on resources like forklifts and automated guided vehicles. RFID tags on fulfilled orders as well. IoT Gateway collects data from motion sensors, RFID tags on resources, and order fulfillment systems and transmits data to the cloud processing. The cloud platform processes and analyzes data and generates optimal travel routes based on start and destination positions.

Warehouse operations overview

You can obtain reports of **key performance indicators** (**KPI**s) based on past data using IoT data.

Key features

The key features of warehouse operations are as follows:

- **Human resource utilization**: This feature provides insights into resource consumption by displaying the number of hours each resource worked daily.
- **Workload tracking**: The system tracks resource workload by queue, helping to visualize the volume of pending work.

- **Distance metrics**: It calculates and presents the total trip distance for each resource and breaks down the distance covered individually for each resource.

Heatmap

The number of physical objects traveling to or from storage bins over a specific period, such as picking or putting away, can be seen using IoT data. To illustrate the goods' motions graphically, a two-dimensional map will have various hues.

You may use the heatmap to identify any sections of the warehouse that frequently experience internal congestion and determine whether you need to move merchandise or provide more resources to these busy locations.

Key features

The key features of heatmap are as follows:

- Look up the quantity of items moved into or out of storage bins.
- Use the warehouse plan to choose a storage bin.
- Details of the storage container.

Resource indoor positioning

Integrating with an IoT service can visualize the location of resources in your warehouse in real time. You may display the paths taken by the resources on the layout of the warehouse, view previously set geofences, and keep track of warning messages. For example, when a resource moves too quickly or comes to a stop, certain issues may arise.

Key features

The key features of resource indoor positioning are as follows:

- View the status of resources on the warehouse layout.
- Visualize the position of resources in real-time on the warehouse layout.
- Keep an eye on warnings, such as when resources exceed speed restrictions or enter forbidden geofenced zones.
- Explore the recent journey route of a given resource.
- Personalized time visualization, view resources with personalized visuals on a warehouse layout.

Case study 2: Smart delivery insights for ordered items

Consider yourself a tiny business owner responsible for procuring raw materials for your production process. When you purchase from a supplier, they provide an estimated delivery date. However, there is a possibility that the materials may exceed your expectations in terms of quality upon arrival. Such delays in production can have a significant impact on your company and may lead to customer dissatisfaction due to delayed order fulfillment.

Although the above example of delivering a product is simple, it is important to consider circumstances with bigger stakes. Consider a situation where an important part of a vital business machine must be carried, or a necessary vaccination or expensive prescription must be delivered to a medical facility. In these situations, the effects of delivery delays or damage can significantly influence the well-being of patients or the success of commercial operations.

Businesses can monitor and optimize their whole supply chain using delivery insights enabled by the **Internet of Things** (**IoT**), to guarantee that raw materials and other supplies are of good quality and delivered on time, lowering the risk of production delays and customer discontent.

With real-time IoT sensor data, the IoT enriches your delivery procedures and offers a comprehensive, transparent perspective of the delivery process. To ensure a seamless user experience, the sensor data is integrated into your current operations.

Using the flexible system configuration technique, you can track various sensor data, such as temperature, humidity, acceleration, position, or radiation. Numerous use cases can be adjusted to your needs.

The system notifies the appropriate stakeholders in ERP when the IoT detects an odd sensor reading, giving them immediate access to information to take appropriate action. Then, you may more effectively respond to urgent supply crises, foresee future quality problems, improve customer happiness, and boost on-time delivery performance. Take a look at the *Figure 4.2:*

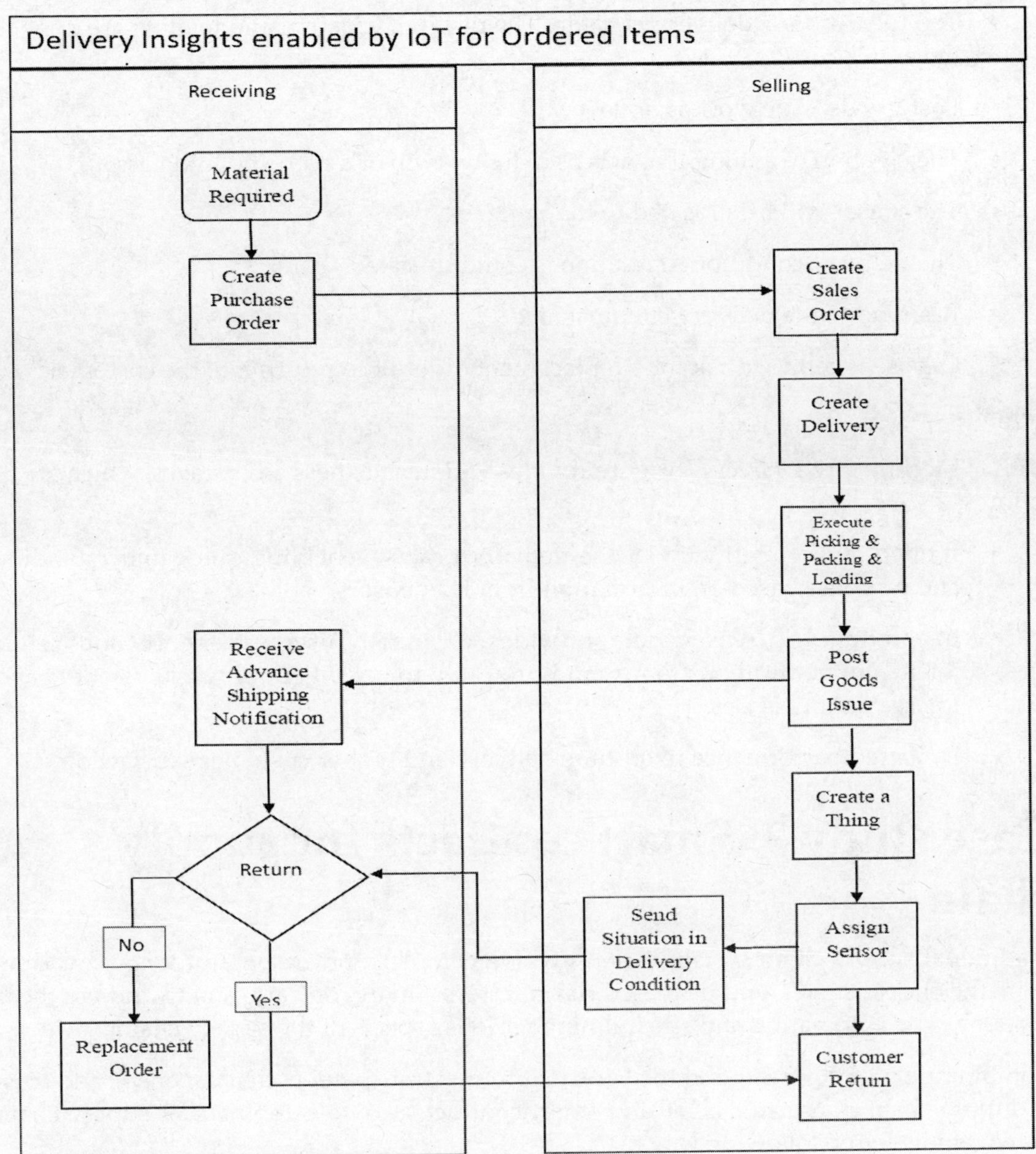

Figure 4.2: Delivery insights enabled by IoT for ordered items

Following is the high-level process flow:

- The process is started by a demand or material requirement.
- A purchase order is made and sent to the supplier.
- The supplier side generates sales orders.

- The sales order's delivery is made. The picking, packing, and loading are done in the warehouse.
- Post-goods issue work is done.
- The creation of a thing that acts as a digital twin of a corresponding asset.
- The sensor will be allocated to the thing.
- The delivery condition's situation is communicated.
- Respond to the delivery circumstance.
- Choose whether to ask for a replacement order or to return it to the customer.

Benefits

With IoT technology, Delivery Insight provides various business advantages, which are as follows:

- It offers a thorough view of the delivery process, enabling quick understanding and response based on information from IoT sensors.
- Integrating IoT sensor data provides a smooth user experience and sends intelligent notifications to respond promptly to urgent supply circumstances and foresee quality issues.
- Increased performance in on-time delivery and higher customer satisfaction.

Case study 3: Smart contracts for supply chain

Traditional supply chain systems often involve complex and manual processes, leading to inefficiencies, delays, and increased risk of errors. Smart contracts aim to address these challenges by automating and streamlining various aspects of the supply chain.

Combining smart contracts and the IoT can improve transparency, effectiveness, and trust in supply chain transactions. IoT and smart contracts can be combined for supply chain management in the following ways:

- **Asset tracking and monitoring:** Goods or shipping containers can have IoT sensors attached to them to track their whereabouts and their temperature, humidity, and other pertinent conditions in real-time. The IoT device can cause a smart contract to carry out activities when predefined circumstances are satisfied, such as a temperature breach. For example, the smart contract can automatically route a shipment to a different location or alert the appropriate parties if the temperature of a perishable item increases above a predetermined threshold.

- **Inventory management:** Smart contracts can be configured to update inventory levels based on information from IoT sensors automatically. The contract can cause orders for replenishment when stock levels reach a predetermined level, ensuring that products are always in stock without human interaction.
- **Quality control:** IoT sensors can collect product quality information during production or delivery. This information can be used by smart contracts to validate adherence to quality requirements. The contract may automatically initiate actions like returns, refunds, or reorders if a product does not satisfy the required standards.
- **Provenance tracking:** From production to delivery, IoT sensors can track every stage of a product's journey for complex supply chains. A blockchain can be used by smart contracts to generate an immutable record of this data, guaranteeing the product's provenance is open and unchangeable.
- **Payment and settlement:** Supply chain payment procedures can be automated using smart contracts. The smart contract may automatically disburse payment to the supplier upon fulfillment of predetermined delivery or quality parameters (as confirmed by IoT data). This lowers the possibility of disagreements and guarantees prompt payments.
- **Regulatory compliance:** IoT data can also aid in ensuring compliance with rules particular to a given industry. When IoT sensors discover compliance issues, smart contracts can be configured to send alerts or initiate actions, assisting businesses in avoiding penalties and legal complications.
- **Real-time updates:** Through IoT devices, supply chain participants, such as producers, suppliers, distributors, and clients, can get real-time updates on the whereabouts of products and shipments. This improves transparency and enables wiser decisions.
- **Security:** IoT and blockchain technology can be combined to create smart contracts to improve security and stop fraud. IoT device data can be hashed and stored on a blockchain, guaranteeing the accuracy of the data.
- **Environmental impact:** IoT data can be utilized to monitor and lessen the supply chain's operations' environmental impact. For example, businesses may improve routes and lower their carbon footprints by tracking fuel use and transportation-related emissions.
- **Auditing and reporting**: Compliance and reporting requirements for supply chain players can be made simpler by smart contracts, which can automatically generate audit trails and reports based on IoT data.

In conclusion, incorporating IoT with smart contracts can improve stakeholder trust, streamline processes, cut costs, and increase transparency. Data privacy, security, and interoperability are a few difficulties that must be properly resolved for a successful implementation.

Case study 4: Smart packaging and monitoring

In recent years, smart packaging supported with IoT-enabled sensors has emerged as a transformative solution for the preservation, monitoring, and delivery of products across multiple sectors, including food, medicine, and pharma. At the heart of this revolution is its ability to provide real-time insights into product conditions during transit, leveraging embedded sensors to gauge temperature, humidity, and even shock levels. This innovation not only underscores the commitment to ensuring product integrity and quality throughout the supply chain but also plays a pivotal role in curbing wastage by optimizing internal conditions for extended shelf life.

Within healthcare, the utility of smart packaging goes a step further. Here, it acts as a guardian of medical devices, ensuring an enhanced user experience while bolstering patient safety. It is instrumental in preserving the potency and efficacy of pharmaceuticals from labs to patients, protecting against external tampering, and introducing intelligent features such as medication reminders and health status monitoring. Even in the beauty and health product sector, this technology facilitates consumer interactions, offering invaluable insights into product quality.

Furthermore, the medical device industry utilizes active packaging materials, intelligent functionalities, and cutting-edge digital technologies to redefine packaging approaches. These advancements collectively spotlight how smart packaging is fast shaping up to be a pivotal quality control platform spanning diverse industries.

Smart packaging implementation process

Implementing smart packaging in the healthcare industry is a multifaceted process that involves understanding the technology components and unique requirements of healthcare products. Here is a step-by-step guide to implementing smart packaging in the healthcare industry:

1. **Needs assessment**

    a. Gain a comprehensive understanding of the healthcare product, including its sensitivity to temperature, susceptibility to light exposure, and any specific humidity level requirements.

    b. **Transportation and distribution:** Assess the challenges associated with the transportation and distribution of healthcare products. Identify critical points in the supply chain where monitoring or intervention may be necessary.

2. **Components of smart packaging**

    a. **Sensors:** These are essential for monitoring conditions such as temperature, humidity, light exposure, and shock.

    b. **Microprocessors:** They analyze data from sensors and make real-time decisions. For example, sending alerts if conditions breach predefined thresholds.

    c. **Communication modules:** These components enable the packaging to communicate data in real-time to central systems or stakeholders.

    d. **Power sources:** Depending on the product's lifecycle, you might need long-lasting batteries or energy harvesting mechanisms.

    e. **Display indicators:** Visual or auditory alerts for immediate feedback. For example, a color-changing label if temperatures go out of range.

Take a look at *Figure 4.3:*

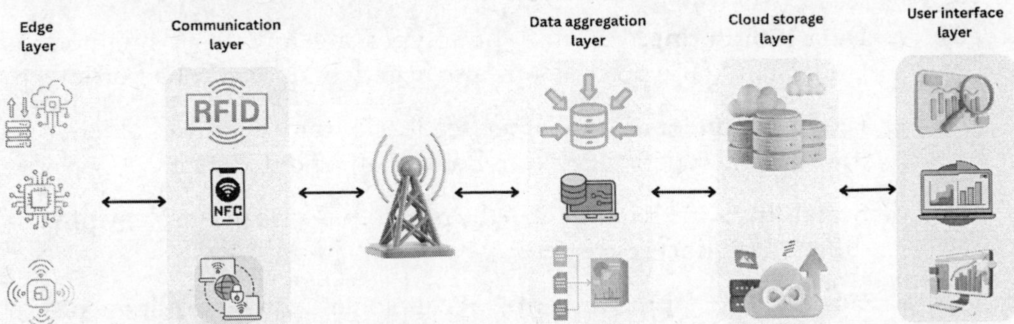

***Figure 4.3:** Smart packaging architecture*

3. **Architecture**

    a. **Edge layer:** The smart packaging itself with embedded sensors, processors, and local storage.

    b. **Communication layer:** Using technologies such as RFID, NFC, Bluetooth, LoRaWAN, or even cellular networks for transmitting data.

    c. **Data aggregation layer:** Central systems or hubs where data from multiple packages is collected.

    d. **Cloud storage and analysis:** Data is sent to the cloud, where advanced analytics, AI, and machine learning can be applied to gain insights.

    e. **User interface layer:** Dashboards, apps, or platforms where stakeholders can monitor product conditions, receive alerts, or analyze trends.

4. **Technologies to be used**

    a. **IoT platforms:** Platforms like AWS IoT, Google Cloud IoT, or Microsoft Azure IoT can be utilized for device management, data storage, and analytics.

    b. **Advanced analytics:** Tools like Tableau and Power BI for visualizing and understanding data.

    c. **Machine learning platforms:** TensorFlow and PyTorch for predictive analytics, for example, predicting when a product might leave its viable conditions.

    d. **Blockchain:** For ensuring data integrity and traceability throughout the product's journey.

5. **Implementation**

    a. **Prototype development:** Start with a small batch of products to test the viability of the smart packaging.

    b. **Data monitoring:** As your prototypes are in transit, monitor the data. Understand false positives or false negatives and adjust accordingly.

    c. **Feedback integration:** Gather feedback from all stakeholders, including transportation personnel, warehouse staff, and end-users.

    d. **Scalability:** Once confident in the prototype, scale the implementation across different products or regions.

    e. **Continuous improvement:** Technologies and requirements change. Regularly review and refine the smart packaging solution based on new data, feedback, and technological advancements.

Healthcare providers and distributors can harness the full potential of smart packaging, ensuring product integrity, improving patient safety, and enhancing operational efficiencies by meticulously planning and leveraging the right technologies.

Benefits of smart packaging

Real-time monitoring of healthcare products during transportation benefits the supply chain in several ways:

- **Enhanced traceability:** Temperature monitoring through IoT and asset management in the cloud helps keep healthcare products safe during transport by automatically tracking temperatures, reducing the chance of temperature problems in the cold chain.

- **Improved patient care:** Transport monitoring systems use wireless technology to send data about patients who are being moved. This helps improve the quality of care during transport and eases the worries of both patients and those taking care of them. It also reduces the stress on caregivers when patients need to be transferred.

- **Greater efficiency:** Real-time monitoring of vital signs and care delivery in remote environments helps improve patient monitoring and reduce workloads and potential errors for medical personnel, improving caregiver efficiency and reducing hospital readmissions.
- **Improved patient safety:** Smart packaging can have temperature sensors that send warnings if the temperature goes outside the safe range. This keeps medicines and vaccines that need specific temperatures working properly while they are being moved or stored.
- **Real-time tracking and monitoring:** One can put RFID tags and NFC tech in packages to track medicines and medical equipment in real-time as they move through the supply chain. This makes the supply chain work better and smoother.

Overall, real-time monitoring of healthcare products during transportation helps ensure the integrity and quality of healthcare products throughout the supply chain, improving patient safety, caregiver efficiency, and supply chain efficiency.

Case study 5: AR in manufacturing

AR has revolutionized the manufacturing industry by integrating technology into the production floor. By blending real-world elements with computer-generated graphics, data, and interactive features, AR creates a heightened reality that enhances the manufacturing process. This innovative approach significantly boosts production efficiency by minimizing labor requirements, providing visibility and control over operations, and enabling easier product customization for a few of the manufacturing industries.

The continuous advancements in AR technology have dramatically reshaped manufacturing practices. Specifically, the global market for augmented reality and virtual reality in manufacturing reached a valuation of USD 5.6 billion in 2021. It is projected to experience a **compound annual growth rate** (**CAGR**) of nearly 30% from this year until 2030.[1]

AR technology helps manufacturers find and fix issues, make production smoother, and keep machinery in good shape. It makes factories more flexible and efficient by changing how production lines work. AR is used in different ways, like remote assembly, giving instructions without using hands, improving quality control, and managing inventory better.

---

1 Augmented Reality & Virtual Reality In Manufacturing Market Size, Share & Trends Analysis Report by Component (Hardware, Software, services), By Technology, By Device, By Application, By Region, And Segment Forecasts, 2023 - 2030.

AR implementation in manufacturing

The stages of implementing AR in an existing manufacturing business are as follows:

1. **Develop and define use cases:** When adding AR to a manufacturing business, the first thing to do is figure out how you will use it. This means looking at how your business works now and deciding which jobs AR can make better or do automatically.

2. **Create a prototype:** Once you map out the use cases, the next step is to craft a prototype of the AR system to test it in a simulated environment. Testing the prototype will allow the team to define potential shortcomings or problems that need addressing before implementing them.

3. **Design and develop the AR system:** After testing and approving the prototype, it is time to design, develop, and implement the existing AR system. It includes identifying the hardware components necessary to run the system, designing and developing custom software solutions to enable the desired features, and integrating them into the enterprise.

4. **Train employees:** Upon creating the AR, employees need to learn to use it effectively. It may involve formalized instruction or hands-on practice sessions with simulated components of the system.

5. **Monitor and maintain:** The final stage of AR implementation is to monitor and maintain the system as needed. It includes regularly evaluating user feedback and adjusting settings to improve performance. Additionally, regular maintenance is essential to ensure the optimal operation of the system.

Use case 1: AR technology for equipment maintenance

AR is revolutionizing the approach to equipment maintenance in manufacturing. By fusing the virtual and real worlds, AR offers technicians precise, step-by-step guidance, enhancing accuracy and efficiency.

A manufacturing facility has multiple complex machineries, each with its maintenance intricacies. Traditionally, technicians relied on bulky manuals, training sessions, or expert intervention to address machinery hiccups, causing prolonged downtimes. Take a look at *Figure 4.4:*

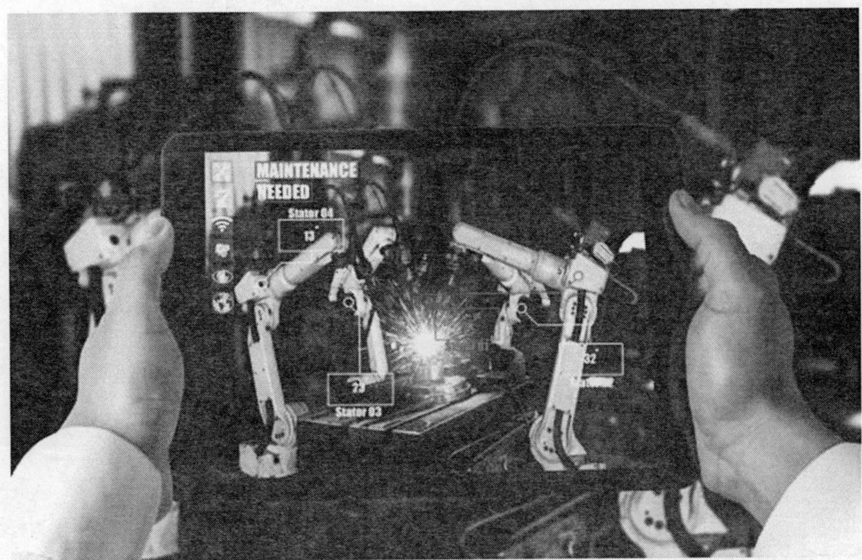

Figure 4.4: AR on the production floor

Solution with AR

The AR technology can bring the following solutions:

- **Instantaneous information:** Upon detecting an issue, the technician does an AR headset. The headset immediately identifies the machinery, retrieving its digital twin and showcasing real-time data, like temperature readings, wear and tear indicators, or performance metrics.
- **Guided repair:** As the technician observes the machinery, the AR system overlays detailed step-by-step repair or maintenance instructions. This is synchronized with the machine's current state, providing contextual advice.
- **3D interactive models:** For complex parts, a 3D animated model appears, guiding the technician on disassembly or replacement procedures. These models can be rotated, zoomed, or even dissected layer by layer, granting a clear insight into the machinery's intricate components.
- **Hands-free operation:** With voice commands or gesture controls, technicians can navigate through the instructions, allowing them to remain hands-on with the repair, thus streamlining the process.
- **Remote expert assistance:** If a technician encounters an unforeseen issue, they can instantly connect with off-site experts. These experts view the technician's live feed, guiding them interactively using AR annotations.

Benefits

The implementation of AR technology in manufacturing can help the industry in the following manner:

- **Efficient repairs:** Reduces the time spent on equipment maintenance, minimizing production downtime.
- **Enhanced accuracy:** The chances of errors during maintenance decrease as technicians receive visual, real-time guidance.
- **Cost savings:** Lessens the dependency on external expert visits or extensive training sessions.
- **Safety enhancement:** Technicians receive immediate alerts if they are about to make a potentially hazardous move, enhancing workplace safety.

AR technology, when integrated into equipment maintenance in manufacturing, not only streamlines the process but also ensures that technicians have all the tools they need to perform tasks safely and effectively. This union of digital information and real-world application holds immense potential for the future of manufacturing maintenance.

Use case 2: AR to transform worker training

In the realm of modern manufacturing, AR stands out as an instrumental tool in facilitating state-of-the-art staff training. This immersive technology synthesizes the virtual and physical worlds, offering an unparalleled interactive training experience that mirrors real-world situations without the traditional constraints of physical equipment or materials.

Envision a trainee about to begin their journey in a large manufacturing facility. Traditional induction methods might involve days of shadowing, physical manuals, or watching older instructional videos. Enter AR, and the entire training paradigm shifts. With AR, the entire training paradigm shifts in the following manner:

- **Intuitive induction:** With AR, newcomers can seamlessly familiarize themselves with the production line. By donning an AR headset, they are instantly surrounded by 3D models, lifelike holograms of machines, and virtual representations of the entire workflow. It is a real-world tour, only enhanced with digital elements highlighting each component's purpose, function, and potential challenges.
- **Role-based learning:** Each worker in a manufacturing setup has a unique role, and AR caters precisely to this. As trainees navigate through the AR-driven manufacturing environment, they get insights into not just their role but also an understanding of their peers' responsibilities. This comprehensive overview ensures that every worker recognizes the interconnectedness of the production line, promoting teamwork and understanding.

- **Instant performance feedback:** Traditional training often requires supervisors to observe, analyze, and provide feedback, which can sometimes be delayed. In contrast, AR systems offer real-time feedback. If a trainee missteps or deviates from the prescribed procedure, visual or auditory cues from the AR system immediately alert them. This immediate feedback loop accelerates the learning curve and ensures errors are corrected instantly, instilling the right practices from the outset.
- **Safety-first training:** Manufacturing setups can be fraught with potential hazards. Rather than learning about these dangers from manuals or after witnessing real-life incidents, AR equips employees with experiential safety knowledge. Trainees can walk through simulated hazardous scenarios, from chemical spills to machinery malfunctions. As they navigate these scenarios, the AR system offers real-time reactions. If a trainee fails to follow a safety protocol, they are instantly alerted through visual warnings or auditory prompts. This immersive form of learning ingrains safety procedures deeply, preparing them for real-world situations without exposing them to real-world risks.

AR is not just a technology; it is an ecosystem that can revolutionize staff training in manufacturing. It strips away the limitations of traditional training methods, replacing them with interactive, real-time, and engaging modules. As manufacturers look toward the future, AR's potential in cultivating a well-trained, safety-conscious, and efficient workforce becomes undeniably evident.

Case study 6: Smart data entry

Cognitive Process Automation is a type of software that utilizes AI and machine learning technologies to automate intricate business processes that involve cognitive skills, such as decision-making and problem-solving. CPA represents an intelligent approach to automation when compared to traditional methods, which usually rely on rule-based automation for repetitive tasks. What sets CPA apart is its ability to handle data, such as emails, voice messages, videos, and other forms of information enabling a comprehensive automation process. It is worth noting that terms like CPA may not be explicitly used by analyst firms like *Gartner*, *Forrester*, or *IDC*. Instead, these firms employ terminologies to describe aspects of cognitive automation such as **intelligent process automation** (**IPA**), **digital process automation** (**DPA**), hyper-automation, and cognitive services. CPA represents an advancement from **robotic process automation** (**RPA**) as it ventures into territories with greater complexity, irregularity, or subjectivity.

Data entry accuracy using CPA

RPA is a technology that employs software robots or *bots* to automate repetitive and rule-based tasks within business processes. These bots are programmed to mimic human interactions with software systems and applications, allowing for the automation of routine tasks, data entry, and workflow processes.

CPA is an extension of RPA. it uses AI, **natural language processing (NLP)**, and machine learning technologies to increase data entry accuracy and efficiency in manufacturing and supply chain activities. This makes it possible to automate various operations, cutting down on manual work and lowering human error. A few ways that CPA improves data entry in manufacturing and supply chain procedures are listed as follows:

- **Intelligent data capture:** CPA uses AI and machine learning to automatically capture, validate, and route data from documents and other sources, streamlining data entry and reducing the potential for errors.
- **Automation of repetitive tasks:** CPA can automate labor-intensive tasks such as data entry, order processing, and inventory management, freeing up human resources for more critical thinking and complex analysis tasks.
- **Real-time insights:** Integration of IoT data with CPA systems provides real-time insights, enabling sensor-based automation and improving decision-making in manufacturing and supply chain operations.
- **Enhanced forecasting and demand planning:** CPA can analyze historical data and current market trends to enable more precise, on-demand forecasting, improving supply chain efficiency.
- **Improved communication and collaboration:** CPA can enhance communication and collaboration between manufacturers, suppliers, and customers, leading to better supply chain performance.
- **Error reduction:** By automating data entry and other tasks, CPA reduces the likelihood of human errors, leading to more accurate data and better decision-making.

Hence, CPA revolutionizes data entry and decision-making in manufacturing and supply chain operations, leading to increased efficiency, reduced errors, and improved overall performance.

Difference between CPA and traditional automation

CPA differs from traditional automation in manufacturing and supply chain processes. Here are some key differences:

- **Technology:** Traditional automation typically uses rule-based automation, which follows predefined rules to perform tasks. In contrast, CPA leverages advanced technologies such as NLP data mining, semantic technology, and machine learning to mimic human thought and action, enabling more intelligent automation.

- **Data handling:** Traditional automation typically works with structured data, such as data in spreadsheets or databases. In contrast, CPA can handle unstructured data, such as emails, voice messages, videos, and other data types, enabling more comprehensive automation.
- **Complementing human workers:** Traditional automation is often used to replace human workers in repetitive tasks. CPA is designed to complement human workers by automating tasks that require cognitive skills, such as decision-making and problem-solving.
- **Timeline for projects:** Traditional automation projects often require significant upfront investment in time and resources to develop and implement. In contrast, CPA can be operationalized in just a few weeks, enabling faster time-to-value.
- **Programming:** Traditional automation requires developers to know and understand the target systems, and users need programming skills to operate it. In contrast, CPA is designed to be used directly by business users without needing support from data scientists or IT.

Hence, CPA represents a more advanced and intelligent approach to automation in manufacturing and supply chain processes, leveraging cutting-edge technologies to enable more comprehensive and efficient automation.

Architecture of CPA IoT-driven manufacturing

The architecture of IoT-driven CPA in manufacturing can be understood by combining the principles of IoT, digital manufacturing, and cognitive automation. While there are no specific search results that provide a comprehensive architecture for this specific combination, we can draw insights from existing IoT and digital manufacturing architectures to understand the key components and their interactions. Here are the main elements involved in an IoT-driven CPA architecture for manufacturing. Take a look at *Figure 4.5:*

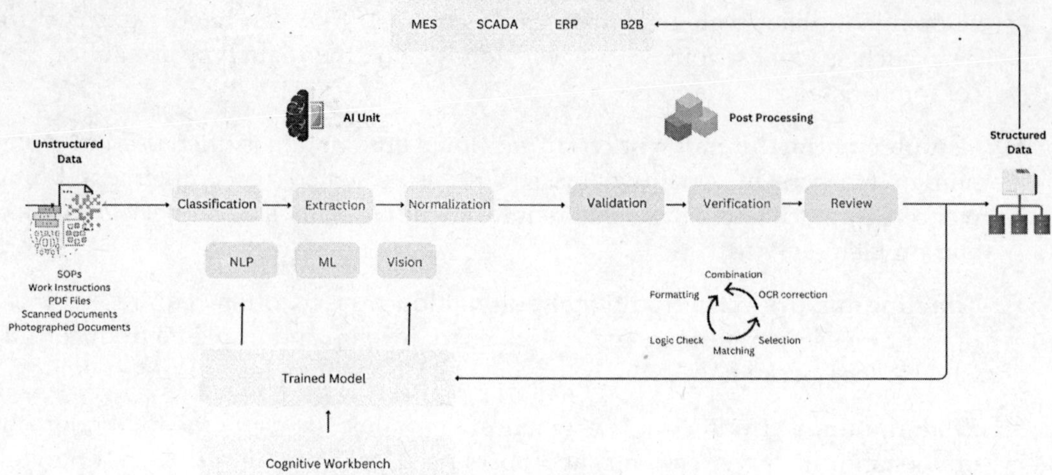

***Figure 4.5:** IoT-driven manufacturing using CPA*

- **Sensing and data collection:** In a factory, there are special sensors placed all around that keep an eye on things like how hot it is, how much pressure there is, if machines are shaking, and whether machines are working or not. These sensors do the important job of finding, sensing, and handling data, which is the main idea behind IoT.

- **Data transmission and processing:** The collected data is transmitted to a central processing unit, which can be a cloud-based platform or an on-premises server. This layer is responsible for data transmission, storage, and initial processing, such as filtering and aggregation.

- **Data analysis and cognitive automation:** In this layer, advanced analytics and machine learning algorithms are applied to the collected data to gain insights, detect patterns, and make predictions. Cognitive automation techniques, such as NLP and machine learning, are used to automate complex tasks that require cognitive skills, such as decision-making and problem-solving.

- **Integration with manufacturing systems:** The insights and recommendations generated by the cognitive automation layer are seamlessly integrated with a range of existing manufacturing systems, including **enterprise resource planning** (ERP) systems, production planning systems, quality management systems, **manufacturing execution systems** (MES), **business-to-business** (B2B) systems, and **supervisory control and data acquisition** (SCADA) systems. This comprehensive integration empowers organizations to make real-time decisions and optimize their processes based on the valuable insights and data-driven recommendations provided by the cognitive automation layer.

- **Feedback loop and continuous improvement:** The architecture should include a feedback loop that allows the system to learn and improve over time. This can be achieved by collecting feedback from operators, monitoring the performance of the implemented recommendations, and updating the machine learning models based on the new data.

While this architecture provides a high-level overview of an IoT-driven CPA system in manufacturing, the specific implementation may vary depending on the industry, company size, and other factors. It is essential to consider the unique requirements and challenges of each manufacturing environment when designing and implementing such a system.

Case study 7: Health and safety compliance monitoring

Industrial environments like factories and plants can expose employees to various potential health and safety hazards, from noise pollution and air contaminants to dangerous machinery and extreme temperatures. This necessitates rigorous **occupational health and safety** (**OHS**) compliance programs in manufacturing organizations. However, traditional manual compliance processes based on periodic inspections have limitations in comprehensively assessing and controlling rapidly changing shop floor risks. Fortunately, the IoT enables a new paradigm for OHS management in smart factories– real-time, data-driven safety compliance.

IoT refers to an ecosystem of connected physical objects, devices, sensors, and systems that can monitor, transmit, analyze, and exchange data over the Internet through embedded computing. In manufacturing, inexpensive IoT sensors can be ubiquitously instrumented across factory environments to track hazardous conditions rather than relying on infrequent inspections continuously. This creates a digital nervous system providing comprehensive visibility. Combined with cloud analytics, it enables intelligent real-time monitoring and preemptive control of health and safety risks.

A variety of IoT sensors can help monitor factory OHS parameters:

- **Gas sensors**: Detect airborne chemicals like **volatile organic compounds** (**VOCs**), combustible gases, and particulates to protect against inhalation risks.
- **Noise sensors**: Track sound levels across machinery and high-decibel areas to avoid hearing damage and comply with regulations.
- **Temperature and humidity sensors**: Ensure workplace air conditions are within limits and not dangerously hot or cold.
- **Air flow sensors**: Monitor ventilation rates for adequate air quality and circulation.
- **Vibration sensors**: Identify excessive vibration that could damage structures or workers' hands.

- **Personnel tracking**: Wearables monitor lone or isolated workers to call for help during emergencies.
- **Panic buttons**: Workers can instantly trigger alerts in case of an immediate threat to safety.

Connected IoT sensors generate far richer OHS data compared to sparse manual sampling. Built-in telemetry also reduces faults. Protocols like **Narrowband Internet of Things** (**NB-IoT**) provide low-power, wide-area connectivity for sensors in remote locations. Gateways collect and process field data before transmitting it to cloud platforms via Wi-Fi or 4G/5G networks.

Cloud-based monitoring and analytics

Ingesting high-velocity sensor streams into cloud IoT platforms like AWS IoT, Microsoft Azure IoT, and Google Cloud IoT provides highly scalable and reliable data management for factory-wide OHS monitoring programs. Cloud databases enable aggregating dispersed sensor data into a unified data lake for analysis.

Big data analytics and machine learning algorithms can then extract key occupational health and safety insights from the massive datasets:

- Identifying trends and anomalies indicating emerging risks or process deviations.
- Correlating hazard data with weather, production schedules, and so on, to find interdependencies.
- Generating real-time alerts when thresholds are exceeded or dangerous conditions are detected.
- Producing risk heat maps to prioritize hazards and guide corrective actions.
- Benchmarking against industry standards to quantify compliance levels.
- Forecasting and optimizing staffing needs based on predictive analytics.

These cloud-enabled analytics transform IoT sensor data into an intelligent occupational health and safety management system. Risks no longer fall through the cracks between manual compliance checks.

Edge computing for real-time response

Latency-sensitive monitoring and hazardous situation response can leverage edge computing resources co-located within factories. This allows pre-processing IoT data and running ML inferencing models at the edge to act on critical OHS threats in milliseconds vs. seconds. Workers can be instantly alerted to dangerous gas build-ups or material leaks detected by edge gateways before the situation escalates. Integrating protocols like **Open Platform Communications Unified Architecture** (**OPC UA**) and **Manufacturing**

Technical Communication Protocol (**MTConnect**) allows connecting to legacy equipment and **supervisory control and data acquisition** (**SCADA**) systems to automate emergency shutdown if required.

IoT solution strategies for OHS management

Intelligently harnessing IoT and cloud analytics delivers significant advantages over traditional occupational health and safety management:

- Continuous monitoring improves risk coverage across the entire facility over time rather than limited sampling.
- Access to rich data like machine vibration and gas concentrations provides early warning of issues.
- Automated compliance reporting reduces manual paperwork and auditing.
- Real-time awareness and alerts to workers about nearby hazards via wearables.
- Rapid incident response by automatically triggering alarms, ventilation, shutdowns, and so on.
- Predictive analytics to anticipate emerging risks and strategize reductions proactively.
- Reduced workplace injuries, illnesses, insurance and liability costs.

The continuous oversight and actionable insights enabled by IoT sensor networks, cloud analytics, and edge intelligence platforms provide a path to proactive, preventative, and data-driven OHS management. By detecting risks in real time and responding quickly and intelligently, manufacturers can protect the most critical asset of all – their workforce. This drives both regulatory compliance and business value. Workplace safety and employee well-being are top priorities for any responsible organization. In the era of smart factories, IoT gives manufacturers new tools to achieve those vital goals effectively.

Case study 8: Smart material handling

Warehouses and fulfillment centers handle immense volumes of diverse products and materials daily that must flow efficiently to meet rising customer expectations on order delivery times. However, the nature of material handling processes poses inherent challenges:

- Large facilities make manually transporting goods time-consuming and labor-intensive.
- Inventory levels fluctuate frequently with seasonal peaks, promotions, and so on, making planning and balancing workloads difficult.

- Sudden disruptions like worker shortages or delayed shipments require rapid adaptation.

This strain on human productivity and warehouse flexibility is exactly where **autonomous mobile robots** (**AMR**s) enhanced by the IoT offer solutions. AMR is a self-driving robotic vehicle that transport, sort, and organize inventory and materials within warehouses or production environments. They autonomously navigate planned routes using techniques like **simultaneous localization and mapping** (**SLAM**), microwave, ultrasonic, or optical sensors. AMRs such as tuggers, forklifts, and pick-and-place robots can take over grueling material handling tasks from human counterparts driven by embedded intelligence.

IoT connectivity and analytics integration unlock the next speed, flexibility, and optimization level for autonomous mobile robot fleets. The key enhancements enabled by IoT include:

- **Real-time tracking**: Connecting AMRs to warehouse management and ERP systems provides end-to-end visibility into material flows. Inventory levels, orders, and logistics activities become more responsive and predictive than manual audits.
- **Coordination and workload balancing:** IoT allows autonomous vehicles to optimize routes dynamically, respond to urgent transfer tasks, and balance work allocation based on real-time needs and constraints.
- **Inventory management:** IoT identification tags and sensors on materials, combined with AMR-mounted barcode and RFID readers, facilitate automated pick-and-place of specific items. This caters to rapidly shifting inventories and orders.
- **Fleet optimization:** IoT telemetry from AMR allows monitoring utilization, energy usage, maintenance needs, and so on, at an individual and fleet level to optimize vehicle performance.
- **Infrastructure integration:** IoT systems provide awareness of the infrastructure state. For example, integrating door and obstruction sensors with AMR navigation algorithms improves routing and safety.
- **Edge analytics:** Onboard IoT edge gateways allow partial compute offloading from AMRs and running latency-sensitive video analytics for object detection and classification. This unlocks more advanced autonomous capabilities.
- **Predictive analytics:** Collecting AMR telemetry and warehouse data over time enables machine learning to optimize future material flows and staff planning.

Case study 9: Last-mile delivery optimization

The last mile of the supply chain is the final delivery from a distribution hub to the end customer. It remains one of the most crucial yet challenging links. Delivery windows continue shrinking while order volumes grow. Dynamic real-world uncertainties like traffic congestion, driver availability, weather delays, and returned shipments further complicate last-mile execution. This makes logistics providers need to maximize the efficiency and flexibility of their last-mile delivery operations. Fortunately, the IoT offers innovative new solutions.

Last-mile delivery must strike an optimal balance between:

- **Agility:** Responding quickly to real-time delivery requests, priority changes, and exceptions.
- **Travel optimization:** Routing vehicles and loads to minimize distance driven and congestion delays.
- **Asset utilization:** Fully leveraging vehicle capacity, storage hubs, and driver availability.
- **Experience:** Meeting customer expectations on order accuracy, visibility, ease of delivery, and pickup.
- **Profitability:** Controlling costs in the low-margin last mile to remain economically viable.

This is challenging to coordinate manually. IoT capabilities can drive the agility, optimization, and transparency needed for robust last-mile operations.

Cost-effective IoT sensors and connectivity empower new levels of real-time visibility:

- **Location tracking:** GPS and RFID tags on trucks and parcels pinpoint current location and speed to estimate delivery times.
- **Condition monitoring:** Sensors track temperature, humidity, vibration, and more inside packages and truck trailers for quality assurance.
- **Driver analytics:** IoT connects driver phones and vehicle sensors to feed telematics data on current activity, hours of service, economy, and maintenance needs.
- **Customer shipments:** RFID-tagged parcels, pallets, and containers provide shipment-level monitoring from the warehouse through customer delivery.

By consolidating data from vehicles, goods, drivers, and recipients, an integrated IoT platform provides a comprehensive understanding of key last-mile processes and resource availability to drive smarter execution.

Advanced analytics extract powerful insights from the richness of last-mile IoT data:

- **Dynamic routing optimization:** It avoids delays by analyzing real-time traffic, weather, road incidents, and delivery densities to adapt routes continuously.
- **Predictive asset maintenance:** It uses vehicle telemetry to forecast maintenance needs and minimize downtime through proactive scheduling.

- **Inventory optimization:** Inventory optimization racks item-level shipment status to refine safety stocks and prevent stockouts.
- **Driver performance and safety:** analyzes driver patterns to provide coaching, incentives, and assistance like fatigue alerts.
- **Automated reporting:** It logs delivery proof-of-service, creates customer-facing transparency, and streamlines regulatory compliance.
- **User self-service:** User self-service allows customers to conveniently reschedule deliveries or redirect parcels using a mobile app connected to the IoT platform.

The overarching benefit of IoT-powered delivery orchestration is agile automation and synchronization from the first mile to the last mile based on real-world conditions. This is the foundation for scalable, reliable, and economical last-mile operations as delivery volumes and demands accelerate. Machine learning unlocks further opportunities like predicting delivery times and optimizing warehouse-vehicle allocations across distribution networks.

An integrated IoT architecture seamlessly orchestrates last-mile flows:

- **Automatic dispatch:** It initiates delivery requests based on inventory systems and route plans. Provides real-time visibility into assigned jobs.
- **Mobile driver apps:** Mobile driver apps provide pickup/delivery instructions, navigation, proof-of-delivery, inventory scans, and more optimized to the location and context.
- **Dynamic optimization engine:** It continuously adjusts routes and schedules based on current hub inventory, traffic, weather, and other IoT data.
- **Web portals:** Web portal allows customers and internal teams to track parcels, report issues, request redirects, and reschedule via a real-time interface.

IoT provides indispensable data and digital tools for tackling the multidimensional complexities of last-mile delivery in the real world. The data visibility, analytics, and automation enabled by IoT platforms empower logistics providers to achieve new levels of responsiveness, reliability, and cost-efficiency in fulfilling the critical last mile.

Case study 10: Smart waste management

The IoT is playing a major role in waste management and recycling optimization. IoT devices can be used to collect data on waste levels, types, and locations. This data can then be used to improve waste collection and recycling rates.

Here are some of the problems that IoT can solve in waste management and recycling:

- **Inefficient waste collection:** IoT devices can be used to track the location of waste bins and trucks. This information can be used to optimize waste collection routes and reduce the amount of time trucks spend on the road.

- **Illegal dumping:** IoT devices can be used to monitor areas where illegal dumping is common. This information can be used to identify and prosecute offenders.
- **Recycling contamination:** IoT devices can be used to identify contaminated recyclables. This information can be used to improve recycling rates and reduce the amount of waste that goes to landfills.

Inefficient waste collection

There are many different types of waste in industries, including:

- **Hazardous waste:** This type of waste can harm human health or the environment. It includes things like chemicals, batteries, and medical waste.
- **Municipal solid waste:** This type of waste comprises everyday items like paper, plastic, metal, and food.
- **Construction and demolition waste:** This type of waste is generated from the construction and demolition of buildings and other structures.
- **Industrial waste:** This type of waste is generated from industrial processes. It can include things like chemicals, metals, and sludge.

The problem of waste in industries is a big one. In the United States, businesses generate an estimated 262 million tons of hazardous waste each year. According to the *Environmental Protection Agency*, an average American generates about 4.4 pounds of trash per day. You can refer to the following for more information: **https://www.epa.gov/emergency-response-research/solid-waste.**

There are several ways that IoT can be used to solve the problem of waste in industries. For example, IoT sensors can monitor waste levels and identify areas where waste is being generated at a high rate. This information can be used to optimize waste collection routes and reduce the amount of waste that is sent to landfills.

IoT can also be used to track the movement of waste through a facility. This information can be used to identify areas where waste is stored for too long or bottlenecks in the waste management process. This can help to reduce costs and improve efficiency.

Finally, IoT can be used to educate employees about waste management and recycling. This can help to reduce the amount of waste that is generated in the first place.

Many companies have successfully used IoT to solve the problem of waste in industries. For example, *Schneider Electric* has developed a system that uses IoT sensors to monitor waste levels and identify areas where waste is generated at a high rate. This information is used to optimize waste collection routes and reduce the amount of waste sent to landfills.

Another example is *Veolia*, which has developed a system that uses IoT sensors to track waste movement through a facility. This information is used to identify areas where waste is stored for too long or bottlenecks in the waste management process. This can help to reduce costs and improve efficiency.

Overall, IoT has the potential to revolutionize the way waste is managed in industries. By collecting and analyzing data, IoT devices can help to reduce waste, improve efficiency, and educate the public.

Illegal dumping

IoT can help to stop illegal dumping in a number of ways. For example, IoT sensors can be used to monitor areas where illegal dumping is common. This information can be used to identify and prosecute offenders. Additionally, IoT can be used to track the movement of waste, which can help to identify illegal dumping sites. Finally, IoT can be used to educate the public about the dangers of illegal dumping, which can help to reduce the number of incidents.

IoT can help governments and industries in several ways. For example, IoT can be used to improve waste management and recycling. Additionally, IoT can be used to reduce costs and improve efficiency. Finally, IoT can be used to protect the environment.

Here are some specific examples of how IoT can help government and industries to stop illegal dumping:

- IoT sensors can be used to monitor areas where illegal dumping is common. This information can be used to identify and prosecute offenders. For example, *San Diego* has installed IoT sensors in areas where illegal dumping is common. These sensors detect when waste is dumped, and alert the city's waste management department. The department then sends a team to investigate and clean up the site.
- IoT can be used to track the movement of waste. This can help to identify illegal dumping sites. For example, the company *Waste Management* uses IoT to track the movement of waste from its collection points to its disposal sites. If waste is found to be diverted from its intended destination, Waste Management can investigate and take action.
- IoT can be used to educate the public about the dangers of illegal dumping. This can help to reduce the number of incidents. For example, the company *Keep America Beautiful* uses IoT to track the number of illegal dumping incidents in a given area. This information is used to create targeted educational campaigns that aim to reduce illegal dumping.

Overall, IoT has the potential to be a powerful tool in the fight against illegal dumping. By collecting and analyzing data, IoT devices can help to identify and prosecute offenders, track the movement of waste, and educate the public about the dangers of illegal dumping.

Recycling contamination

IoT can help recycle contamination in smart factories, government, and the environment in a number of ways.

For smart factories, IoT can be used to monitor the quality of incoming materials and to identify contaminants before they enter the recycling stream. This can help to reduce the amount of waste generated and to improve the quality of recycled materials.

For the government, IoT can be used to track the movement of recyclable materials and to identify contamination at sorting and processing facilities. This information can be used to improve the efficiency of recycling operations and to reduce the amount of waste that is sent to landfills.

For the environment, IoT can be used to monitor the impact of recycling on air and water quality. This information can be used to identify and address potential environmental problems associated with recycling.

Overall, IoT has the potential to play a significant role in reducing recycling contamination and improving the environmental impact of recycling.

Here are some specific examples of how IoT can help to reduce recycling contamination:

- IoT sensors can be used to monitor the quality of incoming materials. For example, sensors can be used to detect the presence of contaminants such as food waste, plastic bags, and glass in paper recycling streams. This information can be used to reject contaminated materials before they enter the recycling stream.
- IoT sensors can be used to identify contamination at sorting and processing facilities. For example, sensors can be used to detect the presence of contaminants such as metals, plastics, and glass in mixed recycling streams. This information can be used to improve the efficiency of recycling operations and to reduce the amount of waste that is sent to landfills.
- IoT sensors can be used to monitor the impact of recycling on air and water quality. For example, sensors can be used to detect the presence of pollutants such as heavy metals and volatile organic compounds in the air and water near recycling facilities. This information can be used to identify and address potential environmental problems associated with recycling.

IoT is a powerful tool that can be used to improve recycling and protect the environment. By collecting and analyzing data, IoT devices can help to identify and address contamination, improve efficiency, and reduce environmental impact.

Case study 11: Smart Product Lifecycle Management

IoT-generated data can be integrated into **Product Lifecycle Management (PLM)** systems to provide valuable insights into product performance, maintenance requirements, and end-of-life considerations. This enables manufacturers to improve product design, extend product lifespans, and optimize aftermarket services.

Here are some specific examples of how IoT data can be used in PLM:

- **Monitor product performance:** IoT sensors can be used to collect data on product usage, such as temperature, vibration, and load. This data can be used to identify potential problems and to prevent failures.
- **Schedule maintenance:** IoT data can be used to track the usage of products and to identify when they need to be serviced. This can help to extend the lifespan of products and to reduce the cost of maintenance.
- **Optimize aftermarket services:** IoT data can be used to provide customers with personalized service and support. For example, manufacturers can use IoT data to identify when a product is about to fail and to offer a replacement or repair proactively.

Overall, IoT data can be a valuable tool for manufacturers who want to improve the quality and lifespan of their products. By integrating IoT data into PLM systems, manufacturers can gain valuable insights that can help them improve their products and services.

A manufacturer of industrial equipment uses IoT sensors to collect data on the performance of its equipment. This data is then used to identify potential problems and prevent failures. For example, the data can be used to identify when a machine is operating at a higher temperature than normal, which could indicate a problem with the cooling system. The manufacturer can then take action to prevent the machine from failing, such as by scheduling a maintenance visit or by replacing a faulty component. Take a look at *Figure 4.6:*

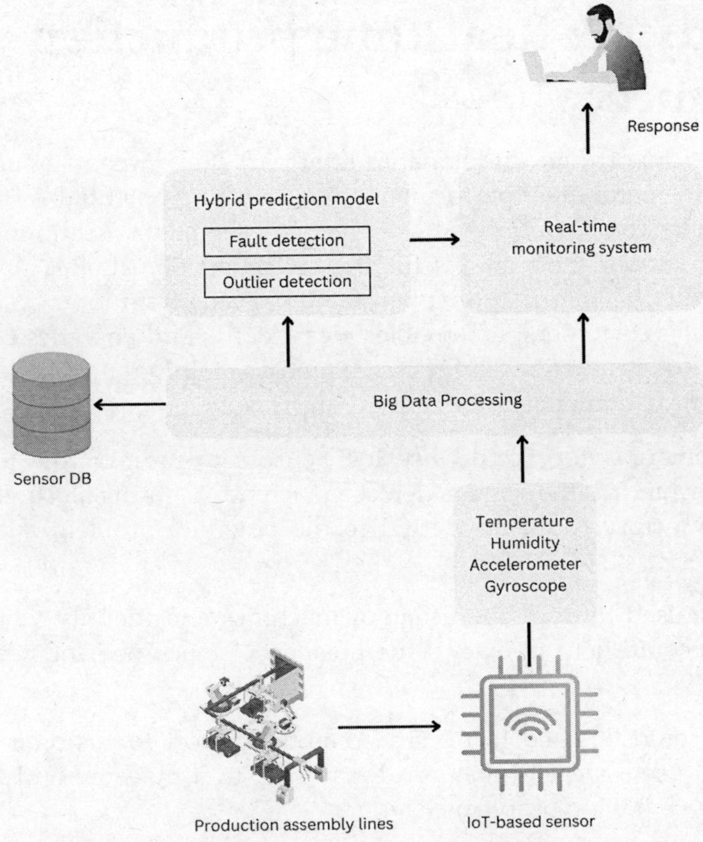

Figure 4.6: *IoT data use in PLM*

As IoT technology continues to develop, we can expect to see even more innovative ways to use this data to improve the quality and lifespan of products.

IoT can be used to improve aftermarket services in smart factories by:

- Monitoring equipment performance and identifying potential problems.
- Scheduling maintenance and repairs based on actual usage data.
- Providing remote support to customers.
- Collecting data on customer usage patterns.
- Providing customers with personalized service and support.

Overall, IoT can be a powerful tool for improving aftermarket services in smart factories. By collecting and analyzing data, IoT devices can help to identify potential problems, prevent failures, provide remote support, and collect data that can be used to improve product design and development.

Case study 12: Real-time production performance

IoT offers various opportunities to enhance aftermarket services in smart factories. This includes monitoring equipment performance and detecting potential issues. Maintenance and repair schedules can be optimized using actual usage data. Additionally, IoT enables remote customer support and allows for the collection of valuable data on customer usage patterns. With this information, manufacturers can offer more personalized service and support to their customers. IoT-enabled dashboards and analytics can provide real-time visualization of production performance metrics, helping managers make informed decisions and identify bottlenecks for process improvement.

For example, a smart factory could use IoT sensors to monitor the temperature and vibration of its machines. If the sensors detect a machine operating at a higher temperature than normal, the factory could be alerted to the potential problem and take action to prevent a failure.

IoT could also be used to track the usage of machines and identify when they need to be serviced. This could help to extend the lifespan of machines and reduce the cost of maintenance.

In addition, IoT could be used to provide remote support to customers. For example, a customer could use a smartphone app to connect to a machine and get help from a technician if they are having problems.

Finally, IoT could be used to collect data on customer usage patterns. This data could be used to improve product design and development, as well as to provide customers with personalized service and support.

Overall, IoT has the potential to revolutionize the way that aftermarket services are provided in smart factories. By collecting and analyzing data, IoT devices can help to improve the quality and lifespan of products, reduce the cost of maintenance, and provide customers with personalized service and support. Based on all contexts above, the following production performance parameters need to be measured in manufacturing-based factories:

- Overall equipment effectiveness
- Machine utilization
- Downtime
- Scrap rate
- Yield
- Cycle time

- First-pass yield
- Safety incidents

IoT can help to measure these parameters by collecting data from sensors and other devices. This data can then be analyzed to identify trends and patterns to improve production efficiency and effectiveness. Machine performance, such as temperature, vibration, and load. This data can be used to identify potential problems and to prevent failures. IoT sensors can also be used to track the movement of materials and products through the production process. This data can be used to identify bottlenecks and to improve efficiency.

IoT can also be used to collect data on customer satisfaction and employee satisfaction. This data can be used to identify areas where improvements can be made to improve the overall quality of the manufacturing process.

Overall, IoT can be a powerful tool for improving production performance in manufacturing-based factories. By collecting and analyzing data, IoT devices can help to identify potential problems, prevent failures, improve efficiency, and improve customer satisfaction.

Based on all contexts above, management can use IoT-based inputs from the production environment in the following ways:

- To improve production efficiency and effectiveness by identifying potential problems and preventing failures.
- To improve quality by tracking the movement of materials and products through the production process and identifying bottlenecks.
- To improve customer satisfaction by collecting data on customer satisfaction and identifying areas where improvements can be made.
- To improve employee satisfaction by collecting data and identifying areas where improvements can be made.
- To improve safety by identifying potential safety hazards and taking steps to mitigate them.
- To improve environmental impact by tracking the use of resources and identifying areas where improvements can be made.

Overall, IoT can be a powerful tool for improving production performance in manufacturing-based factories. By collecting and analyzing data, IoT devices can help to identify potential problems, prevent failures, improve efficiency, and improve customer satisfaction.

One example of a company that has implemented IoT in its production setup is **General Electric** (**GE**). GE has installed sensors and software across its manufacturing plants to collect data on everything from machine performance to energy usage. This data is then used to improve efficiency, identify potential problems, and prevent failures.

GE has seen significant benefits from its IoT implementation. For example, the company has reduced energy consumption by 10% and increased production by 5%. GE has also been able to improve the quality of its products by identifying and addressing potential problems early on.

The success of GE's IoT implementation is just one example of how this technology can be used to improve manufacturing operations. As IoT technology continues to develop, we can expect to see even more innovative ways to use this data to improve the efficiency and quality of manufacturing processes.

Here are some other examples of companies that have implemented IoT in their production setups:

- **Schneider Electric:** *Schneider Electric* has installed IoT sensors in its factories to collect data on energy usage, machine performance, and product quality. The company uses this data to improve efficiency, identify potential problems, and prevent failures.
- **Siemens:** *Siemens* has installed IoT sensors and software in its factories to collect data on production, quality, and maintenance. The company uses this data to improve efficiency, reduce costs, and improve quality.
- **ABB:** *ABB* has installed IoT sensors and software in its factories to collect data on production, quality, and maintenance. The company uses this data to improve efficiency, reduce costs, and improve quality.

As IoT technology continues to develop, we can expect to see even more innovative ways to use this data to improve the efficiency and quality of manufacturing processes.

Conclusion

The proliferation of the IoT is profoundly transforming manufacturing operations, unlocking new potential through connected, intelligent systems. As illustrated throughout this chapter, IoT-enabled solutions deliver tangible value across critical facets of smart factory ecosystems.

Real-time monitoring and predictive maintenance enabled by IoT sensors help boost equipment utilization and lifespan. IoT analytics assist dynamic production planning and scheduling to maximize output while maintaining flexibility. Automated IoT-driven inspection delivers new scales of quality assurance. From shop floors to top floors, data visibility drives informed decision-making and continuous optimization.

Beyond the factory walls, IoT integrates supply chains via unified tracking and coordination. Partners gain transparency into each other's processes and inventories, enabling collaborative planning. Combining IoT with AI, robotics, and other Industry 4.0 technologies magnifies their benefits through hybrid solutions. This convergence will ultimately enable the self-optimizing, resilient factories of the future.

However, IoT adoption has its challenges, from cybersecurity concerns to technology integration hurdles. A holistic approach is essential, aligning IoT deployments with long-term strategic objectives. With careful planning and change management, manufacturers can transform IoT's promise into tangible gains in efficiency, quality, and agility.

As IoT proliferates and matures, its manufacturing impact will intensify. Gaining IoT expertise and cultivating data-driven cultures is imperative to competitive survival. The factory of tomorrow will build upon connected foundational technologies established today. With the power of IoT harnessed responsibly, manufacturers can gain the intelligence, control, and integration needed to excel in the next industrial era.

In the upcoming chapter, we will explore the critical realm of change management in IoT adoption. Beyond technical expertise, successful integration hinges on mastering human dynamics. We will delve into strategies for fostering an IoT-friendly culture, overcoming resistance to change, and nurturing innovation for a future of boundless possibilities.

Points to remember

- IoT refers to a network of interconnected physical objects and devices that collect and share data through embedded sensors and software. IoT enables automation, monitoring, and data analytics in manufacturing.
- The key components of an IoT system architecture include sensors, controllers, cloud platforms, data analytics tools, and communication protocols like MQTT and CoAP. Sensors collect data, controllers process it, while the cloud provides storage and computing capabilities.
- IoT allows real-time monitoring and predictive maintenance in manufacturing plants by analyzing data from sensors on equipment to forecast failures before they occur. This prevents downtime and optimizes maintenance.
- IoT improves production planning and scheduling by providing real-time visibility into inventory, orders, machine performance, and other factors, enabling dynamic adjustments to maximize output.
- IoT enhances quality control by collecting sensor data inline during production to identify defects rapidly using analytics. This facilitates corrective actions before defects multiply.
- Smart packaging with IoT sensors enables real-time monitoring of product conditions like temperature and humidity during transportation. This helps ensure quality and safety.

- Augmented reality provides interactive, contextual training for manufacturing workers by overlaying digital information onto the physical environment.
- IoT-enabled occupational health and safety monitoring using sensors provides continuous, data-driven assessment of hazards like noise, air quality, and radiation.
- Autonomous mobile robots can optimize material flows in warehouses when coordinated in real-time using IoT connectivity and data.
- Last-mile delivery operations can be made more efficient and responsive by leveraging IoT visibility into vehicle location, traffic, weather, and inventory status for dynamic optimization.

Multiple choice questions

1. **What is one of the key benefits of utilizing IoT data in warehouse operations?**
    a. Enhancing customer communication
    b. Reducing empty trip distances by optimizing task assignments
    c. Predicting future market trends
    d. Managing employee payroll
2. **How can IoT data improve warehouse resource management?**
    a. By tracking customer orders in real time
    b. By providing insights into warehouse layout and resource routes
    c. By automating the packaging process
    d. By outsourcing resource management to third-party companies
3. **What is one of the potential consequences of delivery delays and quality issues in supply chain management?**
    a. Increased profitability
    b. Improved employee morale
    c. Disruption of production
    d. Enhanced brand reputation
4. **How does the IoT contribute to supply chain optimization?**
    a. By automating customer service
    b. By reducing labor costs
    c. By providing real-time sensor data for monitoring and insights
    d. By replacing traditional supply chain management software

5. **What types of sensor data can be tracked using IoT systems for supply chain management?**
   a. Only temperature and humidity
   b. Only acceleration and position
   c. A wide range, including temperature, humidity, acceleration, position, and radiation
   d. None; IoT systems do not track sensor data

6. **How does IoT technology benefit businesses in responding to supply chain crises?**
   a. It provides immediate information to stakeholders, enabling effective response.
   b. It prevents all supply chain crises from occurring.
   c. It notifies the media about crises.
   d. It replaces the need for human intervention in crisis management.

7. **How can IoT help improve occupational health and safety management in manufacturing plants?**
   a. By replacing all human workers with robots
   b. By collecting data through manual audits
   c. By enabling continuous real-time monitoring and predictive analytics
   d. By fully automating all processes without human oversight

8. **Which of the following technologies enable CPA to handle unstructured data like emails, voice messages, and videos?**
   a. Rule-based automation
   b. Natural language processing
   c. Edge computing
   d. Computer vision

9. **How can blockchain technology be combined with IoT for supply chain management?**
   a. To replace ERP systems
   b. To enable transparent and immutable provenance tracking
   c. To reduce the need for sensors
   d. To eliminate middlemen

10. How can IoT data help optimize last-mile delivery operations?

   a. By forecasting future order volumes

   b. By providing real-time visibility for dynamic optimization

   c. By automating all delivery tasks

   d. By increasing fuel consumption

Answer key

1. b.
2. b.
3. c.
4. c.
5. c.
6. a.
7. c.
8. b.
9. b.
10. b.

Questions

1. What are the key components of an IoT system architecture?
2. How does IoT enable predictive maintenance and reduce downtime?
3. What manufacturing processes can be optimized using IoT analytics?
4. How can IoT improve quality control and reduce defects?
5. What are the benefits of IoT for supply chain visibility?
6. How can IoT data be used to enhance inventory management?
7. What security measures should be taken when implementing IoT?
8. What communication protocols are commonly used for IoT devices?
9. How can IoT data help optimize production planning and scheduling?
10. How is IoT transforming robotics and automation in manufacturing?

11. What are some challenges faced in adopting IoT solutions?
12. How can manufacturers integrate IoT with legacy systems?
13. How can IoT improve traceability and compliance in supply chains?
14. What skills are required to effectively implement IoT projects?
15. How can digital twin simulation assist IoT system design and deployment?

Key terms

- **Supervisory control and data acquisition:** Systems used to monitor and control industrial processes remotely.
- **Open Platform Communications Unified Architecture:** An industrial M2M communication protocol for interoperability.
- **Manufacturing execution system:** Software systems used to track and document manufacturing processes.
- **Enterprise resource planning:** Software tools that integrate business processes and data flows.
- **Cyber-physical systems:** Networked monitoring and control systems with integrated physical and computational components.
- **Data mining:** The process of analyzing large data sets to identify patterns for actionable insights.
- **Machine learning:** AI algorithms that can learn from data to make predictions without explicit programming.
- **Computer vision:** Technology that seeks to automate analysis of visual data using AI and deep learning.
- **Digital thread:** The flow of data through product lifecycle stages enabled by connected IT systems.
- **Radio frequency identification:** Technology that uses radio waves for Contactless identification and tracking of objects.
- **Smart packaging:** Packaging equipped with sensors and connectivity for real-time monitoring and tracking.
- **Augmented reality:** Technology that overlays digital information and graphics onto the real-world environment.
- **Cognitive process automation:** Software that uses AI to automate complex tasks requiring cognitive skills.

- **Occupational health and safety:** Systems and practices for ensuring workplace safety and compliance.
- **Autonomous mobile robots:** Self-driving robotic vehicles for material handling in warehouses.
- **Dynamic routing optimization:** Continuously adapting delivery routes based on real-time conditions.
- **Blockchain:** Distributed ledger technology providing immutable record of transactions.
- **Digital twin:** Virtual representation of a physical asset or process.

Join our book's Discord space

Join the book's Discord Workspace for Latest updates, Offers, Tech happenings around the world, New Release and Sessions with the Authors:

https://discord.bpbonline.com

CHAPTER 5
Business Factors and Optimization for IoT Implementation

Introduction

In this chapter, we will journey through the intricate landscape of change management within **Internet of Things** (**IoT**) adoption. As the IoT revolution continues to reshape industries and business landscapes, the successful integration of IoT technologies extends beyond mere technical prowess; it hinges on mastering the human dynamics that accompany innovation. Here, we delve into the strategies essential for facilitating a seamless transition into the IoT era. From understanding IoT's profound impact on organizational culture to fostering an environment where innovation and inclusivity thrive, you will gain the knowledge and tools required to inspire your team's embrace of IoT. Navigate the path to overcoming resistance to change and nurturing a culture where IoT innovation becomes second nature, propelling your organization into a future of boundless possibilities.

The outcome of IoT projects frequently proves unpredictable, primarily attributed to the absence of clearly outlined **Key Performance Indicators** (**KPIs**) during the planning stage and the formidable challenges in monitoring the generation of value throughout implementation for manufacturing and supply chain. This chapter also delves into these intricacies, offering insights and strategies to enhance the success rates of IoT projects by addressing the critical elements often overlooked in their planning and execution phases.

Structure

This chapter covers the following topics:

- Strategic objectives for IoT implementation
    - o Aligning IoT Initiatives with business strategy
- Mapping IoT solutions to business cases, benefits, and KPIs
    - o Use cases, benefits, and KPI(s) for embracing IoT in manufacturing
    - o Use cases and benefits of IoT in management
- Mitigating risks with IOT implementation
    - o Regulatory and compliance risks
    - o Device reliability and maintenance risks
    - o Technical risks
    - o Operational risks
    - o Ethical and social risks
- Project planning for IoT implementation
- Change management strategies for IoT adoption
- Impact of IoT on organizational culture
- Facilitating employee adoption and training

Objectives

By the end of this chapter, readers will have a comprehensive understanding of how IoT impacts organizational culture. They will be equipped with strategies for facilitating employee adoption and training. Readers will also possess the tools to overcome resistance to IoT change. Furthermore, they will have insights into fostering an environment where IoT innovation thrives, empowering organizations to integrate and leverage IoT technologies for future success seamlessly.

Strategic objectives for IoT implementation

To guarantee that integrating IoT technologies positively contributes to the overall aims and objectives of the organization, it is essential to align IoT projects with business strategy. By coordinating these endeavors, firms may take advantage of IoT's potential to boost productivity, improve decision-making, and generate new sources of income.

The statement emphasizes the following crucial themes, underscoring the significance of this alignment:

- **Creating new revenue streams:** IoT can provide new business prospects by enabling cutting-edge goods or services. IoT efforts are more likely to concentrate on adding customer value and finding new revenue streams when strongly linked to the organization's business plan. Businesses can gain a competitive edge and increase income by providing IoT-enabled goods or services that address client needs.

  However, it is crucial to note that most IoT implementations require significant investments in devices, analytics, infrastructure, and more. Despite the long-term potential for new revenue streams, the initial phases of IoT adoption may not yield immediate financial benefits. Organizations should be prepared for the upfront costs and consider the long-term strategic value that IoT can bring to their business.

- **Increasing efficiency:** IoT technologies can improve workflows, automate processes, and minimize manual intervention. IoT can increase productivity by automating repetitive processes, reducing downtime, and optimizing resource allocation when integrated with the corporate plan. This can result in reduced costs and increased overall production.

- **Improving decision-making:** Organizations can make more educated and data-driven decisions due to the massive amounts of real-time data generated by IoT devices. Companies may make sure that the data gathered by IoT devices is directly relevant to unique objectives by integrating IoT activities with business strategy. Decisions made with data can be made more quickly, accurately, and strategically.

- **Contributing to organizational goals:** For IoT technologies to be valuable, they must support the broader goals of the enterprise. The effectiveness, productivity, profitability, or customer satisfaction of the business, among other key performance measures, should be directly impacted by IoT projects. By establishing such alignment, businesses can save money on IoT projects that are unnecessary or have little impact.

- **Leveraging IoT potential:** By offering useful data insights, automating procedures, and enabling real-time asset monitoring and control, the IoT can completely change how businesses operate. IoT projects must align with the organization's unique use cases and business requirements to properly utilize this potential. It is due to this alignment that business can use the best IoT solutions for its problems and possibilities.

For businesses to effectively capitalize on the potential advantages of IoT technologies, IoT activities must be coordinated with the overall business plan. It guarantees that IoT projects have a purpose, are pertinent, and ultimately contribute to the business's growth, effectiveness, and success. Businesses can make informed decisions, foster innovation, and maintain a competitive edge in a world that is becoming more networked and data-driven by incorporating IoT into strategic planning. Initiatives related to the IoT should be pursued collaboratively rather than independently. They should be considered essential to the organization's strategic plan instead. IoT projects take on more purpose and have a clearer direction when they align with the business plan, which helps the firm focus on the things most important to its success.

Aligning IoT initiatives with business strategy

IoT has significantly transformed in recent years, opening new possibilities for innovation, efficiency, and data-driven decision-making. To fully benefit from IoT, businesses must incorporate these activities into their overall business strategy. This chapter explores the fundamental practices and concepts required to seamlessly integrate IoT technologies into an organization's strategic strategy. Refer to the following figure:

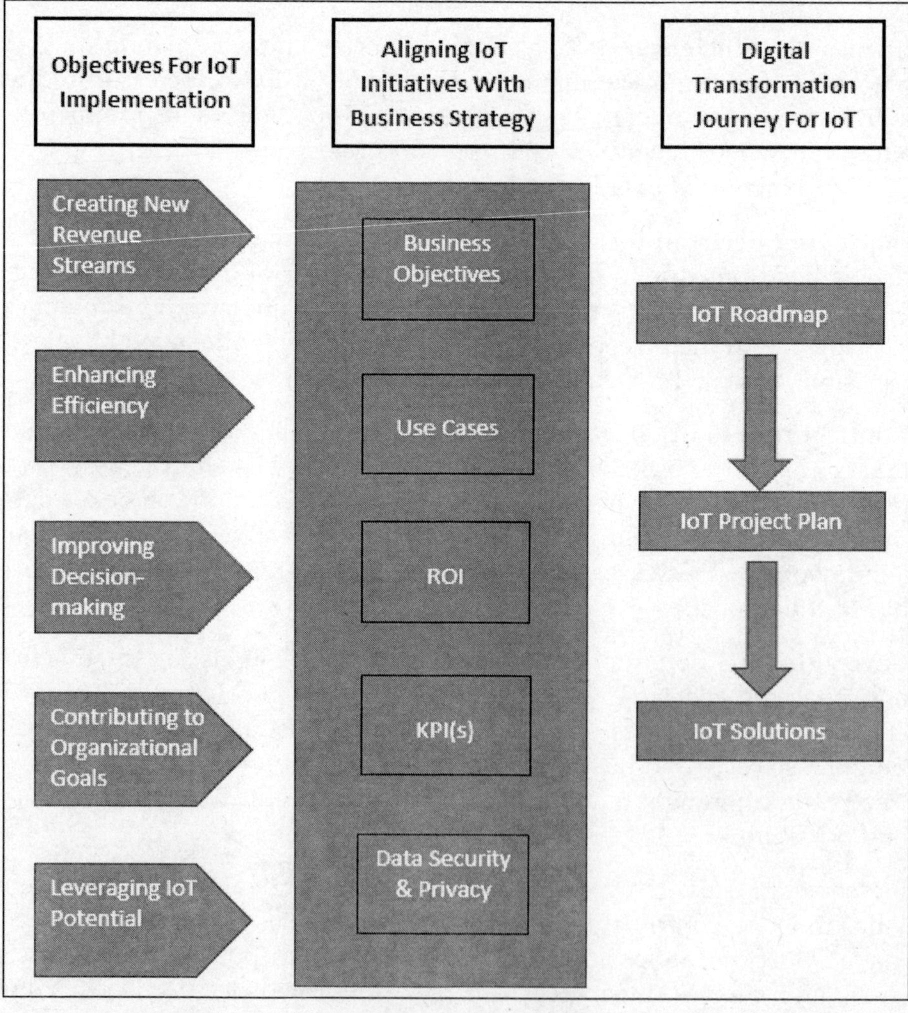

Figure 5.1: Aligning IoT initiatives with business strategy

Business strategy implementation steps for IoT initiatives are given in the following table:

Steps	Descriptions
1. **Defining the business strategy**	It is critical to comprehend the organization's business strategy before using IoT. This involves examining the organization's goals, objectives, and long-term vision. Adapt IoT activities to support and promote these objectives for seamless integration with the broader corporate strategy.
2. **IoT opportunity discovery**	After understanding the company plan, identify chances that align with the corporation's goals. Investigate areas where IoT can enhance operational effectiveness, consumer experiences, or product innovation. Analyze current procedures and identify meaningful IoT use cases.
3. **Return on investment research**	Conduct a thorough **return on investment** (**ROI**) study before allocating major resources to IoT projects. Consider benefits such as cost savings, revenue growth, customer satisfaction, and competitive advantage. Understanding potential ROI helps in selecting projects with the most value.
4.**Key performance indicators**	Use KPIs to assess the efficiency and performance of IoT systems, devices, and applications. These indicators help gauge the success of IoT projects, identify areas for improvement, and make data-driven decisions.
5. **Scalability and flexibility**	Ensure that IoT solutions are flexible and scalable to be future-proof. Choose solutions that can grow and transform the company. Scalability ensures the IoT ecosystem can handle more devices and data, while flexibility enables the company to seize new opportunities.
6. **Collaboration across organization**	IoT implementation requires cross-departmental collaboration as a multidisciplinary project. Business leaders, IT professionals, data scientists, and operational teams must work together to define objectives, manage problems, and ensure successful implementation. Open communication and shared ownership foster a culture of innovation aligned with the company plan.
7. **Data security and privacy**	Since IoT devices generate sensitive data, data security and privacy are crucial. Evaluate IoT adoption-related risks, create effective policies to defend against cyber threats, and ensure compliance with relevant data protection laws. Maintaining trust with customers and business partners is essential.

Table 5.1: *Business strategy implementation steps*

The company's IT infrastructure must be compatible with IoT projects to integrate into the current business environment seamlessly. This calls for a detailed examination of the possibilities for IoT devices and data streams to be integrated seamlessly. Collaboration between IT teams and business divisions is essential to optimize the installation process and minimize disruptions to ongoing operations. Organizations can unleash the full potential of IoT technologies by integrating IoT initiatives with the business strategy. This involves understanding the strategy, identifying opportunities, prioritizing data privacy and security, integrating with existing systems, planning for scalability, evaluating ROI, and encouraging cross-functional collaboration. Through these steps, organizations can drive sustainable growth, boost competitiveness, and achieve a strategic advantage.

Mapping IoT solutions to business cases, benefits, and KPIs

The success of IoT projects is often unpredictable due to a lack of well-defined KPIs in the planning phase and challenges in monitoring value generation during implementation. Many IoT projects focus heavily on technology, leading to low user adoption and difficulty in accurately measuring ROI against business objectives.

Businesses frequently initiate IoT projects to address specific issues, necessitating a recognition of inefficiencies in user acceptance, resource distribution, and scalability. IoT service providers should offer clients standardized methods and tools for planning and tracking IoT initiatives aligned with business objectives. A framework ensures alignment across all phases, from defining strategy to implementing IoT projects.

To evaluate the success of IoT projects, it is crucial to establish a comprehensive set of KPIs that compare predicted business outcomes with actual results. These KPIs, quantitative metrics, play a vital role in assessing the achievement and significance of IoT projects in different domains.

Use cases, benefits, and KPIs for embracing IoT in manufacturing

Leveraging IoT in manufacturing can result in enhanced operational efficiency, predictive maintenance, real-time monitoring, and reduced downtime, while KPIs such as production yield, equipment utilization, and energy consumption provide quantifiable metrics for measuring its impact.

Here is a list of KPIs for various use cases in the manufacturing sector:

- **KPI for use case:** Real-time monitoring and maintenance for IoT-based predictive maintenance.
    - **Reduce maintenance costs**
        - **Mean time between failures:** Measure the average time between equipment failures.
        - **Mean time to repair:** Measure the average time to repair equipment after a failure.

- **Maintenance cost as a percentage of asset value:** Calculate the maintenance cost as a percentage of the total asset value.

- **Enhanced asset utilization**
  - **Asset utilization rate:** Measure the percentage of time that assets are actively used.
  - **Downtime reduction:** Track the decrease in asset downtime due to better utilization and predictive maintenance.
- **Extended equipment life**
  - **Remaining useful life:** Estimate the remaining operational life of equipment based on IoT data.
  - **Asset health index:** Develop a metric that quantifies the equipment's health and tracks improvement over time.
- **Optimize field crew efficiency**
  - **Response time:** Measure the time field crews take to respond to issues after receiving IoT alerts.
  - **First-time fix rate:** Track the percentage of issues field crews resolved during the initial visit.
- **Better safety and compliance**
  - **Safety incidents:** Monitor the number of safety incidents and strive to reduce them through IoT-enabled safety measures.
  - **Compliance adherence:** Track compliance with regulatory requirements and internal safety policies.
- **Effective production lines**
  - **Overall equipment effectiveness:** Measure the efficiency of production lines, considering availability, performance, and quality.
  - **Throughput:** Track the volume of goods produced per unit of time to assess production line efficiency.

- **KPI for use case:** Production planning and scheduling: From manual to IoT-driven.
  - **Reduce the planning cycle**
    - **Planning cycle time:** Measure the time to complete a planning cycle (for example, production planning and resource allocation) before and after IoT implementation.
    - **Planning accuracy:** Assess the accuracy of planning predictions and compare them to historical data before IoT adoption.

- **Increase equipment effectiveness**
  - **Overall equipment effectiveness:** Track equipment efficiency, considering availability, performance, and quality improvements after implementing IoT solutions.
  - **Mean time between failures:** Measure the average time between equipment failures to assess the impact of predictive maintenance through IoT.
- **On-time delivery improvement**
  - **On-time delivery rate:** Measure the percentage of orders or deliveries completed on time after IoT implementation.
  - **Order fulfillment cycle time:** Track the time from order receipt to delivery and compare it before and after IoT adoption.

- **KPI for use case:** IoT-powered solutions to address quality control challenges.
  - **Reduction in defect rates**
    - **Defect rate:** Track the percentage of defective products or units produced before and after IoT implementation.
    - **First pass yield:** Measure the proportion of products passing quality checks on the first attempt, reflecting the reduction in defects.
  - **Faster root cause analysis for quality issues**
    - **Root cause analysis time:** Measure the time taken to identify the root causes of quality issues before and after IoT implementation.
    - **Mean time to identify:** Track the average time taken to detect and pinpoint the root causes of quality problems through IoT data.
  - **Reduction in quality management costs**
    - **Cost of quality:** Calculate the cost associated with maintaining and improving product quality, including prevention, appraisal, and failure costs. Compare it before and after IoT adoption.
    - **Non-conformance cost:** Measure the cost incurred due to non-compliance with quality standards, regulations, or customer requirements.
  - **Higher customer satisfaction because of consistent product quality results**
    - **Customer satisfaction index:** Regularly survey customers to assess satisfaction with product quality and compare it before and after IoT implementation.

  - **Customer complaint rate:** Track the number of customer complaints about product quality and aim for a decrease after IoT adoption.

- **KPI for use case:** Robotic solutions powered by IoT
  - o **Increased productivity**
    - **Overall equipment effectiveness:** Measure the efficiency of production equipment, considering availability, performance, and quality.
    - **Production output:** Track the volume of goods produced per unit of time to assess overall productivity gains after IoT implementation.
    - **Cycle time:** Measure the time to complete a production cycle and look for improvements post-IoT.
  - o **Improved quality and consistency**
    - **First pass yield:** Measure the percentage of products passing quality checks on the first attempt, reflecting improved quality and consistency.
    - **Defect rate:** Track the percentage of defective products or units produced before and after IoT implementation.
    - **Customer returns or complaints:** Monitor the number of product returns or customer complaints related to quality issues and strive for a reduction.
  - o **Worker safety**
    - **Incident rate:** Measure the number of safety incidents or accidents in the workplace and aim for a decrease after IoT implementation.
    - **Near-miss reporting:** Encourage workers to report near-miss incidents, providing insights into potential safety hazards.
    - **Compliance with safety procedures:** Track adherence to safety protocols and ensure workers follow established safety guidelines.
  - o **Competitive advantage**
    - **Time-to-market:** Measure the time taken to bring new products and aim to gain a competitive edge.
    - **Customer retention rate:** Assess customer loyalty and retention due to improved product quality and service facilitated by IoT.
    - **Market share growth:** Monitor changes in market share after IoT implementation to evaluate competitive advantage.

Use cases and benefits of IoT in supply chain

Leverage various use cases, benefits, and KPIs for embracing IoT in the supply chain. Here is a list of KPIs for various use cases in the supply chain sector:

- **KPI for demand forecasting**
  - **Improve the accuracy of demand forecasts**
    - **Forecast accuracy rate:** Measure the accuracy of demand forecasts by comparing actual sales/orders with forecasted values. This can be expressed as a percentage.
    - **Mean absolute percentage error:** Calculate the average percentage difference between actual and forecasted demand values.
  - **Reduce stockouts**
    - **Stockout rate:** Measure the frequency and duration of stockouts, for example, instances when products are not available in inventory when customers demand them.
    - **Fill rate:** Calculate the percentage of customer orders fulfilled from existing inventory.
  - **Improved customer satisfaction**
    - **Customer satisfaction score:** Conduct surveys or feedback mechanisms to gauge customer satisfaction with products/services.
    - **Net promoter score:** Measure customer loyalty and likelihood to recommend products/services to others.
  - **Increase sales**
    - **Sales revenue:** Track overall sales revenue generated over a specific period.
    - **Conversion rate:** Measure the percentage of potential customers who make a purchase, indicating the effectiveness of the sales process.
- **KPI for inventory management**
  - **Improve efficiency**
    - **Inventory turnover:** Measure how quickly inventory is being sold and replaced within a specific period, indicating efficiency in managing inventory levels.
    - **Order fulfillment cycle time:** Calculate the time taken from receiving an order to fulfilling it, reflecting the speed and efficiency of order processing.

- **Improve accuracy**
  - **Inventory accuracy:** Measure the level of accuracy in recording and tracking inventory levels by comparing physical counts with system records. This can be expressed as a percentage or absolute variance.
  - **Order accuracy**: Track the percentage of accurately picked, packed, and shipped orders without errors.
- **Improve security**
  - **Inventory shrinkage rate:** Monitor the rate of inventory loss due to theft, damage, or other reasons to assess the effectiveness of security measures.
  - **Unauthorized access incidents:** Keep track of unauthorized access attempts or incidents related to inventory storage areas or IoT devices.

- **KPI for IoT in stock replenishment:** Real-time inventory monitoring
  - **Reduced cost**
    - **Inventory carrying cost:** Measure the expenses of holding and storing inventory, including warehousing, insurance, and capital costs.
    - **Stockouts cost:** Calculate the financial impact of stockouts, including lost sales, backorders, and potential customer dissatisfaction.
    - **Replenishment cycle time:** Monitor the time taken to restock inventory from the point of order placement to receipt, as shorter cycles can reduce carrying costs and minimize stockouts.
  - **Improved customer service**
    - **Order fill rate:** Measure the percentage of customer orders fulfilled from existing inventory, indicating the ability to meet customer demand promptly.
    - **On-time delivery:** Track the percentage of orders delivered to customers within the promised timeframe or expected delivery date.
    - **Customer complaints:** Monitor the number of customer complaints related to stockouts or delayed order fulfillment to assess improvements in customer service.
- **KPI for intelligent logistics:** Enhancing delivery with IoT
  - **Augmented visibility**
    - **Real-time shipment tracking rate:** Measure the percentage of shipments actively tracked and monitored in real-time through IoT devices.
    - **On-time delivery rate:** Track the percentage of deliveries made within the expected or promised timeframe.

- **Instantaneous insights**
  - **Data processing speed:** Measure the time taken to collect, process, and analyze data from IoT devices to provide valuable insights for decision-making.
  - **Data accuracy:** Assess the accuracy and reliability of data collected through IoT devices, ensuring that insights are based on trustworthy information.
- **Preemptive supply chain management**
  - **Predictive maintenance rate:** Measure the percentage of maintenance and servicing tasks performed proactively. It is based on predictive analytics from IoT devices, reducing the risk of delivery disruptions.
  - **Stockout prevention rate:** Track the effectiveness of IoT-based supply chain management in avoiding stockouts and inventory shortages.
- **Elevated customer satisfaction**
  - **Delivery satisfaction score:** Conduct post-delivery surveys or feedback mechanisms to measure customer satisfaction levels with the delivery experience.
  - **Delivery time variance:** Measure the variance between the expected and actual delivery times, aiming to minimize delays and meet customer expectations.

- **KPI for enhancing fleet management with IoT:** Monitoring and maintenance
  - **Improved efficiency**
    - **Vehicle utilization:** Measure the percentage of time each vehicle uses compared to its total available time, indicating how efficiently the fleet is utilized.
    - **Route optimization:** Track the mileage and travel time reduction achieved through optimized routes, resulting in fuel and time savings.
  - **Reduced cost**
    - **Fuel efficiency:** Monitor the average fuel consumption per mile or kilometer driven to achieve fuel cost savings.
    - **Maintenance cost reduction:** Measure the decrease in maintenance expenses through proactive maintenance enabled by IoT devices, preventing costly breakdowns.
  - **Improved customer service**
    - **On-time delivery rate:** Track the percentage of deliveries made within the promised timeframe, ensuring punctuality and customer satisfaction.

        - **Delivery accuracy:** Measure the percentage of deliveries made to the correct destinations without errors, reducing customer complaints and returns.

- **KPI for smart warehousing**
    - **Inventory accuracy**
        - **Inventory accuracy rate:** Measure the percentage of inventory items that match the recorded quantities in the warehouse management system, indicating the level of accuracy in inventory management.
    - **Order fulfillment**
        - **Order processing time:** Calculate the time taken from receiving an order to its successful fulfillment, indicating the efficiency of the order fulfillment process.
        - **Order accuracy:** Track the percentage of accurately picked, packed, and shipped orders without errors.
    - **Warehouse efficiency**
        - **Order picking productivity:** Measure the number of order lines or items picked per hour by warehouse personnel to improve overall efficiency.
        - **Receiving and put-away time:** Calculate the time to receive incoming goods and place them in designated storage locations to minimize delays.
    - **Real-time visibility**
        - **Real-time inventory visibility:** Measure the percentage of inventory items tracked and visible in real-time through IoT sensors and connected devices.
        - **Warehouse activity monitoring:** Track the utilization and movement of assets (for example, forklifts, pallets) and personnel in the warehouse to optimize workflow and resource allocation.
    - **Space utilization**
        - **Warehouse space utilization rate:** Measure the percentage of warehouse space actively utilized for storage and operational purposes to optimize space usage and reduce wastage.
    - **Error and loss reduction**
        - **Shrinkage rate**: Monitor the rate of inventory loss due to theft, damage, or other reasons to identify areas for improvement and reduce losses.
        - **Error incident rate:** Track the number of errors or discrepancies in warehouse operations to identify root causes and implement corrective actions.

- **IoT device reliability and uptime**
  - **IoT device uptime:** Measure the percentage of time IoT devices used for smart warehousing (for example, RFID scanners, sensors) are operational and connected to the network.
  - **Mean time to failure (MTTF):** Calculate the average time between failures of IoT devices to ensure continuous data collection and monitoring.

- **KPI for reverse logistics**
  - **Visibility of returns**
    - **Return volume tracking:** Measure the number of returned products and assets being tracked through IoT devices to ensure complete visibility of the reverse logistics process.
    - **Real-time return status:** Track the percentage of returns with real-time updates, indicating the level of visibility into return progress and status.
  - **Asset recovery efficiency**
    - **Asset recovery rate:** Measure the percentage of returned assets that are successfully recovered, refurbished, and made ready for resale or reuse.
    - **Average time to recovery:** Calculate the average time to process and recover returned assets, aiming for efficient and timely recovery.
  - **Sustainable practices**
    - **Recycling rate:** Measure the percentage of returned products and materials that are recycled or disposed of in an environmentally friendly manner, promoting sustainability.
    - **Emissions reduction:** Track the reduction in carbon emissions achieved through optimized reverse logistics practices and reduced transportation inefficiencies.

Mitigating risks in IoT implementation

Any IoT project needs to consider risks. Early risk identification and assessment enable organizations to take action to reduce possible issues. IoT initiatives have a few hazards related to system dependability, data security, and data privacy.

Since IoT devices frequently connect to sensitive data sources, data security is a major concern. Data privacy is another issue because so many IoT devices collect personal data. Finally, system reliability is challenging because IoT systems are frequently intricate and interconnected. Organizations can take action to reduce these risks through early risk identification and assessment. This will make IoT projects more likely to succeed and produce the required outcomes.

IoT projects are inherently riskier than conventional IT projects for several reasons. First, IoT projects frequently combine hardware and software, making them more complex and challenging to manage.

Second, IoT initiatives frequently call for creating new technologies or adapting existing ones to a new environment, resulting in unanticipated technical issues.

Finally, IoT initiatives frequently entail gathering and analyzing substantial amounts of data, which can threaten privacy and security. Despite these dangers, IoT initiatives can provide substantial advantages, including higher production and efficiency. Therefore, before deciding whether to move forward with an IoT project, it is crucial to evaluate its risks and advantages properly.

Regulatory and compliance risks

Compliance and regulation are essential aspects of IoT risks. They involve potential difficulties and consequences stemming from IoT projects, devices, or systems not following relevant laws, regulations, industry standards, and guidelines. Governments and regulatory bodies globally have introduced rules and procedures to tackle concerns like data protection, privacy, security, and safety. This is in response to the rapidly evolving IoT technology landscape and the vast data it generates. Individuals and organizations working on IoT initiatives risk facing legal and financial ramifications if they fail to comply with these regulatory requirements. Refer to the following figure:

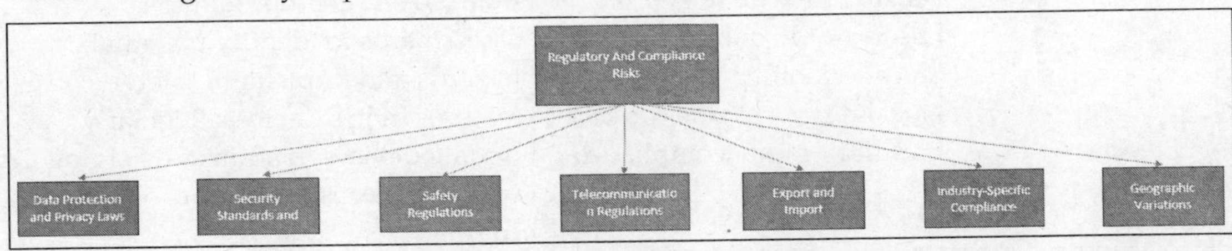

Figure 5.2: Regulatory and compliance risks

Here are some common regulatory and compliance risks and mitigation strategies in IoT:

Risks	Risks description	Mitigation strategies
Data protection and privacy laws	The collection, processing, storage, and sharing of personal data are governed by stringent data protection rules in many jurisdictions, such as the **General Data Protection Regulation** (**GDPR**) in the European Union. Violations of these regulations may incur hefty fines and harm an organization's reputation.	Organizations should prioritize minimal data collection, secure user consent, and employ anonymization techniques. Strong security measures, transparent communication, and continuous monitoring enhance compliance efforts.

Risks	Risks description	Mitigation strategies
Security standards and certifications	Some sectors of the economy or legal systems require specific security standards and certifications for IoT systems and devices. Products may be unable to access the market if certain conditions are not met, and there may be legal repercussions.	Organizations should comprehensively assess applicable requirements, implement a robust cybersecurity framework aligned with these standards, and regularly validate compliance through audits. Maintaining clear documentation and actively staying informed about evolving standards, industry collaboration, and continuous improvement are crucial. Designating a dedicated team for ongoing compliance monitoring ensures adherence, reducing the risk of market access restrictions and legal repercussions.
Safety regulations	IoT devices that interact with physical settings or vital infrastructure may be subject to safety laws to ensure they do not endanger users or the public. Product recalls liability claims, or legal repercussions could result from noncompliance.	Organizations should prioritize compliance with applicable safety laws to address the regulatory risks associated with safety regulations in IoT. Conduct thorough risk assessments to identify potential hazards and implement safety features in IoT devices. Regularly update devices to address emerging safety concerns and ensure ongoing compliance.
Telecommunication regulations	IoT devices frequently use communication networks to transmit data. To prevent network interference problems, adherence to telecom laws, such as frequency utilization and spectrum allocation, is essential.	Organizations should prioritize adherence to relevant laws governing frequency utilization and spectrum allocation to mitigate regulatory risks associated with telecommunication regulations in IoT. Conduct a thorough understanding of the telecommunication regulations applicable to the region of operation and ensure that IoT devices comply with these standards. Collaborate with telecommunication authorities to stay informed about any regulation updates or changes.

Risks	Risks description	Mitigation strategies
Export and import regulations	Laws governing international commerce may impact the import and export of IoT components and devices. These rules must be followed to ensure timely customs and other legal issues.	Organizations should adopt a comprehensive approach to compliance to address regulatory risks associated with export and import regulations in IoT. Stay well-informed about the countries' export and import laws and regulations, including customs requirements and trade restrictions. Establish a dedicated team or work with experts to navigate complex international trade laws and ensure compliance.
Industry-specific compliance	Each industry has its own set of rules for managing data, keeping it secure, and adhering to standards. For example, IoT healthcare devices must follow **Health Insurance Portability and Accountability Act** (**HIPAA**) requirements in the USA.	To mitigate industry-specific compliance risks in IoT, organizations must tailor their strategies to the unique regulations of their respective sectors. Begin by comprehensively assessing industry-specific compliance requirements, such as the **Health Insurance Portability and Accountability Act** (**HIPAA**) in healthcare. Develop and implement specific protocols and security measures that align with these industry standards.
Geographic variations	Due to geographic variations, IoT initiatives deployed across regions may be subject to different regulatory regulations in each jurisdiction. Although it can be difficult, adjusting to these changes is necessary for compliance.	Organizations should adopt a flexible and adaptive compliance approach to navigate regulatory challenges stemming from geographic variations in IoT deployments. Conduct thorough research to understand the specific regulatory requirements in each jurisdiction where IoT initiatives are deployed. Develop a scalable compliance framework that can accommodate variations in regulations across regions.

Table 5.2: *Regulatory and compliance risks and mitigation strategies*

Device reliability and maintenance risks

The potential difficulties and negative effects linked to the dependability and maintenance of IoT devices over lifetimes are covered by the risk associated with IoT device reliability and maintenance. For IoT projects to be successful, IoT devices must be reliable and properly maintained because they frequently interact with the physical world, collect data, and carry out essential functions. Refer to the following figure:

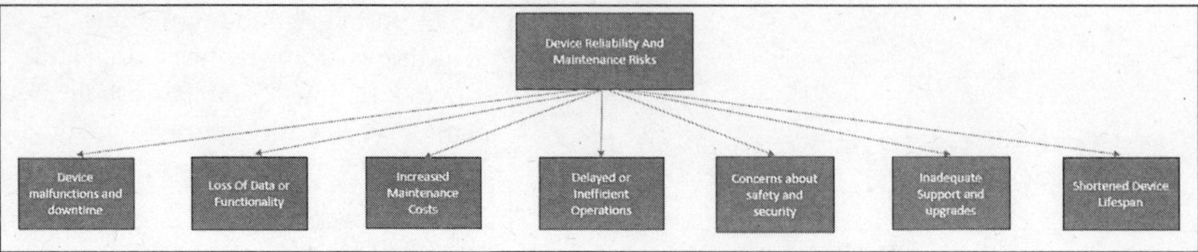

Figure 5.3: *Device reliability and maintenance risks*

Here are some common device reliability and maintenance risk and mitigation strategies in IoT:

Risks	Risks description	Mitigation strategies
Device malfunctions and downtime	Unreliable IoT devices may frequently fail, causing system outages and disruptions to crucial services or procedures.	Organizations should adopt a multifaceted approach to mitigate the risk of device malfunctions and downtime in IoT. Implementing proactive maintenance schedules, utilizing remote monitoring tools, and integrating redundancy and failover systems are critical. Regular firmware and software updates and predictive analytics enhance device performance and reliability.
Loss of data or functionality	Problems with device dependability can result in data loss or inaccurate data capture, which can compromise the integrity and effectiveness of decisions based on data.	Implement robust data backup procedures, ensure data encryption, conduct regular data integrity checks, employ redundancy in data storage, and establish failover systems. Additionally, prioritize device reliability through proactive maintenance, remote monitoring, and quality assurance measures during manufacturing to prevent data loss or inaccurate data capture.

Risks	Risks description	Mitigation strategies
Increased maintenance costs	Increased maintenance costs can lower the cost-effectiveness of IoT systems because unplanned repair and frequent device replacements increase operating costs.	Implement proactive maintenance schedules to identify issues early, utilize remote monitoring for real-time diagnostics, and conduct regular firmware/software updates to enhance device longevity. Strengthen quality assurance in manufacturing to reduce the likelihood of defects and subsequent maintenance needs.
Delayed or inefficient operations	Delayed or inefficient operations can poorly impact productivity and user experience. Device malfunctions and maintenance problems can cause these problems.	Prioritize proactive maintenance and utilize remote monitoring to identify and address potential device malfunctions before they impact operations. Implement redundancy and failover systems to ensure continuous operation in the event of device failure. Regularly update device firmware and software to enhance overall reliability.
Concerns about safety and security	Unreliable devices may jeopardize the security of users and the physical environment in which they interact, creating possible risks or weaknesses.	Prioritize device reliability through proactive maintenance, remote monitoring, and quality assurance during manufacturing to enhance overall security. Regularly update device firmware and software to address vulnerabilities.
Inadequate support and upgrades	Devices may become subject to security risks and unresolved problems if manufacturers fail to provide necessary firmware upgrades and maintenance.	Prioritize vendors with a strong commitment to ongoing support and regular firmware upgrades. Establish clear contractual agreements specifying support and upgrade expectations. Implement a proactive approach to evaluate and address security vulnerabilities promptly.
Shortened device lifespan	The lifespan of unreliable devices may be shortened, requiring more frequent replacements and higher capital costs.	Implement proactive maintenance strategies to extend device lifespan, conduct regular firmware/software updates to address vulnerabilities, and prioritize quality assurance during manufacturing. Utilize remote monitoring for real-time diagnostics to identify and address issues promptly.

Table 5.3: *Device reliability and maintenance risk and mitigation strategies*

Technical risks

In the context of IoT, *technical risks* refer to potential difficulties and problems with the technological components of developing, putting into use, and managing IoT systems. These dangers result from the intricate interconnections and complexity of IoT systems, networks, and applications. Technical hazards can impact IoT initiatives' functionality, performance, scalability, and security. Refer to the following figure:

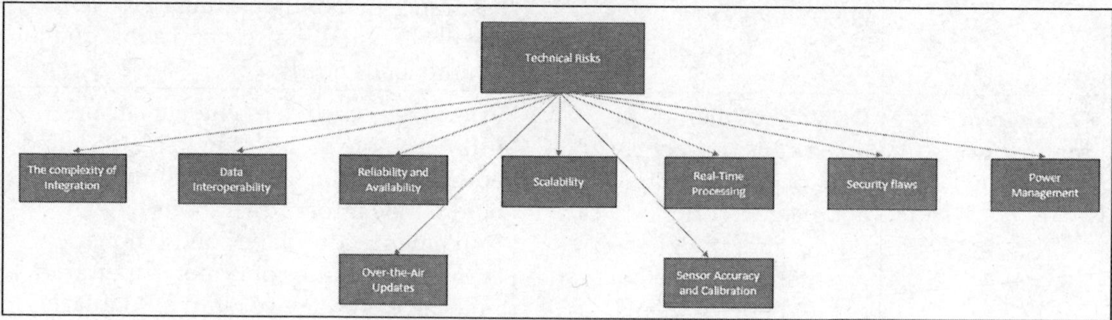

***Figure 5.4:** Technical risks*

Here are some common technical risks and mitigation strategies in IoT:

Risks	Risks description	Mitigation strategies
The complexity of integration	Integrating many IoT devices, sensors, gateways, and platforms from various manufacturers can be difficult and may cause communication and compatibility problems.	Standardize communication protocols to ensure interoperability among diverse devices and platforms. Prioritize the use of widely adopted standards such as MQTT or CoAP. Conduct thorough testing during the integration phase to identify and address compatibility issues. Establish a robust data model and documentation to guide integration efforts.
Data interoperability	Ensuring smooth data transmission and interoperability between them can be difficult because IoT devices and systems use different data formats and communication protocols.	Standardize data formats and communication protocols across the IoT ecosystem to enhance interoperability. Adopt widely accepted industry standards such as JSON or XML for data representation. Implement middleware solutions that can translate and normalize data between different formats and protocols.

Risks	Risks description	Mitigation strategies
Reliability and availability	IoT solutions should function dependably and be accessible when required. Technical problems, including hardware malfunctions, network outages, or software defects, can impact system dependability and uptime.	Implement redundancy and failover mechanisms to ensure continuous operation in the event of hardware malfunctions, network outages, or software defects. Conduct regular hardware and software maintenance to identify and address potential issues before they impact system reliability.
Scalability	Ensuring the IoT infrastructure can support multiple devices and handle rising data volumes without degrading is a huge technical problem.	Design the IoT infrastructure with scalability in mind, using modular and distributed architectures. Employ cloud-based solutions that can dynamically scale resources based on demand. Implement horizontal scaling by adding more servers or nodes to the system to accommodate increasing device and data loads.
Real-time processing	Real-time data processing and analytics are crucial for many IoT applications. Missed opportunities or serious operational problems might result from delays or inefficiencies in data processing.	Implement edge computing solutions to process data closer to the source, reducing latency and enhancing real-time capabilities. Utilize in-memory databases and caching mechanisms to expedite data retrieval and processing. Employ parallel processing and distributed computing architectures to enhance the speed of data analytics
Security flaws	IoT devices are frequently the subject of cyberattacks. Technical hazards include unreliable encryption, lax authentication, and software flaws that unscrupulous actors could use.	Implement robust security measures such as strong encryption protocols, multi-factor authentication, and secure boot processes to safeguard IoT devices. Regularly update firmware and software to patch vulnerabilities and address security flaws.
Power management	Power management is important since many IoT devices, such as batteries, rely on finite power sources. Effective power management is essential to increase device lifespans and lower maintenance requirements.	Implement efficient power management strategies to optimize energy consumption and extend the lifespan of IoT devices. Utilize low-power components and microcontrollers to reduce energy requirements. Implement sleep modes and idle states to minimize power consumption during periods of inactivity.

Risks	Risks description	Mitigation strategies
Over-the-air updates	Implementing secure and dependable over-the-air updates for IoT devices is difficult since updates need to be safely sent to a variety of devices in varied places.	Prioritize secure and encrypted communication channels for over-the-air updates to protect against unauthorized access and tampering. Implement secure boot processes to ensure the authenticity of firmware updates. Utilize digital signatures and certificates to verify the integrity and source of over-the-air updates.
Sensor accuracy and calibration	Sensor calibration and accuracy are essential for IoT applications. For accurate data-driven decision-making, it is essential to ensure sensor accuracy and adequate calibration.	Implement regular sensor calibration schedules to maintain accuracy over time. Utilize certified calibration standards and equipment for precise sensor adjustments. Conduct thorough testing and validation of sensors during manufacturing to ensure initial accuracy.

Table 5.4: *Technical risks and mitigation strategies*

Operational risks

Operational risks are potential difficulties and dangers associated with the regular management and operation of IoT systems and devices. These dangers cover a range of IoT project operational elements, such as project management, maintenance, human factors, and organizational processes. Operational risks can affect IoT systems' effectiveness, stability, and success. Please refer to the following figure:

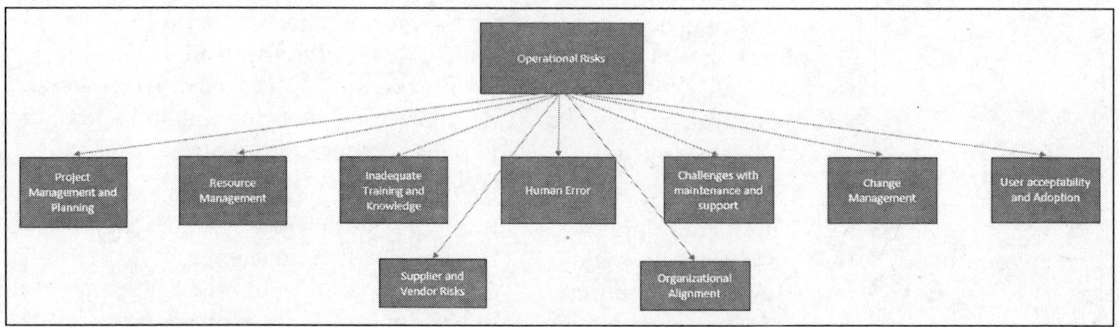

Figure 5.5: *Operational risks*

Here are some common operation risks and mitigation strategies in IoT:

Risks	Risks description	Mitigation strategies
Project management and planning	Project delays, cost overruns, and less-than-ideal results can all be caused by poor project management techniques, such as inadequate planning, unclear objectives, or arbitrary deadlines.	Implement robust project management methodologies, such as Agile or Scrum, to enhance planning and execution. Clearly define project objectives, deliverables, and milestones at the outset. Conduct thorough risk assessments to identify potential challenges and develop contingency plans.
Resource management	Resource management issues can impede project progress and jeopardize deliverables. These issues include inefficient resource allocation and management of employees, budgets, and supplies.	Implement robust resource management tools and systems to optimize the allocation of employees, budgets, and supplies. Conduct regular assessments to identify resource needs and adjust allocations accordingly.
Inadequate training and knowledge	Personnel working on the IoT project may not have received the necessary training, which could result in confusion, mistakes, and ineffective setup, operation, and maintenance of devices.	Prioritize comprehensive training programs for personnel involved in the IoT project, covering device setup, operation, maintenance, and troubleshooting. Establish clear guidelines and documentation to supplement training and provide ongoing reference material.
Human error	This important operational risk is caused by human error. System failures, data corruption, and security breaches can occur due to device installation, configuration, or maintenance errors.	Prioritize comprehensive training programs for personnel to minimize errors during device installation, configuration, and maintenance. Establish clear and standardized procedures, checklists, and documentation to guide employees through critical tasks. Implement role-based access controls to limit access to sensitive systems and data, reducing the risk of accidental errors.
Challenges with maintenance and support	Poor maintenance planning and support can delay problem resolution, more downtime, and diminish system reliability.	Implement proactive maintenance planning, including regular schedules for inspections, updates, and repairs, to minimize downtime and enhance system reliability. Establish clear support processes with designated response times for issue resolution.

Risks	Risks description	Mitigation strategies
Change management	Failure to follow adequate change management protocols while implementing updates or changes to IoT systems can result in compatibility problems, service interruptions, and user resistance.	Establish a comprehensive change management process that includes thorough testing, risk assessments, and communication plans for any updates or changes to IoT systems. Clearly define roles and responsibilities for change management within the organization.
User acceptability and adoption	The successful integration of IoT systems into existing processes can be hampered by user resistance to new IoT technologies or a lack of user acceptability.	Prioritize user involvement from the early stages of IoT system planning and design to understand user needs and expectations. Communicate the benefits of IoT technologies clearly to users, addressing concerns and emphasizing the positive impact on their workflow.
Supplier and vendor risks	Relying on outside suppliers or vendors for essential goods or services might result in operational risks if there are problems with delivery, product quality, or customer service.	Conduct thorough due diligence before selecting suppliers or vendors, assessing their reliability, financial stability, and track record. Establish clear and comprehensive contracts with suppliers, including **service level agreements** (**SLA**s) that outline expectations for delivery, product quality, and customer service.
Organizational alignment	Poor coordination among various departments or stakeholders within an organization can cause coordination issues and inefficiencies in the execution of IoT projects.	Foster cross-functional collaboration by establishing clear communication channels and project governance structures. Implement regular meetings and updates to ensure alignment among different departments and stakeholders involved in IoT projects. Define and communicate clear roles and responsibilities for each department or stakeholder to avoid confusion and enhance coordination.

Table 5.5: *Operational risks and mitigation strategies*

Ethical and social risks

On the IoT, ethical and social risks refer to potential issues and concerns about IoT technologies' ethical ramifications and social impact. As IoT devices become increasingly common and incorporated into daily life, they have the potential to change society significantly. These dangers concern social justice, individual autonomy, data ethics, openness, privacy, and broader societal effects. Please refer to the following figure:

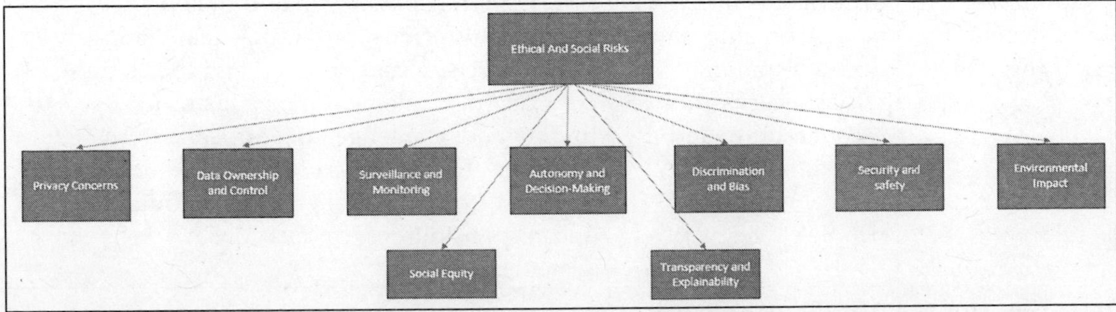

Figure 5.6: *Ethical and social risks*

Here are some common ethical and social risks and mitigation strategies in IoT:

Risks	Risks description	Mitigation strategies
Privacy concerns	The significant data-collecting capabilities of IoT devices pose privacy issues since they may gather sensitive personal data without users' knowledge or consent.	Prioritize privacy by design principles in the development of IoT devices, ensuring that privacy considerations are integrated from the outset. Implement robust data anonymization and encryption techniques to protect sensitive personal data.
Data ownership and control data ownership and control	Determining who owns and controls the data that IoT devices collect can be difficult, which could result in conflicts and abuse.	Clearly define data ownership and control policies in user agreements and terms of service for IoT devices. Provide users with transparent information about how their data will be used, shared, and retained. Implement granular user permissions and controls, allowing users to specify preferences for data sharing and usage.
Surveillance and monitoring	The widespread use of IoT devices with surveillance capabilities may raise concerns about ongoing monitoring and potential privacy violations.	Implement transparent policies and guidelines regarding the use of surveillance capabilities in IoT devices, clearly communicating the purposes and limitations of monitoring. Prioritize user consent by providing clear information about when and how surveillance features are activated.

Risks	Risks description	Mitigation strategies
Autonomy and decision-making	IoT systems that rely heavily on automated decision-making raise concerns about accountability and transparency when choices impact people's lives.	Prioritize transparency in automated decision-making algorithms, providing clear explanations of how decisions are reached and the factors considered. Implement mechanisms for users to understand, challenge, and appeal automated decisions. Establish accountability frameworks within the organization, clearly defining roles and responsibilities for decisions made by IoT systems.
Security and safety	Poorly protected IoT devices might be a safety issue if misused to control physical systems or equipment maliciously.	Implement robust security measures in IoT devices, including secure boot processes, encryption, and regular security updates to protect against malicious activities. Conduct thorough security assessments and penetration testing to identify and rectify vulnerabilities in IoT devices.
Environmental impact	The spread of IoT devices may result in higher energy and electronic waste production, adding to environmental issues.	Prioritize environmental sustainability in the design and manufacturing of IoT devices, considering energy efficiency and recyclability. Implement energy-saving features in IoT devices, such as low-power modes and efficient use of resources.
Social equity	Inequalities in access to IoT technologies might worsen social divisions and disadvantage some groups.	Prioritize social equity in the deployment of IoT technologies, considering the potential impact on diverse communities. Conduct thorough impact assessments to identify and address potential disparities in access and benefits. Engage with local communities and stakeholders to understand their needs and concerns, incorporating their perspectives into IoT planning and implementation.
Transparency and explainability	The public's faith in IoT systems can be damaged by a lack of transparency in how they function and make decisions, and it can be challenging to comprehend the thinking behind automatic judgments.	Prioritize transparency and explainability in the design and deployment of IoT systems, providing clear documentation on how algorithms function and make decisions. Develop user-friendly interfaces that present information about the system's operation and decision-making process in an understandable manner.

***Table 5.6:** Ethical and social risks and mitigation strategies*

Project planning for IoT implementation

Organizations will better match objectives and expectations to the solution if they know the right IoT implementation procedures. Additionally, you may ensure the entire procedure is time-bound, economical, and meets the company's requirements. Refer to the following figure:

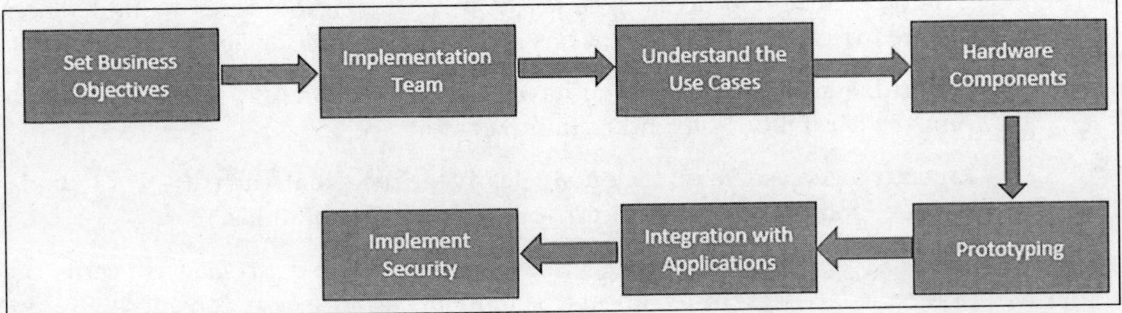

Figure 5.7: *Project planning and execution for IoT implementation*

Here are the steps in planning an IoT project in the organization:

1. **Set business objectives:** To deploy IoT successfully, begin by establishing business objectives through a comprehensive needs analysis with key stakeholders. Identify pain points and opportunities aligned with the overall business plan, setting clear and measurable goals, such as a 20% reduction in manufacturing energy use. Prioritize objectives based on significance, secure stakeholder buy-in through effective communication, and define KPIs to track progress while identifying risks. A collaborative approach with other departments, training, and proactive monitoring ensures project success. Clearly defined business goals serve as a roadmap, guiding decision-making, resource allocation, and project evaluation. This approach, rooted in a thorough assessment and alignment with the overall business strategy, ensures that IoT efforts deliver substantial value and foster growth in the dynamic IoT ecosystem.

2. **Implementation team:** To succeed with an IoT project, follow a strategic approach. First, identify skill gaps in your team and decide whether to hire new talent or provide training. Promote open communication and collaboration within your implementation team. Make sure the IoT solution aligns with business needs and keep your team updated with ongoing training. Use clear communication channels to address issues promptly and set realistic project timelines. Track progress with KPIs and value team members' input for proactive problem-solving. Celebrate milestones to boost motivation. In the end, success relies on a well-chosen, cooperative, and supported implementation team committed to achieving IoT goals.

3. **Understand the use cases:** Before developing and deploying an IoT solution, it is crucial to pinpoint the specific ways you want to use IoT. Here is how to do it:
    - **Talk to stakeholders:** Start by interviewing end users, department heads, and business executives. This helps identify areas where IoT can make a big difference.
    - **Analyze current processes:** Study your current procedures to find places where IoT can optimize operations and remove inefficiencies.
    - **Prioritize use cases:** Once you have data, prioritize use cases based on their impact, feasibility, ROI, and technical complexity.
    - **Specify use case requirements:** Clearly define what each use case needs. Involve end users in this process for user-friendly solutions.
    - **Address security and privacy:** Ensure security and privacy concerns are addressed. Assess the technical feasibility of each use case, considering future growth.
    - **Validation and prototyping:** Work with experts and create prototypes for important use cases to validate assumptions and functions.

    Understanding these use cases is the foundation for a successful IoT implementation, aligning technology with real business needs and realizing its potential to drive positive change.

4. **Hardware components:** To build a reliable IoT system, you need to understand its key parts:
    - **Sensors and actuators:** Sensors collect real-world data like temperature, humidity, motion, and light, while actuators perform actions based on this data, like controlling motors or switches.
    - **Connectivity options:** There are various ways for devices to communicate, like Ethernet for wired connections, Bluetooth for short-range, low-power uses, cellular for broad coverage, LoRaWAN for long-range, and Wi-Fi for high-speed internet in short distances.
    - **Edge computing devices:** Devices like microcontrollers, single-board computers, and gateways handle data processing and communication.
    - **Power sources and protocols:** Choose the right power sources and communication protocols like MQTT, CoAP, or HTTP/HTTPS.
    - **Reliability and compliance:** Ensure reliability by designing redundancy and failover procedures. Follow industry standards, safety rules, and data protection laws.

    Understanding these hardware components helps create a scalable, effective, and dependable IoT system that meets your organization's goals and standards.

5. **Prototyping:** Prototyping is a crucial step in IoT implementation. It involves creating a functional model to test if your idea works well. Here is how it is done:
   - **Set specific goals:** Define what you want to test, like functionality, data accuracy, and user interaction.
   - **Choose the right method:** Decide if you need hardware prototypes to check how things work physically or software simulations for user interfaces.
   - **Create a minimal prototype:** Build a simple version to showcase key ideas.
   - **Test sensors and data:** Check if sensors work accurately and data is reliable.
   - **Evaluate user experience:** Involve users to see if the system is user-friendly and makes them happy.
   - **Performance testing:** Ensure it works well at scale, is responsive, and fast.
   - **Security and privacy:** Protect the system from potential threats.
   - **Iterate and improve:** Make changes based on feedback and tests, and keep good records.
   - **Get stakeholder approval:** Gather input from stakeholders before moving on.

   Successful prototyping reduces risks, confirms ideas, and improves the design, leading to an effective IoT system that meets your goals.

6. **Integration with applications:** Integrating the IoT into your current systems is essential for making the most of the data collected. Here is how it is done:
   - **Define integration needs:** List what needs to connect, like apps and data flow.
   - **Use middleware and APIs:** These tools help connect IoT to other apps.
   - **Consider cloud integration:** Connect to the cloud for a seamless system.
   - **Security and access control:** Protect data during integration.
   - **Real-time data:** Set up data streaming for instant use.
   - **Testing and maintenance:** Check for issues and keep everything running smoothly.
   - **Data governance and compliance:** Follow rules and regulations.
   - **User education:** Help users understand and use the integrated IoT data.

   Successful integration improves your current systems, helps make informed decisions, and gets the most out of IoT for your company's success.

7. **Implement security measures:** Security is a top priority in any IoT setup. With many connected devices and sensitive data, it is crucial to protect against cyber-attacks:

- **Assess risks:** First, identify potential security risks.
- **Control access:** Use strong authentication like two-factor authentication (2FA) to limit who can access devices and data.
- **Encrypt data:** Keep data safe by encrypting it during transmission and storage.
- **Secure devices:** Ensure devices have unique identities and keep firmware and software updated.
- **Monitor for intruders:** Use **intrusion detection and prevention systems (IDPS)** to spot unusual network activity.
- **Protect APIs and interfaces:** Safeguard access points and choose secure cloud providers.
- **Educate staff:** Teach your team about cybersecurity best practices.
- **Plan for incidents:** Have a plan in case of a security breach.

By taking these steps, you can reduce the risk of security breaches, protect data, and make the most of IoT for your business goals. Stakeholders will trust a secure IoT system.

Change management strategies for IoT adoption

Implementing IoT technology involves substantial organizational changes, including new processes, systems, and mindsets. Effective change management strategies are crucial to ensure a smooth and successful IoT adoption. Please refer to the following figure:

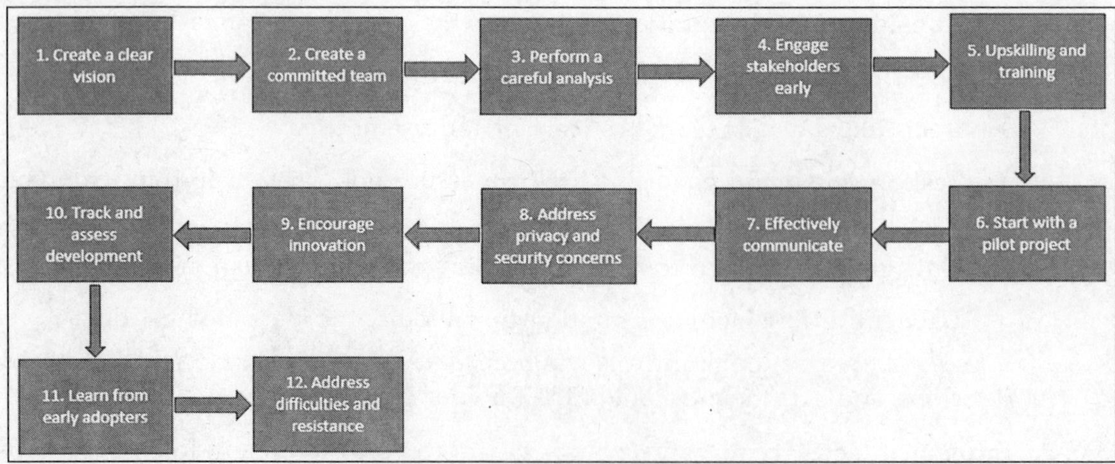

Figure 5.8: Change management strategy

Here are some key strategies to consider:

- **Create a clear vision:** Craft a compelling vision for adopting IoT. Define the objectives, advantages, and anticipated results of the IoT implementation. It will be simpler to implement changes if stakeholders have a common understanding and excitement.
- **Create a committed team:** A cross-functional team of professionals from different areas, such as IT, operations, marketing, and management, should be assembled. This group will manage unforeseen difficulties, oversee the IoT implementation, and ensure collaboration.
- **Perform a careful analysis:** Recognize the organization's existing situation and level of IoT adoption preparedness. Determine any potential weak points, skill gaps, and infrastructural needs. A thorough evaluation will allow us to adjust the change management strategy as necessary.
- **Engage stakeholders early:** Involve stakeholders from various organizational levels early. The IoT effort will get support and ownership if employees, management, and customers are involved. To win support, respond to issues and ask for input.
- **Upskilling and training:** The adoption of IoT frequently calls for new skills and abilities. Provide employees with training programs for the skills they need to work efficiently with IoT devices and technology. Training will increase confidence in using the new technologies and lessen resistance.
- **Start with a pilot project:** To test IoT technology and its effects on the business, start with a smaller-scale trial project. Before a large-scale rollout, this strategy enables you to pinpoint problems, make improvements, and acquire insightful data.
- **Effectively communicate:** Create a strong communication plan to educate all stakeholders on the IoT adoption process. Share information about achievements, milestones, and progress regularly. Transparent communication lowers uncertainty and helps to manage expectations.
- **Address privacy and security concerns:** The adoption of IoT poses new privacy and security issues. Implement security measures, data encryption, and access controls to address these worries proactively. Stakeholders should be reassured that the data is safe.
- **Encourage innovation:** Promote an environment that values innovation and ongoing development. Reward staff members for submitting fresh IoT apps or suggestions for process upgrades. Positive transformation and creativity will be sparked through encouraging innovation.
- **Track and assess development:** Establish KPIs to gauge the effects of IoT usage. Review these KPIs frequently and make any adjustments. The IoT program is continuously evaluated to ensure it continues to track and achieve its goals.

- **Learn from early adopters:** Study other businesses that have successfully implemented IoT solutions to learn from them. Identify the best practices, obstacles they encountered, and solutions they came up with. This information will guide strategy and aid in avoiding typical errors.
- **Address difficulties and resistance:** Prepare ways to address opposition to change in advance. Collaborate with change agents to overcome challenges and underline the advantages of IoT adoption. Celebrate accomplishments to strengthen positive results and create momentum.

Remember that IoT adoption is a continuous process that calls for adaptability and flexibility. Adopt a proactive, team-based approach to change management, and be ready to adjust plans when the organization changes in response to technology.

Impact of IoT on organizational culture

The digital transformation of enterprises is known as IoT. However, more than simply introducing new technologies is required. A methodology that combines the IT team's technical know-how with the operational team's business savvy is necessary for successful IoT implementations. To guarantee the success of IoT projects, this collaborative approach should be ingrained at the executive level. Combining technical and non-technical elements is necessary for an IoT effort to succeed, even at the most fundamental levels. For communication to flow more easily and collaboration to flourish, IT experts and operational team stakeholders must develop a common language that spans differences.

The IoT almost always has a significant impact on the organization's employees. Companies must cultivate a culture that encourages innovation, embraces change, and offers everyone affected by these changes a voice if they want to succeed. It is crucial to foster an atmosphere where workers feel appreciated and heard so they can quickly adapt to change. The cleverest solutions are frequently found when the importance of idea exchange from all organizational levels is stressed.

Roles and duties will inevitably change as the digital transformation process progresses. For employees to recognize that change offers opportunity, transparency is essential. The Internet of Things may remove some occupations while creating intriguing new ones. Encouragement of a change-embracing belief system encourages employees to acquire new abilities and grow nimbler and more effective.

The wide-ranging effects of IoT on industry, education, and government highlight how crucial it is for leaders to foster a culture of collaboration. This is especially clear when the IoT increasingly regularly and quickly brings together business units, knowledge, and technology. Promoting collaboration includes suppliers, integrators, platform providers involved in IoT initiatives, and internal stakeholders.

Technology concerns are only one aspect of creating and implementing an IoT strategy. Businesses must carefully evaluate current procedures and adequately inform staff of the

IoT's effects. Organizations can harness the full potential of people, which is the greatest asset in the IoT world, by creating a culture that embraces these changes.

Facilitating employee adoption and training

By improving the learning experience and making training more accessible, engaging, and efficient, the IoT can considerably facilitate employee adoption and training. IoT can support staff adoption and training in the following ways:

- **Practical training with real-world simulations:** IoT gadgets and simulators can give staff members practical training opportunities. IoT-enabled simulations, for example, can enable workers in manufacturing environments to practice operating equipment or diagnosing typical problems in a secure and regulated environment.
- **Remote collaboration and training:** IoT enables remote collaboration and training. Less physical presence is required for employees to access training materials and take part in virtual seminars or webinars, allowing for more flexible learning.
- **Personalized learning paths:** IoT devices may monitor users' preferences and learning progress. Based on this information, tailored learning paths can be developed that will adapt the training materials to the demands and learning preferences of the employees.
- **Real-time feedback and assessments:** IoT can offer real-time feedback and assessments during training sessions. For example, sensors can track how successfully workers complete specific activities, giving them timely feedback for improvement.
- **Training using augmented reality and virtual reality:** IoT can be combined with **augmented reality** (**AR**) and **virtual reality** (**VR**) technologies to produce engaging training scenarios. Employees can practice skills in realistic environments using AR glasses or VR headsets to visualize complicated ideas.
- **Internet-connected learning management systems:** IoT-capable internet-connected **learning management systems** (**LMS**) platforms can monitor performance metrics, completion rates, and employee progress. Training managers can use this information to pinpoint problem areas and improve the training materials.
- **Remote device monitoring and troubleshooting:** The IoT enables technical or equipment-related training by enabling remote device monitoring and troubleshooting. This can save time and money while guaranteeing workers get support immediately.
- **Real-time performance support:** IoT devices can provide employees real-time performance support while performing routine tasks. For instance, smart wearables can offer detailed instructions or contextual data to support learning while working.

- **Gamified learning experiences:** The IoT can incorporate gamification components into training programs to make learning more interesting and fun. Quizzes, challenges, and leaderboards are examples of gamified aspects that can motivate staff to participate in and excel at training actively.
- **Continuous learning and skill updates:** The IoT allows real-time updating of training materials and resources to stay abreast of the most recent business trends and advancements. This encourages a culture of ongoing education and skill improvement.
- **Lower training costs:** IoT can lower costs by lowering travel expenses, utilizing resources more effectively, and substituting expensive physical training settings with virtual ones.

Organizations may transform training programs into dynamic and adaptable learning experiences by utilizing the IoT's capabilities, giving employees skills and information they need to succeed. Real-time feedback, interactive simulations, remote access, and tailored learning all work together to greatly increase the efficiency of staff training and hasten the adoption of new procedures and technologies.

Nurturing IoT adoption and overcoming resistance: Overcoming apprehension about change and fostering to address the worries and difficulties of employees, IoT adoption necessitates a smart and thoughtful strategy. Here are some methods for creating a welcoming environment for IoT adoption:

- **Communicate the benefits:** Ensure all stakeholders understand IoT's advantages. Describe how it will boost decision-making, streamline processes, increase efficiency, and possibly open new employment prospects. Address any misunderstandings and worries early on.
- **Include staff members early:** Include staff members in the planning and decision-making stages of IoT adoption. Ask for opinions, respond to any inquiries they may have, and take criticism seriously. Employees are more inclined to accept the change if they feel heard and included.
- **Offer comprehensive training and support programs:** Provide in-depth training and support initiatives to assist staff in becoming familiar with IoT technology and applications. Fill the skills gap and give them the tools they need to feel comfortable utilizing new tools.
- **Develop IoT champions:** Find internal IoT champions or advocates passionate about the technology and give them power. These advocates can act as mentors and role models, showing others the advantages of IoT adoption and assisting them in getting over barriers.
- **Begin with pilot projects:** Instead of incorporating IoT across the board, commence with smaller pilot projects. This gradual approach allows employees to acclimate to

IoT progressively, demonstrating its effectiveness through these low-risk activities before widespread adoption.

- **Address security concerns:** The worry about security lapses and data privacy problems is one of the key barriers to IoT adoption. You may proactively address these worries by putting strong security measures in place and training staff in best practices for data protection.
- **Honor successes:** Recognize and honor the organization's various departments' successful adoption of IoT. Employees who have accepted the change should be commended, and success stories should be shared to encourage others.
- **Establish a culture of continuous learning:** Promote a mindset emphasizing lifelong learning and development. Encourage staff members to experiment and learn about IoT technology by encouraging creativity and innovative problem-solving.
- **Speak to organizational procedures and structure:** Sometimes restrictive organizational structures and procedures can cause resistance to change. Analyze whether any changes are required to support IoT adoption adequately.
- **Track and evaluate progress:** Track the development of IoT adoption and gather employee opinions. Utilize metrics to monitor the effect of IoT on important performance indicators and inform the workforce of successful results.
- **Offer resources for problem-solving:** Provide tools and assistance to employees so they can solve any problems they have when using IoT. Frustration and resistance can be reduced with prompt and effective assistance.
- **Set a good example:** The leadership's commitment to IoT adoption is essential. Leaders should show they are open to change by utilizing IoT technologies.

By combining these tactics, organizations can establish an environment where staff members feel encouraged, engaged, and inspired to use IoT technologies. Employee concerns must be considered and helped to understand the significance of IoT in improving work to overcome reluctance to change.

Conclusion

This chapter has provided a comprehensive guide, from identifying strategic objectives and mapping IoT solutions to understanding risks, embracing change, and nurturing a culture of innovation. Its crucial realm of change management within the IoT adoption context equips you with the knowledge and tools to navigate this transformative journey successfully.

The world of IoT is ever-changing, and your organization must continue to adapt and innovate to stay ahead. Keep exploring new use cases, stay attuned to evolving technologies and trends, and foster a culture of continuous learning and improvement. The IoT era offers boundless possibilities, and your organization is well-equipped to seize them.

Points to remember

- The successful integration of IoT technologies hinges on aligning IoT projects with the organization's broader business strategy. This alignment ensures that IoT initiatives are purposeful and directly contribute to the organization's goals and objectives. By integrating IoT with the business plan, companies can create new revenue streams, enhance operational efficiency, and improve decision-making.
- IoT can create new revenue streams by enabling innovative products or services. It can also significantly increase operational efficiency by automating processes, reducing manual intervention, and optimizing resource allocation. This dual benefit of revenue generation and efficiency improvement can give businesses a competitive edge and lead to cost savings.
- IoT generates vast amounts of real-time data that empower organizations to make informed, data-driven decisions. It is crucial to ensure IoT activities are directly aligned with specific organizational goals to maximize this data. Whether it's enhancing productivity, profitability, customer satisfaction, or other key performance measures, IoT projects should directly impact these aspects. This alignment helps avoid unnecessary IoT projects and maximizes their value.
- **Regulatory and compliance risks**
    - o Adherence to data protection and privacy laws, like GDPR, is essential to avoid fines and reputation damage.
    - o Meeting industry-specific security standards and certifications is necessary to access markets and prevent legal issues.
    - o Regularly review and update compliance measures to stay aligned with changing regulations and maintain a competitive edge.
- **Device reliability and maintenance risks**
    - o Carefully choose reliable IoT device suppliers to minimize malfunctions and extend device lifespans.
    - o Implement regular firmware and software updates to ensure device security and performance.
    - o Enable real-time monitoring and diagnostics to identify and address issues promptly, preventing operational disruptions.
- **Technical risks**
    - o Adherence to industry standards and standardized communication protocols enhances device interoperability.
    - o Strong security measures, such as encryption and authentication, must be implemented to protect IoT devices and data.

  - Design IoT infrastructure with scalability to accommodate future growth without compromising performance.

- **Operational risks**
  - Thorough project planning, including clear goals and resource allocation, helps prevent delays and budget overruns.
  - Provide training programs to improve the knowledge and proficiency of personnel working on IoT projects.
  - Establish proactive maintenance plans and support procedures to resolve issues and ensure system availability quickly.
- Successful IoT implementations require collaboration between IT teams with technical expertise and operational teams with business acumen. This collaboration should start at the executive level and bridge the gap between technical and non-technical aspects.
- IoT significantly impacts organizational culture, requiring a culture that encourages innovation, embraces change, and values input from all levels of the organization to succeed.
- IoT can enhance employee adoption and training through practical training, remote collaboration, personalized learning paths, real-time feedback, augmented/virtual reality, IoT-capable learning management systems, gamified learning experiences, continuous learning, and reduced training costs.

Multiple choice questions

1. **Why is aligning IoT projects with an organization's business strategy important?**
   a. To increase the number of IoT devices used in the organization.
   b. To reduce the costs associated with IoT implementation.
   c. To ensure IoT initiatives contribute to the organization's goals and objectives.
   d. To create a separate IoT department within the organization.
2. **How can IoT technology enhance operational efficiency within a business?**
   a. By adding more layers of complexity to existing processes.
   b. By automating processes, reducing manual intervention, and optimizing resource allocation.
   c. By increasing downtime and resource wastage.
   d. By focusing solely on revenue generation.

3. **What is a key benefit of data generated by IoT devices for organizations?**
   a. It allows organizations to avoid data-driven decision-making.
   b. It can be sold to third-party data providers for profit.
   c. It empowers organizations to make informed, data-driven decisions.
   d. It has no impact on organizational decision-making.
4. **What is a key consideration in addressing regulatory and compliance risks in IoT projects?**
   a. Adherence to industry-specific security standards
   b. Frequent firmware updates
   c. Extensive data collection
   d. Avoiding user training
5. **How can organizations mitigate device reliability and maintenance risks in IoT initiatives?**
   a. Selecting IoT devices from unverified suppliers
   b. Implementing regular firmware updates
   c. Avoiding remote monitoring and diagnostics
   d. Ignoring user training
6. **What is crucial in managing technical risks in IoT projects?**
   a. Avoiding standardized communication protocols
   b. Minimizing data security measures
   c. Prioritizing scalability in infrastructure design
   d. Ignoring firmware updates
7. **Which action helps address operational risks in IoT projects?**
   a. Providing inadequate training to project personnel
   b. Avoiding proactive maintenance plans
   c. Conducting thorough project planning
   d. Disregarding user feedback
8. **According to the provided information, what is a key requirement for successful IoT implementations?**

   a. Technical expertise within IT teams.

   b. Strict separation between IT and operational teams.

   c. Lack of collaboration between IT and operational teams.

   d. Executive-level involvement in technical aspects.

9. **How can organizations foster a culture that embraces IoT-induced changes effectively?**

   a. By limiting input to top-level executives.

   b. By discouraging innovation and change.

   c. By valuing input from all organizational levels.

   d. By keeping employees in the dark about IoT initiatives.

10. **How can IoT support employee adoption and training, as mentioned in the content?**

    a. By ignoring the need for training and support.

    b. By excluding employees from the planning stages.

    c. By providing practical training, personalized learning paths, and real-time feedback.

    d. By making training inaccessible and expensive.

Answer key

1. c.
2. b.
3. c.
4. a.
5. b.
6. c.
7. c.
8. a.
9. c.
10. c.

Questions

1. What is the primary advantage of aligning IoT projects with an organization's business strategy?
2. How can IoT technologies create new revenue streams for businesses?
3. In what way does IoT contribute to improved decision-making within organizations?
4. What should be the relationship between IoT projects and an organization's strategic plan?
5. How can IoT technologies help reduce operational costs within a business?
6. Which of the following is a common consequence of failing to comply with data protection laws in IoT projects?
7. How can organizations enhance the security of IoT devices to mitigate technical risks?
8. What does proactive maintenance planning aim to achieve in IoT projects?
9. In addressing ethical and social risks in IoT, what does *data minimization* refer to?
10. What role do IoT champions or advocates play in fostering IoT adoption?
11. Why is addressing security concerns crucial for successful IoT adoption?
12. How can organizations create a culture of continuous learning in the context of IoT adoption?

Key terms

- **Internet of Things:** Ensuring that IoT projects are closely linked to and support the broader business strategy.
- **New revenue streams:** Utilizing IoT technology to create innovative goods or services that generate additional sources of income.
- **Efficiency improvement:** Leveraging IoT to optimize workflows, automate processes, and enhance operational efficiency.
- **Data-driven decision-making:** Using real-time data from IoT devices to make informed and strategic decisions.
- **Contributing to organizational goals:** Ensuring IoT projects directly impact key performance measures and support organizational objectives.
- **IoT potential:** Harnessing the transformative potential of IoT by aligning projects with specific use cases and business requirements.

- **IoT strategy:** Develop a comprehensive plan for integrating IoT technologies into the overall business strategy.
- **ROI analysis:** Conduct a thorough **ROI** study to assess the value of IoT projects.
- **Key performance indicators:** Metrics used to evaluate the effectiveness and success of IoT systems, devices, and applications.
- **Scalability and flexibility:** Ensuring that IoT solutions can adapt and grow to accommodate changing needs and technologies.
- **Cross-functional collaboration:** Collaboration among different departments and teams to define objectives and ensure successful IoT implementation.
- **Data security and privacy:** Implementing policies and measures to protect sensitive data generated by IoT devices.
- **Business case:** Identifying areas where IoT can enhance operational effectiveness, consumer experiences, or product innovation.
- **Real-time monitoring:** Using IoT for continuous monitoring and predictive maintenance of assets.
- **Production planning and scheduling:** Applying IoT to improve operational responsiveness and reduce planning cycle times.
- **Quality management:** Leveraging IoT for automated inspection and data-driven quality control.
- **Robotic solutions:** Using IoT to enhance productivity, quality, and safety in manufacturing through robotics.
- **KPI metrics:** Specific metrics used to measure the success of IoT initiatives in various use cases.
- **Customer satisfaction:** Evaluating the impact of IoT on customer satisfaction through improved product quality.
- **Competitive advantage:** Assessing how IoT can contribute to gaining a competitive edge in the market.

Join our book's Discord space

Join the book's Discord Workspace for Latest updates, Offers, Tech happenings around the world, New Release and Sessions with the Authors:

https://discord.bpbonline.com

CHAPTER 6
Challenges and Solutions

Introduction

This chapter will cover numerous difficulties while implementing the **Internet of Things (IoT)**. Due to the possibility of breaches and illegal access, security and privacy are essential. Interoperability and standards must be established to facilitate seamless communication across various devices. A strong infrastructure is needed to scale IoT implementations to handle increasingly connected devices. The enormous amount of created data must be handled with effective data management and analytics. Optimizing power and energy efficiency is necessary, especially for devices with limited resources. A stable network architecture should support increased traffic. It can be challenging to integrate IoT with existing systems. It is necessary to address ethical and legal issues relating to data ownership, permission, and privacy. For frameworks and best practices to be developed, stakeholders must work together to prioritize security, interoperability, scalability, and privacy while guaranteeing the implementation of the IoT responsibly.

Structure

This chapter covers the following topics:

- IoT cybersecurity concerns
  - Identifying security vulnerabilities in IoT
  - Manufacturing and supply chain IoT security threats

- Solution strategies for mitigating security risks
- IoT security in medical devices

- Overcoming integration challenges
  - Challenges of IoT integration
  - IoT integration in supply chain and manufacturing
  - IoT integration in connected supply chain
  - Future of IoT integration in manufacturing
- Ensuring reliable connectivity
  - Reliable connectivity for IoT applications
  - Common connectivity challenges and their impact
  - IoT connectivity in healthcare systems
  - Future of IoT connectivity
- IoT and data privacy
  - Understanding data privacy concerns
  - Balancing data utilization and privacy
  - Strategic approach to IoT and data privacyResponsible data innovation
- Architecting scalable and interoperable IoT
  - Scalability challenges in IoT implementations
  - Interoperability considerations for IoT systems
  - Strategies for scalable and interoperable IoT solutions
- Addressing latency issues with edge computing
  - Introduction to edge computing and its benefits in IoT
  - Edge computing in manufacturing and supply chainImplementing edge computing for IoT
- Data analytics and machine learning
  - Leveraging data analytics in IoT for predictive insights
  - ML for anomaly detection and optimization
  - Data analytics and machine learning in IoT

- Energy efficiency and sustainability in IoT
    - o Optimizing IoT energy use
    - o Green IoT practices for sustainable supply chains
    - o Energy efficiency and sustainability goals with IoT

Objectives

This chapter will equip readers with solution strategies to overcome key technical challenges in scaling and deriving maximum value from the IoT deployments. It covers managing inherent IoT cybersecurity risks, integrating with existing systems, ensuring reliable connectivity, addressing data privacy, architecting for scale and interoperability, and reducing latency through edge computing. By providing comprehensive guidance on surmounting these hurdles, this chapter seeks to enable smoothly transitioning IoT proof-of-concepts to full-fledged implementations that transform operations, products, and business models. The readers will gain insight into proactively tackling the multidimensional complexities of IoT adoption to accelerate returns on IoT investments. Whether you are starting early on a greenfield deployment or introducing IoT incrementally into brownfield environments, the chapter outlines practical approaches to avoid common pitfalls as manufacturing ecosystems get increasingly connected, data-rich, and intelligent.

IoT cybersecurity concerns

The growth of IoT deployments in smart factories introduces transformational visibility and automation capabilities. However, this also expands the attack surface and data vulnerability risks exponentially. A breach disrupting manufacturing operations or stealing sensitive intellectual property could have major financial, reputational, and safety impacts. With connectivity woven into the core of how modern factories function, IoT cybersecurity becomes an indispensable priority.

Identifying security vulnerabilities in IoT

While IT teams are accustomed to managing endpoints like computers and servers, IoT introduces a new class of heterogeneous connected devices and protocols. Many embedded sensors and legacy industrial systems lack native security capabilities. The scale and diversity make device-by-device cyber hardening implausible for most organizations. Holistically addressing IoT infrastructure and data flows is key.

The following scope requires enterprises to take a comprehensive view of the IoT ecosystem and cyber risks rather than just individual components.

Many IoT cyber risks stem from inherent vulnerabilities at different levels:

- **Device:** Many sensors and embedded systems lack cryptography, access controls, and mechanisms for secure updates, while weak default passwords often remain unchanged, leaving industrial environments susceptible to cybersecurity breaches through physical tampering of devices.
- **Networking:** Data flows between field devices, gateways, and cloud platforms rely on wireless or ethernet protocols, many of which lack encryption, exposing industrial data capture via man-in-the-middle attacks, risks further amplified by poor network segmentation across the production environment. Network segmentation creates protected enclaves for critical assets and data flows, limiting lateral pathways for attackers. It also aids monitoring, access control, and incident response.
- **Platform:** IoT platforms powering device connectivity, data aggregation, and application enablement create central data repositories. Insufficient access controls, activity logging, and system hardening introduce data theft or manipulation risks.
- **Application:** The apps and dashboards accessing IoT data require security measures against threats like code injection, DDoS attacks, and hijacking user sessions.

While cybersecurity incidents create disruptions across all industries, IoT ecosystems face uniquely severe business impacts, given the tight integration with physical systems and processes. Breaches within IoT environments can threaten safety, availability, liability, intellectual property, and corporate reputation in the following critical ways:

- **Safety:** Shutting down sensors or manipulating control systems could result in dangerous malfunction of heavy machinery, industrial processes, and autonomous vehicles.
- **Availability: Denial-of-service (DoS)** attacks that disable manufacturing operations could mean significant revenue loss from stalled production.
- **Liability:** Tampered IoT medical or automotive systems could severely injure end users, resulting in major legal and regulatory consequences.**Intellectual property:** Theft of proprietary data on equipment settings, custom manufacturing processes, or product designs via breached IoT systems erodes competitive advantage.
- **Reputation:** Cyber incidents undermine customer trust and corporate image, especially when reliability and safety are paramount.

The scale of disruption was demonstrated in real-world attacks like *Stuxnet* in 2010, which destroyed uranium centrifuges by manipulating control systems. Once inside a system, it specifically targeted Siemens **Programmable Logic Controllers (PLCs)** that controlled the speed and operation of centrifuges used in uranium enrichment. Hence, a proactive cybersecurity approach is mission-critical.

Manufacturing and supply chain IoT security threats

Manufacturers need to safeguard against a range of hostile actors:

- **Malware attacks:** Viruses, worms, spyware, and ransomware could infiltrate networks or IoT devices, denying system access or shutting down operations. Attackers may camouflage malware as legitimate software updates.
- **Data exfiltration:** Hackers may target proprietary data on equipment settings, manufacturing methods, product designs, customer orders, and pricing, which can be sold or used against the company. Breached IoT data removes any internal/external barriers.
- **DoS:** Flooding systems like IoT platform APIs or public-facing apps with excessive requests can cause outages and disruption. The lack of availability has dire financial impacts on factories.
- **Man-in-the-middle**: By intercepting insecure IoT sensor data flows, attackers can steal information or manipulate operational parameters, resulting in damage. Thus, encryption is essential.
- **Insider risks**: Even authorized users like disgruntled employees or compromised vendors with stolen credentials can tamper with IoT configurations or destroy data.
- **Physical manipulation:** Unsecured physical access allows altering sensor readings, device settings, or tampering to sabotage production.

Solution strategies for mitigating security risks

Managing cyber risks across complex manufacturing environments requires a multi-layered defense combining people, processes, and technology. A cybersecurity strategy is crucial for securing interconnected IoT infrastructure. The core elements of such a strategy include:

- **Network segmentation:** Logically separate IoT networks using **virtual local area networks** (**VLANs**) and **access control lists** (**ACLs**) to restrict traffic between operational, corporate, and guest zones. This prevents lateral movement across networks with differing security levels. Furthermore, authentication mechanisms should be implemented to control which IoT field data is allowed into critical applications, providing an additional access management layer.
- **Access controls:** Implement role-based access for users and devices to allow only authorized access. Mandate multi-factor authentication, single sign-on, and encryption of passwords to strengthen identity management. Automatically

disable any dormant accounts to prevent unauthorized use.

- **Data protection:** Encrypt sensitive IoT data flows end-to-end as transmitted and at rest. Additionally, anonymize or mask data wherever possible to limit exposure. Typically, the data encryption for IoT devices is handled by a separate security module or application, not by the IoT devices themselves. The constrained nature of most IoT devices means they lack computing resources to handle intensive encryption. Another component in the architecture provides encryption to protect the data flows and at-rest storage. The decryption would then happen only at the target analyzing application.

- **Monitoring and auditing:** Diligently track all granted and denied access attempts. Continuously monitor networks, endpoints, and system logs using SIEM solutions to identify anomalies in near real-time. While sophisticated SIEM tools allow larger enterprises to gain unified threat insight, these prove complex and costly for smaller manufacturers with limited security budgets.

  A well-suited entry point for industrial IoT players to attain core SIEM capabilities on limited budgets is to deploy integrated threat detection features within their existing firewalls and secure routers.

  Many advanced network security appliances designed intentionally for mid-sized organizations now embed basic analytics and reporting to aggregate key events, identify known **malicious patterns**, spotlight suspicious anomalies, and log activity trails for investigation. While lacking the full sophistication of enterprise-class SIEM solutions, leaning on the unified visibility these purpose-built devices provide out-of-the-box provides a pragmatic starting point to gain a footprint into baseline behaviors, risk exposures, and security incidents without overstretching limited resources. The fundamentals are built to provide an upgrade path to augment capabilities over time via cloud services or managed providers as needs evolve.

- **Asset management:** Maintain a complete inventory of all approved IoT devices, their firmware versions, and baselines to detect any unauthorized shadow IT and enable prompt security updates.

- **Software hardening:** Disable any unnecessary ports and protocols to minimize vulnerabilities. Continuously patch firmware and application vulnerabilities to limit the attack surface.

- **Physical hardening:** Use tamper-resistant casings for any IoT hardware deployed in insecure public locations. Also, restrict physical access to data centers to protect critical infrastructure.

- **Incident response:** Have a detailed action plan for investigation, containment, and recovery from cybersecurity incidents to limit impact and prevent recurrence. Involve public relations and legal teams as appropriate.

- **Training:** Provide comprehensive education for all employees on risks, policies, and their role in prevention. Avoiding phishing links, device misuse, or unauthorized access is imperative.

For highly vulnerable IoT systems, additional controls like custom firmware, whitelisting, and air-gapped operation might be warranted where feasible. Partnering with specialized IoT cybersecurity firms also brings valuable assessment and implementation expertise to complement internal IT.

Ultimately, organizations must architect security into the foundation of any IoT rollout rather than leaving it as an afterthought. This necessitates the involvement of cybersecurity teams from initial design through technology selection, deployment, and ongoing operation.

IoT security in medical devices

Healthcare offers an exemplary case study of IoT cyber risk impact and mitigation. If compromised, networked medical devices like MRI machines, pacemakers, insulin pumps, and other embedded systems are vulnerable to life-threatening manipulation.

Attackers could tamper with device functionality, falsify diagnostic data, or deny access in ransomware scenarios; all potentially fatal for patients. In 2020, suspected ransomware resulted in a German hospital being unable to access IT systems, resulting in a patient's death en route to another hospital.

The **Food and Drug Administration** (**FDA**), USA, now recommends that medical device makers consider cybersecurity throughout product lifecycles. These measures include:

- Developing threat models during design to systematically identify risks and controls.
- Validating that software properly restricts access and validates input data.Ensuring deployment procedures deactivate unnecessary hardware ports, protocols, and services.
- Monitoring systems through methods like device syslog analysis to detect anomalies.
- Designing devices to fail and recover from potential attacks safely.
- Making cybersecurity capabilities a competitive advantage over less secure products.

Continuous network segmentation, authentication, encryption, and monitoring are vital for healthcare organizations to prevent infiltration from adjacent IT systems. Ensuring manufacturers deliver secure-by-design devices is imperative.

Medical IoT systems warrant the utmost cyber caution, given the high stakes involved.

The lessons also apply to any field where IoT drives critical infrastructure - energy, transportation, or manufacturing.

As factories get smarter, cyber risks grow exponentially. However, with the diligent application of security-in-depth principles, the disruptive potential of IoT data vulnerabilities can be tamed. The key is devising a comprehensive cyber strategy spanning governance, infrastructure safeguards, partnerships, and employee training. By investing in sustainability IoT security from day one, manufacturers can realize the full benefits of connectivity and data visibility while safeguarding their most vital assets: intellectual property, operations continuity, and public trust.

Overcoming integration challenges

The rapid proliferation of IoT sensors, devices, and systems hold immense potential for supply chain and manufacturing organizations to gain unprecedented visibility, automation, and analytics. The value of merely deploying more IoT endpoints without strategy is limited. The key to successfully harnessing IoT is integrating it effectively into the people, processes, and legacy environments that define factories and fulfillment centers. This integration unavoidably poses multi-dimensional technical and organizational challenges that companies must navigate for smooth and successful IoT deployments.

Challenges of IoT integration

Several characteristics inherent to IoT ecosystems increase integration complexity:

- **Heterogeneity of endpoints:** IoT environments comprise a heterogeneous mix of sensors, machines, vehicles, wearables, and appliances. Each has unique communication protocols, data formats, interfaces, and platforms. It is difficult to integrate and normalize data across this diversity.
- **Legacy systems:** Factories contain legacy production equipment, operational technology systems like SCADA, and logistics infrastructure that lack native connectivity to emerging smart factory IT landscapes yet hold invaluable data. To maximize the potential of Industrial Internet of Things initiatives, ensuring interfaces between existing operational assets and new IoT platforms for consolidated data visibility and insights is vital. Integrating sensors, collectors, and translators capable of tapping into output from conventional machines as input for enterprise IoT analytics and applications can enrich visibility into overall manufacturing processes. Careful bridging of legacy environments with modern smart infrastructure unlocks fuller optimization.
- **Data scale and speed:** As IoT endpoints multiply, generated data compounds quickly - from millisecond readings to billions of signals daily. While individual sensors seem manageable, such volume and velocity at scale overwhelm traditional infrastructure. However, edge analysis and efficient data transportation condense

noisy inputs to relevant essences. So, while immense data represents IoT's growing reality, smart architectures temper scale through filters and compression. Still, compressed formats stretch limits over time as devices spread across the enterprise. Legacy data warehouses built for gigabytes break under immense petabyte loads. Velocity spikes, too, as predictive analysis calls for all readings from all inputs continuously. This inevitable flood from success must have room to flow safely – for example, capacity set aside in flexible big data lakes.

- **Analytics complexity:** Collecting huge machine or sensor data volumes provides little direct business value. Making sense of the data requires complex analytics and data science expertise.
- **Organizational silos:** Data science, OT, IT, and business teams have limited experience collaborating across domains. Aligning objectives proves to be challenging.
- **Continuous change:** Additional sensors, new software versions, and replaced machinery result in constant flux. The integrations must adapt and scale dynamically.
- **Security requirements:** With critical infrastructure and processes at risk, security, access controls, and regulatory compliance cannot be compromised while integrating IoT.

These challenges make IoT integration far more complex than traditional IT projects. Greenfield deployments have the luxury of engineering for IoT from the ground up. However, brownfield environments with existing processes, machines, and culture require methodical software and organizational integration.

IoT integration in supply chain and manufacturing

IoT deployments span software, hardware, and organizational domains. Successfully navigating the multidimensional integration challenges relies on blending architecture, technology, and culture. However, the effort enables realizing the promise of connected factories and supply chains.

Following are the ten strategies for effective IoT integration:

- **Architect a connectivity blueprint:** Create a high-level outline mapping the various systems, data types, interaction patterns, and required capabilities like security, analytics applications, redundancy planning, and so on, to provide an architectural understanding of the end-to-end ecosystem to help guide integration projects.
- **Phase rollouts via use cases:** Rather than attempting a large complex *big bang* integration all at once, select high-value applications like predictive maintenance

or warehouse optimization to implement first via IoT pilots. These narrowly scoped projects deliver a quicker return on investment while providing working integration capability templates for wider reuse later.

- **Engineer infinitely scalable pipelines:** Design data ingestion mechanisms, transformation engines, and analytic computing pathways anticipating exponential increases over time in sensors and data volumes. So, the integration architecture continues to perform without interruptions or infrastructure bottlenecks as IoT usage grows.
- **Adopt interoperable protocols:** Seek out device hardware, platform services, and communication mechanisms following standard published protocols like MQTT or REST rather than proprietary APIs to avoid single vendor dependency and enable substituting components as needed.
- **Modularize via microservices:** Componentize distinct integration functionality into standalone, independently upgradeable modules interacting through well-defined interfaces to simplify ongoing updates and avoid change-rippling impacts.
- **Centralize on an integration platform:** Set up a common centralized middleware layer using **extract, transform, and load (ETL)** tools, streaming data hubs, and conversion frameworks that standardize and connect all the modules that need to interact so dispersed teams do not create one-off custom connections.
- **Bridge legacy systems:** Provide gateways capable of translating proprietary legacy protocols into modern IoT communication standards; build in hooks to push data into legacy systems from IoT apps where viable to make interaction bi-directional.
- **Foster cross-domain collaboration:** Break down organizational silos and knowledge gaps, impeding end-to-end system visibility via initiatives like unified IT/OT teams, training boot camps, and online technical support forums focused on systems integration.
- **Embed cybersecurity checks:** Incorporate identity and access management, hardened hosts, end-to-end encryption, activity and anomaly detection monitoring within the integration flows to address increased cyberattack surfaces.
- **Expect continual change:** Architect for modularity and abstraction via APIs and datastores to limit internal component coupling so that change impact remains localized; adopt modern automated toolchain and culture capabilities from DevOps.

IoT integration in connected supply chain

Global brewer *Anheuser-Busch InBev* [1]provides an instructive case study on the transformative value IoT integration offers supply chains. AB InBev launched a connected

[1] **https://www.iot-now.com/2021/10/04/113929-weissbeerger-part-of-ab-inbev-builds-next-gen-beverage-analytics-system-with-aws-iot/**

supply chain initiative spanning over 150 facilities and distribution centers to provide fresher beer faster to retailers and consumers.

It installed internet-connected sensors in beer kegs to continuously track temperature, humidity, motion, and other attributes through brewing, filling, distribution, and retail. IoT gateways consolidated and transmitted the field data to the cloud. Combining this real-time sensor data with brewery systems and distribution data provided end-to-end supply chain visibility.

Integrating the IoT data with inventory systems allowed for the proactive refilling of retail shelves based on consumption rather than fixed schedules. Shelf life predictions reduced spoilage. The company also built mobile apps to help distributors efficiently manage inventory and placements using IoT data during deliveries.

Future of IoT integration in manufacturing

As Industry 4.0 gains traction, manufacturing plants must integrate internal equipment and processes via IoT and synchronize operations globally across suppliers, logistics partners, and customers. Collaboration powered by interconnected, intelligent systems will define competitiveness.

Developments like low-power wide area networks, 5G, and edge computing will proliferate hyper-connected smart factories. Companies also need integration strategies spanning cloud architectures, data science, change management, and cybersecurity. With robust integration, manufacturers can harness the oncoming tidal wave of big data to maximize efficiency, quality, and responsiveness.

Integrating technology is just as vital as integrating human stakeholders within and across organizations to focus on collective value. As connections multiply between people, processes, devices, and analytics, integration skills will be the glue enabling Industry 4.0 to fulfill its promise.

Ensuring reliable connectivity

Connectivity is the lifeblood of IoT ecosystems. Without reliable, real-time data flowing from the field into enterprise systems, the promise of data-driven visibility, automation, and intelligence cannot be realized. However, the scale and variety of connected endpoints make attaining robust connectivity highly challenging across global assets, systems, and mobile users. From network availability to device management, many factors impact IoT connectivity. For supply chain, logistics, and manufacturing organizations where operations critically rely on real-time IoT data, having contingency plans to ensure connectivity resiliency becomes pivotal.

Reliable connectivity for IoT applications

Loss of connectivity, even temporarily, negates the benefits of IoT across these scenarios. While users have come to expect occasional web outages, mission-critical industrial IoT use cases necessitate extremely high availability, redundancy, and failover mechanisms to avoid disruptions.

The critical need for always-on connectivity and reliable IoT connectivity enables:

- **Real-time analytics:** IoT analytics derives instant insights from fresh data versus static datasets. Disconnected assets starve applications of key data.
- **Situational awareness:** Tracking people, equipment, and inventory locations requires constant updates to provide accurate views for monitoring and coordination. Gaps introduce dangerous blind spots.**Rapid response:** Alerting, troubleshooting, and damage control require immediate data for shedding light on emerging problems. Latency costs money and safety.
- **Predictive maintenance:** Continuously monitoring asset telemetry is foundational for predicting failures before they occur. Missing data has ripple effects downstream.
- **Process automation:** With processes directly controlled by sensor data, gaps break the real-time feedback loops needed for dynamic adjustments and performance.

Common connectivity challenges and their impact

Without connectivity resilience, the return on investment (ROI) of IoT deployments remains limited despite their scale. These seven key factors result in data delays and gaps that degrade situational awareness, analytics fidelity, process efficiency, and service levels:

- **Sparse networks:** Remote assets, vehicles, and infrastructure exist where cellular and WiFi coverage can be weak or absent altogether. This causes blackout regions.
- **Interference:** Equipment congestion and physical obstructions can cause interference despite adequate coverage.**Bandwidth constraints:** HD video feeds from cameras and drones may saturate network capacity. Lower-priority data becomes delayed or lost.
- **Power issues:** Battery-operated endpoints like sensors may deplete prematurely or lack consistent supply. This results in compromised data flow.
- **Device failures:** Physical damage, misconfigurations, or software crashes in the field can make endpoints unreachable. Detecting outage sources grows difficult.
- **User errors:** Improper device usage in the field of IT misconfigurations on the backend impacts uptime. Troubleshooting interactions slows resolution.
- **Security attacks:** External threats like DDoS attacks or internal risks like unauthorized IoT devices being added can disrupt connectivity.

IoT connectivity in healthcare systems

Preemptively building connectivity resilience at the edge and system levels provides insurance against real-world variability accompanying IoT scale. Addressing the risks requires a combination of network design, device management, and redundancies:

- **Adaptable networks:** Hybrid networks combining LAN, cellular, LPWAN, and satellite dynamically route packets based on link quality and application data importance. Edge computing reduces backhaul reliance.
- **Power options:** Battery optimization, energy harvesting, and PoE provide endpoints supplementary power sources to sustain operation.
- **Heartbeat monitoring:** IoT platforms periodically check device connectivity status and alert if unresponsive. It helps to pinpoint outage locations.
- **Redundancy:** Backup networks, SIMs, endpoints, and communication paths provide failover when the primary goes down. Deploying redundant gateways avoids a single point of failure.
- **M2M protocols:** Lightweight messaging protocols like MQTT, CoAP, and AMQP allow assets to share small data packets with resiliency features efficiently.
- **Edge intelligence:** Having edge nodes pre-process data and run lower-priority tasks locally preserves network capacity for critical data transfers and control.
- **Configuration automation:** Tools remotely configuring at scale help roll back problematic changes and rapidly optimize settings. It also minimizes technician dispatches.
- **Security:** Network segmentation, firewalling, and authorization limit connectivity threats. Encryption prevents content hijacking.

Future of IoT connectivity

As supply chains, logistics networks, and smart factories become increasingly interconnected, resilient, and adaptable, connectivity within and between organizations will define their cyber-physical efficiency.

Several technology trends will diversify how scalable, global connectivity gets delivered:

- New wide-area networking options like LPWANs and 5G provide low-power, long-range, high-bandwidth connectivity suited for IoT.
- Expanding edge intelligence allows producing insights and automation closer to assets rather than relying solely on cloud data centers. This improves response times and reduces backhaul bottlenecks.

- The rise of mesh architectures where devices relay through local peers provides an organic growth path for dense connectivity and redundancy between endpoints.
- The growth of satellite connectivity promises low-latency global coverage anywhere. *SpaceX*'s *Starlink* constellation promises low-latency satellite connectivity anywhere globally, a boon for transportation.

These advances will enhance industrial and supply chain connectivity's reliability, responsiveness, and reach.

Holistic connectivity resilience also requires a cultural commitment to treat connectivity as a profit-driving capability rather than a cost center. Networking teams must partner strategically with the business to ensure the availability and responsiveness of connectivity to optimize operational outcomes and productivity.

As factories embrace Industry 4.0 transformation built on complete interconnectedness, resilient IoT connectivity within and between global assets, systems, partners, and customers will become more vital. The stakes grow exponentially higher as operations digitally reinvent themselves through the physical-digital fusion promised by the IoT.

IoT and data privacy

The proliferation of IoT deployments across industries is driven by the promise of extracting powerful insights from machine and sensor data. However, the same IoT data that unlocks optimization also introduces customer and employee privacy risks. As IoT permeates the enterprise, proactively addressing data privacy becomes integral to sustaining trust and managing compliance.

Understanding IoT data privacy concerns

IoT data is especially prone to privacy abuse at scale compared to traditional systems. Unlike traditional systems, IoT data remains essential for core operations.IoT intensifies data privacy concerns due to:

- **Data sensitivity:** IoT provides intimate visibility into equipment, systems, products, and users through detailed telemetry and embedded sensors. This data sensitivity makes protection imperative.
- **Lack of consent:** IoT data gets continuously collected from endpoints like devices, cameras, and wearables. However, user notice or consent is often limited compared to web apps.
- **Pattern discovery:** Advanced analytics on aggregated IoT data may uncover sensitive inferences like health conditions that individuals did not actively provide or intend.

- **Data persistence:** IoT data gets amalgamated into cloud data lakes for perpetual analysis. Information lives on indefinitely instead of being deleted.
- **Lack of transparency:** IoT ecosystems' scale and integration complexity obscures what data gets shared with which systems and applications. Users lose visibility into downstream usage.
- **Third parties:** Specialized analytics software, predictive maintenance firms, and cloud service providers may get access to IoT data, multiplying the risk of misuse. As such, vendor management becomes pivotal.**Cybersecurity:** Breaches of IoT platforms or endpoint devices expose personal data like factory floor access control systems logging employees. Encryption and access controls provide protection.

Balancing data utilization and privacy

The following strategic balancing act allows for deriving essential operational value from IoT data for visibility and optimization while proactively managing privacy pitfalls. Organizations can manage IoT data privacy strategically through:

- Conducting privacy impact assessments for planned projects to quantify risks specific to the IoT data type, analytics, and use case.
- Minimizing data collection to the essential IoT sensors for required analytics rather than maximizing data volume alone. Judicious data selection reduces exposure.
- Anonymizing IoT datasets to remove personal identifiers like device IDs that could link back to individual users. This preserves aggregate insights without attribution.
- Analyzing data sets locally on devices vs. the cloud using edge intelligence to avoid widespread data transfer.
- Encrypting IoT data flows during transmission and at rest to avoid interception or breach risks. The use of access keys by authorized applications maintains security.
- Abstracting raw data through aggregation and normalization techniques to mask potential personal details when sharing widely.
- Restricting data access to specific apps and analytics use cases via permissions and API keys. Avoid wide-open data lakes.
- Providing transparency to users on what IoT data gets collected and how it gets used. Enabling user control options builds trust.
- Assessing third-party data-sharing policies through security and privacy audits. Staying current on evolving regional regulations like the EU's GDPR and tailoring data practices and disclosures accordingly.

Strategic approach to IoT and data privacy

Global wholesaler *Costco* provides an instructive example of strategically leveraging IoT data while respecting privacy. Costco outfitted store freezers and warehouses with IoT sensors to monitor appliance temperature, power consumption, door open frequency, and foot traffic past freezers. This data helps optimize energy usage and place high-demand items in high-traffic locations to boost sales.

However, to mitigate privacy concerns, Costco adopted several safeguards, which are as follows:

- No cameras or identifiers that could link appliance data to individual shoppers. The analysis relies on aggregated anonymized data.
- Analytics are run on-premises rather than in the cloud to limit external data sharing. Only aggregated insights get transferred.
- Public notices inform customers of appliance monitoring and excluding personally identifiable data.
- Strict contractual terms prohibit its IoT platform vendor from reselling or misusing the collected data.
- Fine-grained access controls limit data visibility to authorized teams. No wide-open data lakes.

This demonstrates how IoT can focus on operational insights without intrusive personal tracking, even for public-facing environments.

Responsible data innovation

The IoT revolution is driven by organizations' ability to extract value from connected data. In the process, maintaining customer and employee trust through ethical data practices separates sustainable businesses from shortsighted entities. Companies must architect systems to collect and share only necessary data, restrict downstream usage, provide transparency, and keep apprised of emerging best practices as IoT-scale data privacy management remains an evolving landscape.

With a foundation of responsible data handling that protects people's interests, businesses can build their reputations and competitive advantage on extractive IoT analytics responsibly and sustainably. Getting data privacy right helps the IoT revolution scale new heights.

Architecting scalable and interoperable IoT

The transformational potential of the IoT relies on an organization's ability to seamlessly scale systems as new sensors, data sources, and use cases are added continuously. Similarly, harnessing insights across heterogeneous devices, protocols, and platforms requires careful interoperability considerations from the outset. Without planning for scalability and interoperability, the impact of IoT gets constrained despite heavy investment.

Scalability challenges in IoT implementations

IoT solutions often begin as small pilots before expanding enterprise-wide. Each dimension needs strategic architectural decisions like cloud adoption, containerization, and modular design to prevent IoT sprawl. This requires planning for scale across:

- **Data velocity and storage:** As an IoT system expands to add more endpoints, the volume of generated data can outpace current infrastructure capabilities. Thoughtful architecture planning accounts for substantial future growth in data velocity and storage needs.

  A modular, cloud-based platform offers flexibility to scale up ingestion pipelines, filtering processes, and compression techniques as new data sources emerge.

- **Analytics complexity:** Algorithm and dashboard complexity increases as new analytics use cases emerge from more data signals.

- **Integration:** Interfaces between IoT systems and business applications multiply as adoption spreads. API and code maintenance burdens amplify.

- **Management overhead:** Monitoring, administering, and securing diverse endpoints becomes unwieldy over time. Automating provisioning, updates, and accessing controls is key.

- **Changing dependencies:** Hardware refresh cycles, operating system upgrades, and app migrations keep integration in flux.**Traffic spikes:** Temporary peaks from seasonal demand shifts or multi-year data builds require capacity buffers for headroom.

- **Machine learning models:** Machine learning retraining needs like migrating to new frameworks necessitate reusable model packaging and deployment workflows.

Interoperability considerations for IoT systems

Integrating IoT data across the multifaceted manufacturing and supply chain environment necessitates interoperability foundations through:

- **Avoiding proprietary ecosystems:** IoT architectures should emphasize flexible, accessible data pipelines. Open standards that ease connections with various systems prevent lock-in. Most importantly, the scalable design accommodates future sensors and use cases.

- **Designing for backward compatibility:** New IoT software versions should not break integration with existing assets and data schemas where possible.
- **Using middleware:** Tools like *Apache Camel* enable routing data across diverse formats and interfaces in brownfield environments via translation and message brokering.
- **Seeking cloud portability:** Multi-cloud and containerization approaches prevent cloud vendor dependencies as needs evolve.
- **Building modular microservices:** Breaking monoliths into mix-and-match components accessed via APIs avoids cascading failures and eases upgrades.
- **Implementing common data lakes:** Unifying disparate data streams into shared repositories enables unified analytics across silos.
- **Federation over consolidation:** Creating alignment between distributed systems allows interoperation without forcing unwieldy centralization.

Interoperability between devices and systems needs to expand alongside business growth. Enterprise architecture leadership plays a critical role in guiding the strategic evolution of this increasingly interconnected environment.

Strategies for scalable and interoperable IoT solutions

In healthcare, the number of connected staff, patients, wearables, and medical devices is exploding. This exponential growth requires concurrently managing the expanding scale and increasing diversity of connected devices and systems.

The massive growth in connected devices and systems in healthcare necessitates strategies to handle scale.and diversity. The core approaches include:

- **Distributed data management:** Gateways pre-process edge device data before routing higher-value subsets to cloud IoT platforms for cost efficiency.**Containers and orchestration:** Device logic and analytics models are containerized using Docker for portability across on-premises and cloud. Kubernetes orchestrates at scale.
- **Cloud analytics:** Cloud platforms like Apache Spark and Kafka enable distributed analytics at scale. However, they do not interface directly with edge devices - instead, IoT architectures rely on gateways and pipelines to ingest and consolidate data before feeding cloud servers for processing.
- **Open APIs and standards:** FHIR interfaces and protocols like MQTT allow medical devices to share data despite vendor differences.**Security:** Role-based access control, identity management, and cryptography applied at device, network, application, and data layers establishes robust protection.

Proactive design thinking prevents a lack of scalability or interoperability from stifling healthcare IoT outcomes despite exponential adoption.

Maximizing ROI through design principles

Ultimately, scalability and interoperability determine the growth trajectory and ROI of IoT. Constraining IoT's reach due to lack of planning undercuts transformation potential despite sunk costs. Organizations must implement key design principles focused on the following:

- **Modularity:** Modularity favors loosely coupled components that can be added and upgraded independently without cascading changes.
- **Abstraction:** It hides the complexity behind interfaces and processes, enabling technology integration.
- **Interoperability:** It prioritizes data accessibility and interchange over proprietary solutions to prevent silos.
- **Elasticity:** Systems are designed for workload fluidity through on-demand resource allocation, autoscaling, and load balancing.
- **Automation:** Tools and infrastructure as code allow programmatic management of device rollout, configurations, and software updates at the IoT scale.

With a focus on these technical fundamentals augmented by architecture leadership navigating complex enterprise dynamics, organizations can maximize business transformation through IoT.

Addressing latency issues with edge computing

The responsiveness of IoT applications depends heavily on analyzing data as close as possible to where it originates. Sending IoT data to faraway centralized clouds before processing can introduce lags that hurt use cases needing real-time response. Edge computing solves this issue by distributing processing capacity within the local data ecosystem. For manufacturers and supply chain companies relying on IoT for latency-sensitive applications, strategic use of edge computing is crucial. It enables processing on or near production equipment, vehicles, warehouses, and other field locations where milliseconds matter. Carefully placing analytic power at the edge allows insights to be derived and acted on faster. This edge analytics keeps businesses nimble by avoiding the delays of cloud transmission.

IoT connectivity accelerates data generation and collection from assets and systems. However, to turn this data into true business value requires additional capabilities such as:

- **Real-time processing:** Real-time processing is better suited for time-critical applications rather than just storing data. This extracts timely insights.
- **Rapid response:** It implies taking immediate actions based on analytics, like shutting down failing equipment.
- **Local optimization:** Local processing allows customizing actions per asset versus generic centralized decisions.**Autonomy:** Assets can operate semi-autonomously using on-site data rather than awaiting cloud directions.
- **Bandwidth conservation:** Analyzing close to the source reduces communication bandwidth needs.
- **Cost efficiency:** Distributing processing reduces cloud data and infrastructure costs.

For such needs, the round-trip to distant centralized clouds results in prohibitive latency from transmission, queueing, and execution delays. Edge computing overcomes this through distributed deployment.

Introduction to edge computing and its benefits in IoT

Edge computing refers to locating processing power physically closer to IoT data sources rather than sending everything to the centralized cloud. This is achieved by installing mini-data centers with compute resources at the *edge*, near local data generation and consumption points. Various edge deployment models exist, including:

- **On-device:** Processing on intelligent IoT devices like robots and vehicles. It provides ultimate low latency, but computing is limited.
- **On-premises:** The organization's on-site edge data center for processing data from nearby devices before sending it to the central cloud.
- **ISP-located:** Edge computing resources can be located inside **internet service provider** (**ISP**) networks to enable low-latency connectivity. In these cases, the edge infrastructure is owned and managed by the ISP rather than the customer. Positioning computational power deeper in the network topology minimizes communication delays. This ISP-provisioned edge computing allows businesses to leverage the scale and reach of large telco networks for distributed real-time processing.
- **Cloud provider edge:** Public cloud providers like *AWS Outposts* offer edge appliances installed on-premises. It combines local control with cloud vendor management.

Each model offers tradeoffs between latency, control, ease, and costs that inform deployment decisions for specific use cases.

Edge computing in manufacturing and supply chain

Edge computing allows manufacturing companies to unlock emerging IoT use cases needing instant data-to-action turnarounds.

The key manufacturing use cases benefitting from edge computing include:

- **Predictive maintenance:** Monitoring vibration, temperature, and other sensor data to quickly detect anomalies and avoid disruptive equipment failures.
- **Quality inspection:** Rapidly analyzing product images to detect defects and adjust processes in real-time using computer vision edge models.
- **Operations monitoring:** Tracking assembly line throughput, inventory, and other metrics to optimize production flows using local edge data.
- **Autonomous robots:** Allowing robots to sense environments and navigate themselves safely using localized edge data vs. waiting for cloud direction.
- **Augmented reality and virtual reality (AR/VR):** Providing real-time augmented views by overlaying context data on users' visual fields to assist maintenance, training, and so on.

Implementing edge computing for IoT

This edge architecture complements rather than replaces the cloud- critical for hybrid analytics and data aggregation. Implementing edge computing includes:

- **Edge hardware:** Deploying mini-data centers on-premises with storage, computing like GPUs, and networking capabilities.
- **Edge software stack:** OS, containers, analytics runtimes like TensorFlow execute models and applications locally.
- **Local data collection:** IoT gateways aggregate and preprocess data from nearby sensors before forwarding it to the edge for analysis.**Data prioritization:** Metadata tagging routes higher priority data, like alerts, to the edge while bulk sensor data goes to the cloud.**Cloud integration:** Seamlessly synchronizing insights, actions, and learnings between edge and centralized cloud.
- **Management/monitoring:** Tools to remotely manage, update, and monitor distributed edge environments.
- **Security:** Local data protection plus secure connectivity protocols like SSL/TLS/VPN between edge and cloud.

Edge computing in action: Optimized delivery

Edge computing allows organizations like third-party logistics provider GlobeX to optimize operations by processing data closer to the source. For example, GlobeX improved delivery and asset utilization through the following edge computing implementations:

- Installed edge data centers at dispatch centers to process data from nearby delivery trucks and cargo.
- Edge analytics optimize truck routing and load factors for lowest latency deliveries by location.
- Assets self-optimize based on edge data instead of awaiting centralized direction.
- Performance data aggregated across edge gets analyzed in the cloud to refine global logistics.
- Predictive maintenance leverages edge data to minimize downtime.

By optimizing logistics intelligence at the edge, *GlobeX* accelerated responsiveness across its operations.

Edge computing shifts processing physically closer to where data is produced and consumed. This powerful paradigm reduces transmission bottlenecks and cloud dependency that can throttle IoT outcomes. With connectivity and analytics permeating every facet of modern factories and supply chains, the edge is pivotal for localized intelligence. Combining cloud scale and flexibility with edge speed and autonomy provides the ultimate IoT innovation and transformation platform.

Data analytics and machine learning

The promise of actionable insights that justify massive IoT investments relies heavily on advanced analytics. While connecting devices and collecting data is crucial, making sense of the data is where much of IoT's business value lies. Technologies like data analytics and **machine learning** (**ML**) extract powerful insights from IoT data to optimize performance. Developing analytics capabilities is as pivotal for manufacturers as deploying sensors.

Leveraging data analytics in IoT for predictive insights

IoT data has unique characteristics compared to traditional business data, such as high velocity, time series nature, high variety in formats, and large volumes with low-value density. Specifically, IoT data arrives with high velocity due to frequent reporting from sensors. It is a time series in nature, with temporal continuity. IoT data also shows high variety, as it encompasses diverse structured and unstructured formats from different devices. IoT typically involves large data volumes but with low-value density, requiring extracting insights from vast streams of sensor readings.

Advanced analytics overcomes these big data challenges to unlock IoT value:

- **Descriptive analytics:** Aggregate, visualize, and report on current IoT data for monitoring and alerts.**Diagnostic analytics:** Mining IoT data helps determine why something occurred through correlation, clustering, regression, and so on.
- **Predictive analytics:** Statistical modeling and machine learning identify trends to forecast future occurrences and conditions.
- **Prescriptive analytics:** Optimizes decisions and actions based on predictive insights from IoT data.

Evolving from descriptive to predictive and prescriptive analytics allows systematic improvement of business performance through data-driven intelligence.

Robust analytics architecture for industrial IoT includes:

- **Data ingestion:** Scalable pipelines collecting, cleaning, and processing high-velocity sensor data streams using Apache Spark, and so on.
- **Data storage:** Optimized time-series databases like *InfluxDB* and cloud data lakes provide retention and query ability at scale.**Data visualization:** Tools like *Grafana* allows rapid creation of dashboards of operational metrics for monitoring.
- **Analytics platform:** Managed platforms like SAS Databricks simplify developing and deploying analytics models at scale.
- **Machine learning:** ML frameworks like *TensorFlow* empower training algorithms on industrial data for prediction.**Application integration:** APIs and microservices architecture enable the distribution of insights derived from analytics on IoT data across operational systems that can take action based on those insights.
- **Edge analytics:** Deploying stream processing and ML inferencing on gateways or on-asset reduces latency and bandwidth needs.

This foundation allows systematically aggregating data, applying analytics, and driving action.

ML for anomaly detection and optimization

Applied intelligently, machine learning is a competitive differentiator for manufacturers. IoT data combined with ML delivers high-impact use cases:

- **Predictive maintenance:** Continuously monitoring asset sensor data allows predicting failures before they occur based on similar preceding patterns and anomalies. This avoids downtime.

- **Quality optimization:** ML models trained on production line sensor data related to product quality can guide parameter tuning to minimize defects and waste.
- **Energy efficiency:** Finding correlations between machine workload sensor data, environmental conditions, and energy consumption enables optimizing equipment usage.
- **Inventory optimization:** Time series forecasting algorithms applied to consumption patterns allow optimally aligning stock levels across supply chains.
- **Threat detection:** Anomaly detection identifies risks like cyber intrusions by detecting unusual network traffic or login patterns.

Data analytics and machine learning in IoT

Pioneer Energy leveraged IoT analytics and ML to optimize its shale oil production and equipment health:

- Sensor instrumentation across wells, pipelines, negative pressure vapor recovery units, heat exchangers, and so on.
- Statistical analysis identified wells with decreasing yield for proactive maintenance. Sensor data correlated with operating conditions enables tailored equipment parameters per well.ML predictive maintenance maximizes equipment lifespan.
- Reduced downtime and optimized production increased yields by over 12% compared to reactive approaches.

By tapping into data, Pioneer increased productivity through prescriptive actions.

The proliferation of smart, connected products and processes generates unprecedented data volume, velocity, and variety across manufacturing. Companies now have a choice to let this data deluge go to waste or extract value from it. Thoughtful application of analytics and machine learning provides a structured path to data-driven decision-making. Companies that invest in collecting IoT data and making sense of it position themselves for agile, efficient, and sustainable manufacturing powered by intelligence. The analytics journey requires patience but pays continuous dividends, scaling into the future.

Energy efficiency and sustainability in IoT

The IoT growth brings potential for enhanced operational efficiency and agility. It also risks increasing energy usage and sustainability impacts from additional hardware and network demands. With climate change accelerating, manufacturers must minimize IoT's own resource footprint while harnessing it to optimize broader environmental performance. Comprehensive energy management and sustainability practices enable ecologically conscious IoT adoption.

Optimizing IoT energy use

The key facets of green IoT include:

- **Energy-efficient devices:** IoT hardware can be optimized by selecting devices with processors, transmission components, sleep modes, and power consumption metrics designed for efficiency. Innovations like ARM's M33 processor help enable hardware-level energy optimization for IoT endpoints and gateways.
- **Renewable or harvested power:** Using solar, vibration, thermoelectric generators, and other creative means to self-power wireless sensor nodes rather than just batteries.
- **Optimized data transmission:** Minimizing network communication needs through edge processing, data aggregation, and transmission scheduling. 5G and LPWAN help here.
- **Power optimization algorithms:** Intelligent power management of nodes based on harvested energy, workload scheduling, variable duty cycling, and climate.
- **Efficient cloud usage:** Adopting approaches like auto-scaling, resource hibernation, carbon-neutral clouds, and renewable energy help reduce computing demands.

Green IoT practices for sustainable supply chains

Anticipating and optimizing IoT's footprint is the first step towards green operations. IoT also offers tools to drive broader ecological improvements across supply chains:

- **Fleet electrification:** Monitoring EV charging infrastructure usage enables rightsizing installations while analyzing vehicle telemetry optimizes range.
- **Route optimization:** Using IoT fleet data to minimize transit distances, congestion, and fuel waste through intelligent routing and load planning.
- **Predictive maintenance:** Sensors monitoring asset wear reduce downtime, allowing greener remanufacturing of parts versus replacements.
- **Food spoilage prevention:** Supply chain sensors monitoring perishable food transit conditions like temperature minimize spoilage and waste.
- **Circular supply chains:** Product lifecycle data aids designed for durability, disassembly, and recycling to retain value.

IoT data provides visibility into optimizations that reduce supply chain environmental impact.

Energy efficiency and sustainability goals with IoT

To drive progress on corporate sustainability goals, IoT can:

- **Water conservation:** Manufacturing facilities optimize water usage by monitoring flow, quality, and leak sensors across sinks, machines, sprinklers, rainwater harvesting, and so on.**Waste reduction:** Tracking trash levels in bins optimizes pickup routes, while scrap sensors minimize manufacturing byproducts through quality improvements.
- **Energy management:** Combining smart meter data analytics with HVAC, lighting, and machinery telemetry optimizes energy consumption across buildings and processes.
- **Environmental compliance:** Distributed sensors enable continuous emissions monitoring and incident control rather than manual sampling alone.
- **Triple bottom line accounting:** IoT data quantifies environmental and social costs for inclusion in financial reporting and incentives, enabling balancing sustainability with profit.
- **Carbon tracking:** End-to-end visibility allows calculating carbon emissions across product and distribution lifecycles to manage offsets.

Thoughtfully deployed, IoT enables tangible improvements against ESG goals as metrics.

The IoT **Total Addressable Market (TAM)** [2]forecasts published by *Transforma Insights* in May 2020 estimates global IoT devices will nearly triple to 24.1 billion+ by 2030. These warrants ensuring adoption aligns with ecological priorities. By combining smart devices and networks with a culture of conservation, manufacturers can minimize IoT's footprint while leveraging its insights to create intelligent, resilient, and sustainable operations. With climate action more urgent than ever, leading organizations recognize IoT's role in building a cleaner future - not undermining it.

Conclusion

As factories continue digitally transforming into increasingly automated, data-rich, and connected environments through IoT adoption, cyber risks pose severe threats. However, the diligent and proactive application of multilayered security-in-depth principles can help manufacturers confidently harness IoT capabilities without compromising safety, reliability, or intellectual property. Architecting comprehensive safeguards into IoT solutions is as crucial as the underlying connectivity capabilities. Combining savvy strategy, vigilant culture, and adaptable protections enables manufacturers to progress securely into the era of interconnected supply chains and smart infrastructure.

---

2 The IoT in 2030: 24 billion connected things generating $1.5 trillion - IoT Business News

Points to remember

- IoT environments introduce new cybersecurity vulnerabilities from connected devices, data flows, and partners that require comprehensive mitigation strategies.A multilayered defense spanning access controls, encryption, network segmentation, monitoring, training, and resilience capabilities reduce IoT attack risks.
- Ensuring security gets embedded into IoT solutions from initial design stages rather than as an afterthought is pivotal.Ongoing vigilance via asset management, activity tracking, vulnerability patching, and incident planning builds sustainable data protection as deployments evolve.
- Cross-functional collaboration between security, IoT platform, and engineering teams coupled with executive support establishes a culture of shared responsibility.

Multiple choice questions

1. **What type of attack involves disabling systems by flooding them with excessive requests?**
    a. Man-in-the-middle
    b. Denial-of-service
    c. Code injection
    d. Data exfiltration
2. **What approach helps secure IoT data flows during transmission?Access controls**
    a. EncryptionBug fixingLog files
3. **How can organizations restrict access to IoT data?**
    a. Through permissions and API keysBy using blockchain
    b. With predictive analytics
    c. Through edge computing
4. **What helps manufacturers maintain an inventory of approved IoT devices?Version control systems**
    a. Asset management tools
    b. Backup power sources
    c. Remote configuration

5. **What security measures help protect physical IoT devices?**
    a. Encryption
    b. User training
    c. Tamper-resistant casings
    d. Firewalls
6. **What helps detect unusual patterns indicative of a cyber-attack?**
    a. Real-time monitoring
    b. Access controls
    c. Data encryption
    d. Using proprietary hardware
7. **What security approach focuses on company-wide safeguards?Defense-in-depthPrinciple of least privilegeSecurity by obscurity**
    a. Perimeter security
8. **What helps prevent disruption from impacting an entire IoT ecosystem?**
    a. Internal firewallsExternal firewalls
    b. Intrusion detection systems
    c. Network segmentation
9. **What requires strict oversight when accessing or sharing IoT data?Third partiesEmployees**
    a. Devices
    b. Applications
10. **What strategy aims to limit the impact of a successful cyber-attack?**
    a. Compartmentalization
    b. Security misdirection
    c. Automated recovery
    d. Obfuscation

Answer key

1. b.
2. b.
3. a.
4. b.

5. c.
6. a.
7. a.
8. d.
9. a.
10. a.

Questions

1. What key vulnerabilities can make IoT ecosystems prone to cyber-attacks?
2. How can a lack of encryption impact the security of IoT data?What are the risks of unauthorized physical access to IoT devices and infrastructure?Why is it important to have an incident response plan for IoT cybersecurity breaches?
3. How can organizations implement the principle of least privilege for IoT devices and data access?
4. What security risks are introduced by third-party IoT system vendors and service providers?Why is ongoing employee cybersecurity training important for IoT environments?
5. What warning signs of an IoT cyber-attack should companies monitor for?
6. How can network segmentation and compartmentalization limit the impacts of an IoT system breach?What cultural factors influence an organization's IoT cybersecurity readiness?

Key terms

- **Defense-in-depth:** Company-wide layered safeguards spanning people, processes, and technology.
- **Encryption:** Encoding data to prevent unauthorized access during transmission and storage.**Role-based access control:** Managing user access to resources based on assigned roles.**Third-party risk:** Vulnerabilities introduced by partner and vendor ecosystems.
- **Network segmentation:** Logically separating networks into zones based on sensitivity.
- **Monitoring and auditing:** Tracking systems and user activity to identify security issues.
- **Compartmentalization:** Isolating subsystems to limit the cascading impacts of outages.
- **Security culture:** Organization-wide training, vigilance, and support needed for readiness.

Join our book's Discord space

Join the book's Discord Workspace for Latest updates, Offers, Tech happenings around the world, New Release and Sessions with the Authors:

https://discord.bpbonline.com

CHAPTER 7

Artificial Intelligence in Manufacturing

Introduction

Driven by the integration of **artificial intelligence** (**AI**) and the **Internet of Things** (**IoT**), the manufacturing industry is in the midst of a digital revolution. AI and advanced analytics translate this data into valuable insights, enabling smart, self-optimizing production environments known as **Industry 4.0**. This chapter explores AI's diverse applications in manufacturing, from shop floor operations to supply chain coordination, encompassing predictive maintenance, dynamic scheduling, defect detection, demand forecasting, and sustainability. Industrial IoT platforms, computer vision, natural language processing, and edge computing underpin this intelligent, interconnected manufacturing ecosystem. Successful adoption requires infrastructure upgrades, workforce reskilling, and change management, offering manufacturers the potential for increased throughput, cost reduction, improved quality control, and real-time market responsiveness. These technologies pave the way for factories that continuously self-optimize through data-driven learning and decision-making.

Structure

The chapter covers the following topics:

- Introduction to AI systems
    - International perspective on AI adoption

- Applications of AI in manufacturing
  - Enhancing worker safety using AI
    - Real-time monitoring using vision cameras
    - Hazard recognition powered by AI
    - Case study: Monitoring beyond human capacity
  - Supply chain optimization using AI
    - Demand forecasting using AI
    - Inventory management and procurement
  - Quality control and inspection using AI
    - Automated visual inspection using AI
    - Defect detection and classification
    - Enhancing product quality and reducing defects
  - Process optimization and production planning
    - AI-driven process optimization
    - Adaptive production planning with AI insights
    - Just-in-time manufacturing and resource utilization
- Case studies and success stories
  - AI in automotive manufacturing
    - Automotive design using AI
    - Challenges of using AI
    - AI use cases in the automobile industry
  - AI in electronics manufacturing
    - LG case study
    - Samsung case study
  - AI in pharmaceutical manufacturing
    - Drug discovery and research using AI-powered language models
    - Regulatory compliance and documentation improvement

Objectives

This chapter comprehensively examines how AI and the IoT are transforming manufacturing operations, processes, and strategies. It covers the essential technologies powering this transformation, including industrial IoT infrastructure, advanced analytics, computer vision, and edge computing. The discussion highlights key applications of AI and IoT across the manufacturing value chain, from design and planning to production, quality control, maintenance, inventory management, and supply chain coordination. The goal is to convey a holistic understanding of how these disruptive technologies enable intelligent, interconnected, and highly optimized manufacturing powered by data and analytics. By the end of this chapter, readers will grasp the immense potential of AI and IoT to bring unprecedented efficiency, flexibility, and competitive advantage to modern manufacturing.

Introduction to AI systems

The manufacturing industry is on the transition of a new era driven by AI and advanced data analytics. The way IoT connects today's factories with rich streams of data, AI systems are enabling unprecedented levels of insight, automation, and optimization across the manufacturing value chain. This convergence of operations data and AI promises to revolutionize how products are designed, produced, and serviced.

AI refers to computer systems or software that can perform tasks that would otherwise require human intelligence, such as visual perception, speech recognition, decision-making, and language translation. AI solutions can generate actionable insights, automate processes, and enable self-optimizing production by analyzing data from connected IoT sensors, cameras, and enterprise systems.

The manufacturing industry generates vast amounts of data across the product lifecycle, from R&D and **computer aided design** (**CAD**) models to supply chain signals, production line variables, quality testing, and after-sales servicing data. AI allows all of this data to be fully leveraged. Machine learning algorithms can continuously analyze data streams in real-time to spot inefficiencies, while deep learning identifies hard-to-detect product defects and anomalies.

To fully unlock the potential of AI, manufacturers need to assess processes suitable for AI integration and ensure the right data infrastructure. AI model development requires multi-disciplinary teams spanning production, IT, and data science. Ongoing model governance and maintenance is also crucial to sustain value.

AI is a journey that will transform work on the factory floor. Various skill sets, from robotics operations to quality control and data analytics, will be augmented by AI rather than replaced. This presents an opportunity to upskill employees and create new hybrid roles that combine human expertise with AI.

With the right strategy, talent, and data foundations, manufacturers can realize immense efficiency, quality, and throughput benefits from infusing intelligence throughout their operations. AI promises to play an integral role in taking manufacturing into a new era defined by self-optimization, predictive intelligence, and maximum flexibility. The factories of the future will continuously learn, adapt, and get smarter over time.

International perspective on AI adoption

While the manufacturing industry as a whole is embracing AI, adoption patterns differ across geographies and cultures. In Asia, manufacturers in countries like China, Japan, and South Korea are heavily investing in AI and automation to optimize large-scale production. Europe is taking a balanced approach, augmenting existing workforce skills with AI. North America sees nimble adoption of AI innovations but faces legacy infrastructure challenges. Trends also differ within regions. Developed markets focus more on predictive maintenance and quality inspection use cases. Emerging markets prioritize automation for workforce reduction and boosting production volumes efficiently. Regulatory and social acceptance of technologies like automation also play a role in global AI adoption. Cultural perspectives on human vs. machine balance in manufacturing impact the speed of implementation. Ultimately, manufacturers worldwide recognize AI's benefits but are charting adoption roadmaps aligned to their priorities and constraints.

Applications of AI in manufacturing

In manufacturing, the transformative power of AI extends far beyond the factory floor, touching every facet of the industry. We will cover the AI-driven revolution in manufacturing, how cutting-edge technologies are propelling the industry toward unparalleled levels of precision, productivity, and sustainability.

Enhancing worker safety using AI

In the realm of manufacturing, workplace injuries are an ever-present concern. Strains, slips, and falls are not only painful for employees but can also lead to substantial financial burdens in the form of medical expenses and lost work hours. Given the ongoing challenges associated with labor shortages, it becomes even more critical for companies to prevent these injuries from occurring in the first place.

The evolution of AI-equipped wearables has paved the way for significant advancements in ergonomic safety. These wearable devices serve as early warning systems, instantly notifying workers when they assume high-risk postures or engage in improper lifting techniques that could result in injury. Remarkably, these wearables have demonstrated the potential to reduce high-risk postures by up to 50 percent. However, it is worth noting that the effectiveness of these devices hinges on the commitment to *compliance* from both employees and employers. Workers must consistently wear and maintain these devices, and once potentially dangerous activities are identified, they should be addressed through a combination of training, education, and the employee's own initiative.

In the manufacturing sector, integrating AI, which replaces once-manual tasks with highly automated mechanized processes, prompts excitement and concern. High-profile incidents involving self-driving cars and malfunctioning robotic tools have raised questions about how the manufacturing industry can effectively balance the adoption of AI with its steadfast commitment to employee and customer safety.

Regarding ensuring employee safety, the cornerstone legislation is the **Occupational Safety and Health** (**OSH**) Act of 1970. This law empowers the **Occupational Safety and Health Administration** (**OSHA**), an agency under the *U.S. Department of Labor*, with the responsibility for creating policies and enforcing regulations related to workplace safety among private-sector employers. While manufacturers have long been cognizant of safety concerns, introducing AI technology gives rise to additional, less well-known considerations related to OSHA compliance.

Real-time monitoring using vision cameras

Real-time monitoring using vision cameras is a crucial application of AI in enhancing worker safety in manufacturing. This technology involves using cameras equipped with advanced computer vision capabilities and AI algorithms to analyze visual data from the factory floor continuously. Furthermore, it is worth noting that real-time monitoring is essential not only for worker safety in manufacturing but also for tracking the progress of new employees who are still gaining proficiency in their roles. Here is a detailed explanation of how real-time monitoring using vision cameras works and its significance in improving worker safety:

- **Continuous surveillance:** Vision cameras cover work areas, capturing real-time footage for ongoing monitoring.
- **AI-powered analysis:** Real-time video is processed by AI algorithms trained to recognize patterns, objects, and behaviors.
- **PPE detection:** AI identifies compliance with **Personal Protective Equipment** (**PPE**) like safety gear like helmets, gloves, or vests, triggering alerts for violations.
- **Behavior analysis:** AI spots unsafe actions like proximity to machinery or improper lifting techniques, alerting supervisors.
- **Environmental conditions:** AI assesses factors like temperature and air quality, issuing alerts for deviations from safety thresholds.
- **Immediate alerts:** The system notifies safety personnel instantly when safety violations or hazards are detected.
- **Data logging and analysis:** Safety-related data is logged for post-incident analysis, aiding in safety protocol improvement.

- **Deterrent effect:** Continuous monitoring deters workers from risky behavior, promoting a safer work environment.

This is a proactive approach to worker safety in manufacturing. It provides a robust layer of protection by detecting non-compliance with safety regulations, identifying risky behaviors, and monitoring environmental conditions. The ability to provide immediate alerts and data-driven insights empowers safety managers to address potential hazards swiftly, reducing the risk of accidents and ensuring a safer workplace for all employees.

Hazard recognition powered by AI

Hazard recognition is a critical component of worker safety in manufacturing. AI, especially computer vision technology, plays a significant role in improving this aspect. Here is a more detailed explanation of how AI enhances hazard recognition and its importance in ensuring workplace safety:

- **Continuous surveillance:** Hazard recognition using AI relies on the continuous surveillance of the manufacturing environment through strategically placed cameras. These cameras capture high-resolution video footage in real-time, covering various areas of the factory floor.

- **Computer vision technology:** Computer vision is the core technology that enables the AI system to see and interpret visual data from the cameras. It involves training AI algorithms to recognize specific patterns, objects, and anomalies within the video feeds. These algorithms can be specifically designed to identify safety hazards.

- **Identification of safety hazards:** The AI system is programmed to recognize many safety hazards. These hazards can include but are not limited to:

    - **Slip and trip hazards:** The system can identify wet or oily surfaces, spilled liquids, loose objects, or uneven flooring that may lead to slips or falls.

    - **Blocked emergency exits:** AI can detect obstructions or objects blocking emergency exit paths, ensuring these routes remain clear and accessible in emergencies.

    - **Inadequate lighting:** AI can assess lighting conditions and identify areas with poor illumination, which could pose a risk to workers.

    - **Improper storage of materials:** The system can recognize instances where materials are stored unsafely, such as heavy objects stacked precariously or improperly secured loads.

    - **Machinery malfunctions:** AI can detect abnormalities in machinery operation or signs of equipment failure, which could lead to accidents if not addressed promptly.

- **Real-time alerts:** When the AI system identifies a safety hazard, it generates real-time alerts. These alerts are sent to safety managers or designated personnel, ensuring that potential hazards are addressed immediately. For example, if the AI system detects a liquid spill, it can send an alert so that the spill is cleaned up promptly to prevent slip hazards.
- **Assisting safety managers:** Hazard recognition AI systems are valuable tools for safety managers. They help safety professionals pinpoint safety hazards more effectively than relying solely on human observation. By leveraging AI's ability to analyze video footage continuously, safety managers can focus their efforts on addressing identified hazards proactively.
- **Data collection and analysis:** The AI system logs and stores data related to identified safety hazards. This data can be used for further analysis, allowing safety managers to identify trends and patterns in hazard occurrences. This information is invaluable for making informed decisions about safety protocols and improvements.
- **Enhanced workplace safety:** The primary goal of hazard recognition with AI is to create a safer work environment. Identify potential safety hazards that may go unnoticed by human workers due to oversight, fatigue, or other factors. AI helps prevent accidents and injuries, ultimately reducing workplace risks.

Hazard recognition powered by AI and computer vision technology enhances worker safety in manufacturing by continuously monitoring the environment for safety hazards. It identifies potential risks that might escape human detection, providing real-time alerts to safety managers. This proactive approach ensures a safer workplace, reduces the likelihood of accidents, and supports data-driven safety improvements.

Case study: Monitoring beyond human capacity

In today's contemporary workplace, the prioritization of employee health and safety emerges as a prominent concern. Workplace accidents wield profound impacts on individuals and their families, with the potential to adversely affect a company's reputation and lead to substantial financial losses. According to data from the **National Safety Council** (**NSC**), the annual cost of workplace injuries is an astonishing $167 billion in 2021.[1] However, there is a hopeful prospect emerging through the integration of technologies such as AI, ML and IoT. Take a look at *Figure 7.1:*

1 Work injury cost by National Safety Council - **https://injuryfacts.nsc.org/work/costs/work-injury-costs/**

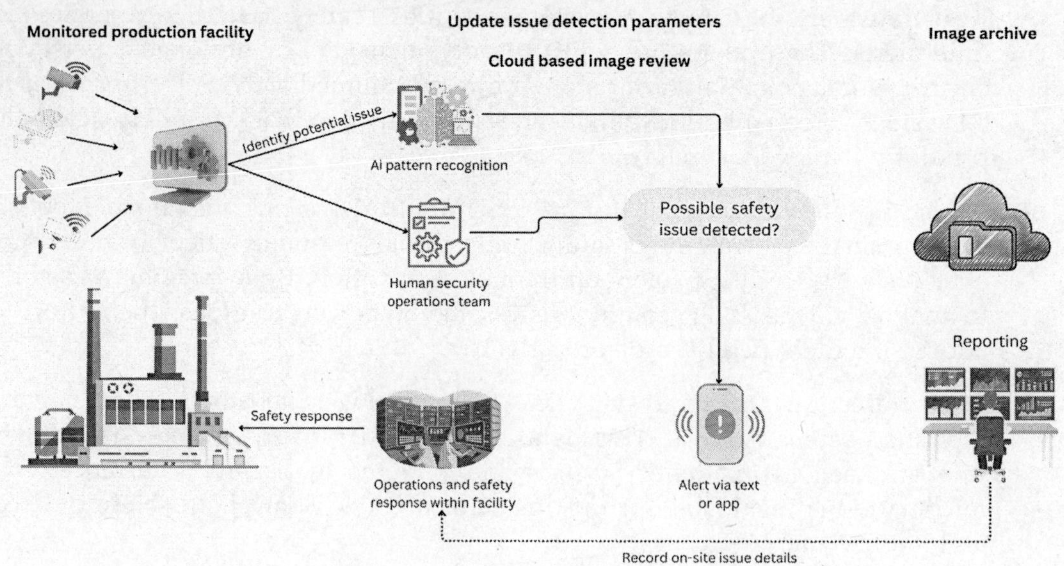

Figure 7.1: Worker safety monitoring using AI

Constant monitoring is a crucial element in ensuring workplace safety, yet it is impractical for managers to personally oversee employees around the clock to ensure they perform their tasks safely and correctly. This is where technology steps in. An AI remote-monitoring solution tailored to various industries and environments using IoT-enabled devices offers an effective solution. Here is how this technology works:

- **Wireless camera surveillance:** Strategically positioned wireless cameras capture continuous footage of critical areas within a workplace, such as factory floors or hospital hallways. This ongoing surveillance helps spot potential hazards.
- **Cloud-based AI analysis:** The captured images are transmitted to the cloud, where advanced AI technologies analyze them for unusual patterns and anomalies. This analysis is a pivotal part of identifying potential safety risks.
- **Human verification by team:** Trained team members review the alerts generated by the AI system. Human involvement ensures that potential safety issues are accurately recognized and assessed.
- **Instant alerts to local safety representatives:** When the AI system detects a potential safety concern, the SOC verifies it. If confirmed, an immediate alert is sent to the local safety representative stationed at the facility.
- **On-site investigation and intervention:** The local safety representative responds swiftly by going to the actual site to investigate and intervene, preventing potential accidents from occurring.

- **Confirmation and automation:** Following the incident's resolution, the local safety representative confirms the accuracy of the system alert. Subsequently, the cameras and AI technology are programmed to monitor specifically for those identified issues, with the goal of increasing automation over time.
- **Data storage and reporting:** Images captured by the cameras are securely stored for future reference. Later in the day, comprehensive reports are generated, justifying new equipment purchases, improving training practices, and providing evidence of safety efforts to auditors, insurers, potential employees, and other stakeholders.

By integrating generative AI, ML, and IoT into workplace safety, organizations can proactively address hazards, minimize accidents, and cut costs. AI safety solutions prioritize employee well-being, boost productivity, protect reputations, and showcase a strong commitment to safety. This tech-driven approach benefits everyone, fostering safer workplaces in collaboration with technology.

Supply chain optimization using AI

AI's expertise is essential for simplifying supply chain processes in three key areas. It first improves demand forecasting by carefully examining historical data, market trends, and external variables to produce more precise projections. This enables businesses to successfully manage their inventory, reducing excess or insufficient supply instances. Second, by considering elements like fluctuating demand, lead times, and storage costs, AI helps optimize inventory management. Reordering points and amounts, cutting carrying expenses, and assuring product availability are all advised. Finally, AI contributes its experience to optimizing distribution networks, modes of transportation, and delivery routes, thereby reducing transportation costs by considering traffic, fuel prices, and delivery windows.

The typical steps for integrating AI into supply chain optimization are as follows:

1. **Data integration:** Gather and combine information from many sources, including ERP systems, IoT sensors, market data, and archived documents.
2. **Model training:** Use your specific supply chain data and objectives to train an AI-based model, then fine-tune it for optimization tasks.
3. **Implementation:** Include the model in your supply chain management systems to provide decision-makers with recommendations and insights.
4. **Continuous improvement:** Improve the model in response to fresh information and changing supply chain dynamics.

It is critical to recognize that while AI and comparable AI models provide insightful analysis and recommendations, they should be used with human judgment and skill to accomplish successful supply chain optimization. Additionally, ethical issues and data protection must be considered when using AI in supply chain management.

Demand forecasting using AI

An effective strategy for supply chain optimization's demand forecasting is AI. Using AI's capabilities, forecasts that can guide inventory management, production planning, and distribution plans can be created by analyzing historical data, market trends, and relevant information. A top-level procedure for applying AI to demand forecasting in the context of supply chain optimization is provided below. Take a look at *Figure 7.2:*

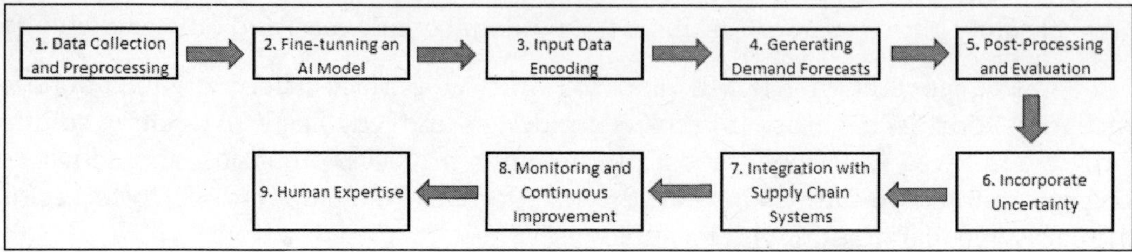

Figure 7.2: *Process flow of demand forecasting optimization using AI*

Here are the process steps for demand forecasting optimization using AI:

1. **Data collection and preprocessing**
    a. Compile historical information on sales, demand, and other relevant factors. This data set might include information on sales, market trends, customer opinions, and more.
    b. Preprocess the data to remove outliers, deal with missing values, and correct anomalies. Split the data into training and testing datasets after standardizing it and converting it to an appropriate format.
2. **Fine-tuning an AI model**
    a. Start the procedure using pre-trained AI models. Use the data from your specific supply chain and demand projections to finetune this model.
    b. Create a bespoke fine-tuning dataset with input (such as past sales data or market conditions) and target (such as future demand) sequences.
    c. Use this dataset to train the model, paying great attention to loss and validation performance indicators.
3. **Input data encoding**
    a. Appropriate input data formatting is essential for AI-based demand forecasting. This can entail converting historical information into a text sequence the model can understand.
    b. Include relevant background data, such as seasonality, promotions, or other forces influencing demand.

4. **Generating demand forecasts**

    a. Use the model to produce demand forecasts when the final adjustments have been made. Provide the model with previous data and background knowledge.

    b. Utilize the model to forecast future demand for different items or SKUs over a specified period.

5. **Post-processing and evaluation**

    a. Post-process the model's output for improved actionable demand projections. This could involve managing negative data, rounding predicted figures, or turning them into order quantities.

    b. Utilize measures like **mean absolute error** (**MAE**), **mean squared error** (**MSE**), or Forecast Bias to assess the model's performance. Continue to enhance model accuracy ensures more reliable and precise demand projections, aiding better decision-making, cost savings, and customer satisfaction. It optimizes operations and helps maintain a competitive edge in dynamic markets.

6. **Incorporate uncertainty**

    a. Given the inherent uncertainty in supply chain management, including uncertainty estimates or confidence ranges to consider demand changes is crucial.

7. **Integration with supply chain systems**

    a. Effortlessly integrate your supply chain management systems with the demand forecasting model. Based on the forecasts produced, this integration might involve automating order placing, improving inventory management, and expediting production scheduling.

8. **Monitoring and continuous improvement**

    a. Please keep track of the model's performance and retrain it occasionally with new data to adjust to changing market conditions and demand trends. For continuous system improvement, keep up with the most recent developments in AI and demand forecasting approaches.

9. **Human expertise**

    a. Even though AI can automate many aspects of demand forecasting, it is still crucial to work with subject-matter experts who can analyze the forecasts, come to informed conclusions, and adjust the model's output as needed.

Utilizing AI for supply chain optimization's demand forecasting can greatly improve accuracy, expedite procedures, and enable quick reactions to shifting market conditions.

However, it is important to approach this technology with a clear understanding of its limitations and the need for constant human supervision.

Inventory management and procurement

For any firm, inventory management and procurement are crucial elements of supply chain management. Utilizing cutting-edge AI models or comparable technologies can provide priceless insights and support different portions of these processes. They should be seen as complementary rather than stand-alone solutions. They should improve decision-making, streamline processes, and increase productivity. An explanation of how AI can be used in procurement and inventory management can be seen below:

- **Supplier choice:** A crucial aspect of procurement is selecting the correct suppliers, and AI may significantly help with this process in several ways, including:
  - **Data analysis:** AI has the expertise to thoroughly examine a wide range of supplier-related data, including past performance indicators, reviews, certifications, and financial stability. To assess the supplier's standing, it excels at concluding unstructured data sources, such as customer comments and reviews.
  - **Scoring and ranking:** Based on dependability, quality, pricing, and prior performance, AI can rank and score potential providers. This rating method gives supplier evaluations objectivity.
  - **Recommendations:** AI can suggest which providers best match the buying needs. Cost-effectiveness, proximity to the customer, and product accessibility are considered.
  - **Risk assessment:** The AI model is adept at determining the risks associated with each supplier, considering variables like geopolitical stability, potential interruptions, and regulatory compliance.
- **Create purchase orders:** With AI's support, you may efficiently generate purchase orders that specify product details, quantities, delivery schedules, and contractual terms:
  - **Automatic drafting:** Using input data, including demand projections, inventory levels, and established supplier relationships, AI may automatically write purchase orders. These purchase orders created by AI are thorough and organized.
  - **Natural language processing:** AI can facilitate more human-like interactions with suppliers by utilizing **natural language processing** (**NLP**). For transmitting purchase orders and receiving acknowledgments, generate emails or messages.

- **Order optimization:** AI can recommend the best order quantities and timing to save expenses while meeting demand needs. Lead times, order cycles, and **economic order quantities** (**EOQ**) are considered.

- **Effective supplier communication:** Supplier communication is essential for seamless procurement, and this is where AI may make a significant contribution in:
  - **Automated correspondence:** AI can send suppliers automated emails, messages, or notifications for a variety of reasons, such as placing orders, updating suppliers on the progress of their orders, or asking about potential delays in shipments.
  - **Negotiation support:** Based on prior experience and current market situations, AI can provide talking points, pricing benchmarks, and alternate terms during supplier discussions.
  - **Handling disruptions:** In the event of an interruption in the supply chain, AI can speed up communication with suppliers, evaluate the resulting impact, and provide alternate solutions or backup plans.
  - **Documentation management:** AI can help effectively manage and organize communication records, ensuring that important details and agreements are routinely documented for use as a source and for compliance requirements.

- **Inventory optimization:** AI's contributions can greatly help with inventory optimization initiatives that attempt to match inventory with customer demand while reducing carrying costs:
  - **Demand forecasting:** AI uses historical data analysis, market trend monitoring, and other assessments to produce accurate demand projections. Decisions about the optimum inventory level to keep are based on these forecasts.
  - **Reorder points:** AI can determine reorder points, which cause replenishment orders to be placed when inventory levels fall below predetermined levels. These calculations take lead delays and demand fluctuations into account.
  - **Safety stock:** The AI model can suggest appropriate safety stock levels for unanticipated demand swings or supply disruptions.
  - **Just-in-time:** By providing real-time insights into inventory levels and demand, AI can help **just-in-time** (**JIT**) inventory techniques be implemented. This allows for more exact ordering procedures.

AI can dramatically improve inventory management and procurement processes, from choosing suppliers to creating purchase orders, optimizing inventories, and communicating with suppliers. It accomplishes this by utilizing its data analysis and NLP capabilities, enhancing efficiency and cost-effectiveness in these crucial supply chain operations.

Quality control and inspection using AI

Quality control and inspection are crucial to ensure products meet specifications and customer requirements. Traditionally, these processes have been manual and tedious. However, with recent advances in AI and computer vision, automating quality control and inspection is becoming more viable. AI and automated visual inspection can enhance product quality, improve efficiency, and reduce costs.

Automated visual inspection using AI

Manual visual inspection by human workers has been the norm for quality control and inspection. However, this approach has several downsides, including:

- It can be slow, tedious, inconsistent, and prone to human error. Workers get tired and miss defects.
- A large number of workers are required on the production line to keep up with output volumes.
- Minor cosmetic defects may be missed, which impacts customer perception of quality.
- Testing 100% of products may not be feasible with manual inspection.

Automated visual inspection using AI and computer vision overcomes these challenges. AI-powered systems can:

- Inspect products at high speeds matching production output. They are consistent and do not fatigue over time.
- Detect defects quickly and accurately. AI models can be trained on visual characteristics of defects.
- Replace large teams of human inspectors with a single AI system integrated into the production line. This reduces labor costs.
- Inspect 100% of products rather than sampling, improving overall quality.
- Go beyond cosmetic inspection and check functional and performance attributes.

Automated inspection is applicable across many industries, including:

- **Electronics manufacturing:** AI systems can check for defects in circuit boards, microchips, display screens, and so on.
- **Automotive:** AI can inspect body panel gaps, paint defects, and component assembly.
- **Pharmaceuticals:** Tablets, capsules, vials, and packages can be checked for defects and incorrect labeling.

- **Food and beverage:** Visual inspection of food and beverage items for quality and safety issues.
- **Aerospace:** Checking for tiny cracks, dents, or imperfections in aircraft components.

Defect detection and classification

A key capability of AI-powered visual inspection is accurately detecting and classifying defects. By learning from product images labeled with defects, deep learning algorithms can be trained to identify faults ranging from scratches, dents, and assembly issues to label misprints.

Defect detection involves locating where faults are present in a product image or video frame. This allows for generating bounding boxes around the defect or highlighting defective regions. Object detection algorithms/libraries like **you only look once** (**YOLO**), **single shot detector** (**SSD**), or **region-based conventional neural network** (**R-CNN**) can perform this type of localization. In addition to open-source models like YOLO, SSD, and R-CNN mentioned, the major cloud providers offer pre-trained and customizable computer vision services leveraging advanced deep learning algorithms for object localization tasks. Amazon uses LSTM networks, Microsoft leverages Residual Networks, and Google employs EfficientNets and Neural Architecture Search Networks. These advanced deep learning algorithms provide major cloud platforms with accurate off-the-shelf and customizable computer vision for simplified object localization.

Accurately localizing defects in product images is critical for automated inspection systems. Defect detection frames this as an object detection problem in computer vision. Some common algorithms used include:

- **YOLO:** Uses a single neural network to predict bounding boxes and class probabilities directly from images in one pass. It applies anchor boxes of different scales and ratios to detect objects of various sizes. YOLO is optimized for speed and real-time processing.
- **SSD:** It also uses a single feedforward CNN with anchor boxes of varying aspects to detect objects. It captures features from multiple scales using convolutional feature layers of decreasing size. SSD achieves a balance of accuracy and speed.
- **Faster R-CNN:** Uses a two-step process: generating region proposals likely to contain objects with a Region Proposal Network, then classifying and refining the boxes with a CNN. It provides very accurate localization but is slower than single-shot methods.

In automated inspection, there is a trade-off between localization accuracy, inference speed, and model complexity. For optimal performance, a two-step approach is often used. A fast model like YOLO is employed for initial defect screening, followed by a more precise but slower model like Faster R-CNN for accurate localization. Training these models requires abundant labeled data with bounding box coordinates, and data augmentation techniques such as random crops and flips help prevent overfitting.

Defect classification takes it a step further, categorizing defects like scratches or dents. This relies on image classification algorithms, particularly deep learning models, which excel at recognizing visual patterns. Recent advances in deep learning address challenges in manufacturing defect inspection, such as attention-based transformers to improve detection accuracy and self-supervised learning for better generalization with limited labels. Meta-learning, active learning, multimodal learning, federated learning, and reinforcement learning techniques further enhance defect inspection in real-world scenarios, going beyond traditional **convolutional neural networks** (**CNNs**) and optimizing neural architectures for embedded devices.

By combining defect detection and classification, an AI system can find multiple defects present in a product and identify the type of each automatically. This provides valuable information for quality control and root cause analysis. The system output highlights the following:

- Number and location of defects on a product item.
- Categorization of each defect type, for example, scratch, dent, assembly fault, and so on.
- Severity assessment- minor cosmetic issue, major functional fault, and so on.
- Trends and frequency of defects.

This granular data enables operators to take appropriate action depending on the defect. Minor cosmetic defects may just need buffing, while major faults require halting production and fixing the process.

Obtaining reliable defect detection and classification results requires careful training of AI models on high-quality labeled images collected under diverse real-world conditions. Data augmentation techniques can expand limited training data by applying rotations, crops, brightness changes, and so on.

Overall, automating the tedious task of inspecting and classifying defects with AI allows the focus of human effort on assessing root causes and implementing systemic quality improvements.

Enhancing product quality and reducing defects

Adopting AI-based automated visual inspection solutions provides many benefits for enhancing product quality and reducing defects:

- **Earlier detection of defects:** AI systems can perform inspection earlier in the production process and closer to manufacturing steps where defects originate. This enables correction before additional value is added.

- **Reduced defect escape:** With automated inspection, defects are less likely to pass undetected into finished products shipped to customers. This improves outbound quality and reduces returns/servicing.
- **Inspection of 100% output:** Manual inspection is typically done on samples for practicality. AI systems can cost-effectively inspect every manufactured item.
- **Consistency:** AI maintains consistent performance over time, unlike humans who fatigue. Variability in inspection is reduced.
- **Objectivity:** Bias, emotions, or distractions do not affect AI like human inspectors.
- **Faster feedback:** AI enables collecting and analyzing defect data in real time to identify quality issues faster.
- **Data-driven improvements:** By highlighting defect trends, problematic processes and equipment can be pinpointed and fixed at the source.
- **Reduced costs:** Automation reduces manual inspection labor while scrap is lowered by catching defects early.
- **Reallocating workers:** Workers can be shifted from inspection roles to more value-added functions and operating AI systems.

With a thoughtful implementation approach, manufacturers can utilize AI-powered automated visual inspection to achieve the next level of product quality, efficiency, and cost competitiveness. The result is defect-free products that exceed customer expectations.

Process optimization and production planning

Effective process optimization and production planning are critical for maximizing manufacturing productivity, quality, and profitability. Traditionally, these activities relied heavily on industrial engineering principles, linear programming, and operations research techniques. However, with the emergence of artificial intelligence and machine learning, there are new opportunities to optimize manufacturing operations. AI-driven solutions can analyze data from multiple sources, model complex production environments, adapt dynamically to changing conditions, and enable proactive, just-in-time planning.

AI-driven process optimization

Manufacturing processes involve many interdependent variables- from equipment parameters and tooling configurations to material flows and quality control factors. The goal of process optimization is to find the ideal combination of these variables to maximize performance objectives like throughput, quality, yield, and cost-effectiveness. However, the complex relationships between all the different process elements make it challenging to determine the optimal settings manually. This is where AI has transformative potential.

AI-driven process optimization works by collecting and analyzing data from all process aspects. Industrial IoT sensors continuously monitor key parameters like temperature, pressure, speed, and vibration. This data combines process logs, quality metrics, and downtime incidents. Powerful AI algorithms uncover patterns in this data to model the complex inner workings of each process digital twins and deep learning models leverage data to provide actionable insights. The AI system leverages these models to identify superior process configurations and control policies. It runs simulations to preview how changes will impact metrics like output rate or defect rate before implementation. This enables rapid tuning of processes for ideal performance. In operation, the AI applies adaptive control logic, dynamically adjusting process parameters in real-time based on live data. This maintains optimal conditions despite external variability. By continuously optimizing based on data insights, AI systems can maximize throughput, quality, uptime, and efficiency across even the most complex manufacturing processes. The tight integration of data, modeling, simulation, and control is the key to enabling intelligent optimization.

Adaptive production planning with AI insights

Production planning involves determining the schedule of tasks, materials, and resources required to manufacture products. This planning must align supply with demand while optimizing efficiency and costs.

Traditional production planning relied on forecasting demand and then scheduling activities using manual calculations or linear programming. However, forecasts are rarely accurate and cannot adapt to changing requirements. This leads to problems like shortages, excesses, delays, and poor resource utilization.

AI and machine learning enable a more adaptive approach to production planning that continually optimizes activities based on real-time data and insights:

- **Demand forecasting:** AI can analyze market trends, sales data, macroeconomic indicators, and other signals to produce a probabilistic demand forecast across multiple time horizons. This provides inputs for planning.
- **Inventory optimization:** AI models can determine optimal inventory policies and position target levels based on demand patterns, lead times, variability, and other constraints. This balances availability with inventory costs.
- **Adaptive scheduling:** As actual demand unfolds, AI can dynamically reschedule production tasks, materials, and capacity to fulfill orders in a timely and efficient manner.
- **Supply chain coordination:** AI facilitates collaborative planning with suppliers and customers for synchronized activities and rapid transmission of requirements.
- **Constraint management:** Machine learning algorithms can optimize complex production activities subject to multiple resource constraints and business rules. This maximizes output.

- **Continuous improvement:** AI identifies pain points in planning and helps assess the system impact of changes through simulation before implementation.

An AI-driven planning approach is highly responsive to variability and changes in the production environment. It enables leveraging large amounts of data from sensors, ERP systems, supply chains, and so on, to make optimized decisions. The result is manufacturing plans that maximize profitability and customer service in dynamic real-world conditions.

Just-in-time manufacturing and resource utilization

JIT manufacturing, which aims to produce and deliver goods precisely when needed without maintaining large inventories, can be optimized through AI and machine learning techniques. These technologies offer several key advantages in achieving JIT production:

AI plays a pivotal role in manufacturing optimization, excelling in predictive maintenance by analyzing sensor data to forecast equipment failures and proactively schedule maintenance, thus averting disruptions. It facilitates real-time adjustments in capacity and materials for efficient order fulfillment through AI-driven demand forecasting. Intelligent scheduling ensures smooth workflows and on-time deliveries by prioritizing activities and optimizing resource allocation. AI dynamically adapts parameters to maintain target cycle times and production throughput rates. Quality optimization is achieved by AI systems that detect and correct deviations, avoiding downstream delays.

Furthermore, AI enhances supply chain coordination by aligning activities and synchronizing component deliveries across the network, while automation and robotics under AI control boost manufacturing flexibility and reliability. Resource optimization continually optimizes the allocation of personnel, machinery, tools, and inventory, minimizing waste and maximizing utilization, culminating in comprehensive manufacturing process enhancement.

By orchestrating the entire production environment in response to real-time data, AI systems enable true, JIT manufacturing. This provides advantages, including reduced work-in-process, lower inventories, flexible capacity, rapid fulfillment, lower costs, and better customer service. AI transforms theory into reality.

AI and ML drive step-function improvements in manufacturing process optimization and production planning. By intelligently analyzing data to model complex systems, adapt dynamically, provide insights, and optimize decisions, AI enables levels of productivity and flexibility that are not possible with traditional methods. Companies that leverage AI for process improvement and JIT production will gain sustainable competitive advantages in their industries. With thoughtful strategy and implementation, manufacturers can unlock the full potential of AI to enhance efficiency, quality, and profitability.

Case studies and success stories

These are diverse case studies and success stories that showcase AI's transformative power across various applications.

AI in automotive manufacturing

The automotive industry, renowned for its innovation and adoption of cutting-edge technologies, is at the forefront of the integration of AI. Here are the benefits of using AI in the automotive industry:

- **Customer service enhancements:** AI has paved the way for highly intuitive chatbots. These bots streamline customers' inquiries, ensuring rapid and accurate responses. The automation facilitated by AI aids dealerships in managing a vast influx of leads, efficiently handling inquiries, and consequently, elevating customer satisfaction levels. This is a leap towards modernizing the customer service experience in the car industry.

- **Revolutionizing design and engineering:** The vast data-processing capabilities of AI offer valuable insights drawn from customer feedback. These insights can be pivotal in refining vehicle designs and functionalities. Beyond data analysis, AI accelerates technical documentation and 3D modeling processes. This automation allows engineers to dedicate their expertise to intricate tasks such as conceptual designing, ensuring vehicles are both efficient and aesthetically pleasing.

- **Manufacturing and production efficiency:** AI's precision in identifying production inefficiencies can lead to optimized assembly line structures, ensuring smoother and faster vehicle production. AI plays a crucial role in workforce training, offering tailored instructions for intricate assembly tasks. This ensures employees remain updated with the latest manufacturing methodologies, ensuring peak operational efficiency. Predictive maintenance can identify potential machinery failures or wear-and-tear, ensuring timely interventions. This not only translates to cost savings but also ensures longevity and quality in vehicle production.

- **Enhanced vehicle safety:** AI tools, when integrated within vehicles, can significantly amplify safety measures. For example, AI can handle various driver queries, ensuring drivers remain focused on the road. The collaboration of AI with a vehicle's infotainment system can lead to a more interactive and user-friendly experience. This not only augments vehicle safety but also enhances the overall driving experience, making it seamless and enjoyable.

The automotive realm is witnessing a transformative phase powered by AI. With tools like AI, the industry is poised to redefine customer interactions, design paradigms, manufacturing efficiency, and on-road safety, steering towards a future where vehicles are not just modes of transport but intelligent companions.

Automotive design using AI

Generative AI, with its ability to produce new content from existing datasets, holds transformative potential for the automotive industry. The design process stands to benefit immensely from the capabilities of generative AI. Here is a detailed look into how it can play a pivotal role in automotive manufacturing:

- **Generating new design concepts:** Traditional design brainstorming sessions, although effective, can be time-consuming. Generative AI takes this to the next level by proposing novel design concepts. With rudimentary inputs, like a few sketches or prompts, the AI can suggest many design variations, speeding up the ideation phase and enriching the design pool.
- **Creating virtual prototypes:** The age of physical prototyping is seeing a paradigm shift. Generative AI can craft sophisticated 3D vehicle models. These intelligent virtual prototypes allow designers to visualize concepts tangibly, making iterative refinements more streamlined and effective.
- **Optimizing the manufacturing process:** The manufacturing intricacies in the automotive domain are vast. Generative AI simplifies this by simulating myriad design scenarios. Generating multifaceted design options for complex systems such as engines or lightweight structures provides designers with a sandboxed environment. This iterative design-testing cycle fosters innovative solutions and optimizes manufacturing blueprints.
- **Improving safety:** A vehicle's safety is not about its structure; it is about the meticulous design decisions that precede the manufacturing. By testing various design configurations and parameters, Generative AI can predict and optimize a vehicle's safety quotient. This proactive design approach could significantly expedite R&D phases, ensuring vehicles are both innovative and safe.
- **Enhancing existing designs:** Automotive designs are seldom static; they evolve based on feedback, technological advancements, and market demands. Generative AI aids in enhancing these existing designs. By analyzing previous models and industry trends, it offers intelligent insights. This leads to vehicles that are not just aesthetically refined but are also optimized for performance, safety, and efficiency.

The union of generative AI and automotive design leads to a future where vehicles are conceptualized and manufactured with unprecedented precision and innovation. Through machine learning and data-driven insights, generative AI promises a future of automotive design that is aesthetically appealing and functionally superior, aiming for optimal safety and user experience.

Challenges of using AI

Generative AI is a promising technology that can significantly advance the automotive industry. However, its implementation is not without challenges. Here is a detailed breakdown of the potential hurdles and their implications in the context of automotive manufacturing:

- **Ethical issues:** One of the foremost concerns surrounding generative AI is the ethical implications it may carry. For example, there is a risk that AI-generated car designs might unintentionally mimic existing intellectual properties, leading to copyright infringements. Additionally, there is the concern that AI might generate designs that could be deemed unsafe or not in line with ethical manufacturing standards.
- **Data quality issues:** For generative AI to be effective, it requires vast high-quality datasets. The crux of the problem lies in ensuring this data is accurate and comprehensive. If the AI works off incomplete data, the resulting designs could be less than optimal or even flawed, affecting the vehicle's performance.
- **Regulatory issues:** The automotive industry is heavily regulated, especially concerning safety and environmental impacts. If an AI-generated design does not adhere to these stringent regulations, it poses significant legal and safety risks. Manufacturers must ensure AI designs are in compliance with all industry regulations.
- **Security issues:** With the integration of AI into the design process, there arises a concern about the security of these designs. There is potential for designs to be hacked, stolen, or tampered with, posing intellectual and safety risks.
- **Manufacturability:** An innovative design is of little use if not manufacturable. Generative AI might produce designs that might be challenging or costly to produce in real-world manufacturing environments.
- **Resistance to change:** Any industry, over time, develops its tried and tested methods. In the automotive industry, certain traditional design processes are deeply rooted. Introducing AI in the design process might face resistance from those accustomed to these traditional methods. This could be due to a lack of understanding, fear of the unknown, or reluctance to change established methods.

While generative AI holds immense potential to reshape the automotive design landscape, manufacturers need to recognize and navigate these challenges. By proactively addressing these concerns, the industry can harness the full potential of AI, leading to designs that are not only innovative but also safe, efficient, and in line with industry standards.

AI use cases in the automobile industry

The introduction of generative AI to the automotive sector is on the verge of inaugurating a revolutionary phase in design and manufacturing. The impact that generative AI is set to have on the automotive industry cannot be overstated. Market forecasts indicate a meteoric rise in its adoption, with predictions suggesting that the generative AI in the automotive market size will burgeon to an impressive \$2.105 billion by 2032, marking a substantial leap from its valuation of $271 million in 2022. This growth trajectory, boasting a CAGR of 23.4%, reflects the technology's transformative potential.[2] To understand this profound impact more vividly, let us delve into real-world applications by leading automotive giants:

- **Toyota Research Institute**[3]
    - **Approach: Toyota Research Institute (TRI)** has harnessed generative AI to embed the initial design sketches and the essential engineering constraints directly into their creative design workflows.
    - **How it works:** By utilizing accessible text-to-image generative AI tools, TRI's technique streamlines the design process, minimizing the iterative adjustments often necessary to marry design with engineering requirements.
    - **Outcome:** This integration has dramatically reduced the number of design iterations, resulting in a more efficient and harmonized design process.
- **BMW**[4]
    - **Approach**: BMW integrates generative AI through a sophisticated AI model tailored to its design objectives.
    - **How it works:** When provided with specific parameters such as weight optimization, load capacity, and connection points, the model generates a plethora of design variations. Each proposed design meets the stipulated criteria, often suggesting innovative solutions.
    - **Outcome:** Incorporating generative AI has expedited BMW's design process, providing a range of design alternatives optimized for efficiency, aesthetics, and function.
- **Faraday Future Intelligent Electric**[5]
    - **Approach: Faraday Future Intelligent Electric (FF)** has pioneered the Generative AI Product Stack, a comprehensive software suite to enhance the in-cockpit experience.

---

2 Generative AI in Automotive Market by Enterprise Apps Today - **https://www.enterpriseappstoday.com/news/generative-ai-in-automotive-market-will-forecasted-to-boost-usd-2105-mn-expanding-at-a-cagr-of-23-4-by-2032.html?utm_content=cmp-true**

3 The Groundbreaking Influence of Generative AI in the Automotive Industry - **https://www.marktechpost.com/2023/07/03/the-groundbreaking-influence-of-generative-ai-in-the-automotive-industry/**

4 Optimizing automotive manufacturing with Industrial Generative AI - **https://zapata.ai/bmw-generative-ai-case-study/**

5 From Pixels To Pavement: Generative AI Use Cases In Automotive Industry - **https://www.forbes.com/sites/sarwantsingh/2023/05/17/from-pixels-to-pavement-generative-ai-use-cases-in-automotive-industry/?sh=50ace5c27666**

- o **How it works:** This software suite offers various personalized services and features, including intelligent search, text queries, instant translations, and tailored content recommendations.
- o **Outcome:** By offering a personalized cockpit experience, FF ensures a tailored driving experience, enhancing comfort, entertainment, and driver satisfaction.

These instances underscore the transformative power of generative AI in the automotive realm. Beyond just design enhancements, it is evident that generative AI plays a pivotal role in optimizing vehicle safety and performance, and in providing a richer driving experience. As automotive brands continue to innovate, generative AI stands out as a cornerstone technology, shaping the industry's future.

AI in electronics manufacturing

AI is rapidly transforming the electronics manufacturing industry, with the potential to solve a wide range of problems.

The general concept is to capture data on the process and system where the inefficiency lies. With the help of machine learning and artificial intelligence, the improvements are performed.

The framework of AI-based electronics manufacturing is as follows:

- AI-powered sensors are attached to equipment to collect data about its performance. This data can include things like temperature, vibration, and noise levels.
- The AI software analyzes the data to identify patterns and trends. This allows the software to predict when equipment is likely to fail.
- The alerting system alerts the manufacturer of the potential failure. This gives the manufacturer time to take preventive action, such as replacing or repairing the equipment.

By taking preventive action, manufacturers can avoid costly downtime. Downtime is when equipment is not operational. This can happen for various reasons, such as equipment failure, power outages, or natural disasters. Downtime can be costly for manufacturers, leading to lost revenue and productivity.

AI plays a pivotal role in transforming manufacturing in several crucial ways. Predictive maintenance, for instance, enables manufacturers to forecast equipment failures, proactively preventing costly downtime. Foxconn's implementation of AI resulted in a remarkable $1 billion in savings in 2018, showcasing its effectiveness.

Quality control benefits greatly from AI, as it can identify even the most subtle product defects that might elude human inspectors. Intel's reliance on AI prevented a significant recall of 1 million processors in 2019, highlighting the technology's capacity to ensure product integrity.

AI's impact extends to process optimization, helping manufacturers identify and resolve bottlenecks, ultimately enhancing efficiency and reducing costs. Qualcomm's implementation led to savings of $500 million in 2020, a testament to its effectiveness.

Furthermore, AI contributes to design optimization, enabling companies like Samsung to create more efficient, reliable, and cost-effective products. In 2021, Samsung released a line of AI-designed smartphones that outperformed previous models in these aspects.

AI aids in supply chain management by predicting demand and ensuring the timely availability of essential components. Apple's successful management of its supply chain during the 2022 COVID-19 pandemic, thanks in part to AI-driven optimization, illustrates its potential to mitigate disruptions and maintain efficiency.

These are just a few ways AI is being used to revolutionize electronics manufacturing. As AI technology develops, we can expect to see even more innovative applications.

In addition to the applications mentioned above, AI is also being used in electronics manufacturing for a variety of other tasks, such as:

- **Automating tasks:** AI can be used to automate tasks that are currently performed by humans, such as inspecting products or loading and unloading machines. This can free up human workers to focus on more complex tasks.
- **Making decisions:** AI can be used to make decisions about manufacturing processes, such as which products to produce, how many to produce, and when to produce them. This can help manufacturers to optimize their production and reduce costs.
- **Learning from data:** AI can learn from data to improve its performance over time. This means that AI can become more accurate at identifying defects, optimizing processes, and making decisions as it is exposed to more data.

LG CNS case study

LG CNS is a South Korean IT company that provides a wide range of services, including electronics manufacturing. The company was looking for a way to reduce the time and cost of manual inspection of products. Manual inspection is a time-consuming and labor-intensive process, and it can be error-prone. LG CNS used Google Cloud Vision AI to inspect products for defects. Google Cloud Vision AI is a cloud-based AI service that can analyze images and videos. The service can be used to identify objects, text, and faces in images, and it can also be used to detect defects. LG CNS trained Google Cloud Vision AI to identify defects in its products. The company used a dataset of images of products with defects. The service was able to learn to identify the defects in the images, and it was able to achieve an accuracy rate of 99.99% based on the test data available from the company, which reflects real-life conditions.

LG CNS then deployed Google Cloud Vision AI to inspect products in its manufacturing plant. The service was able to reduce manual inspection time by 90%. This resulted in significant savings in time and cost, and it also improved the quality of the products.

Here are some of the benefits that LG CNS realized by using Google Cloud Vision AI:

- **Reduced manual inspection time:** Manual inspection is time-consuming and labor-intensive. Google Cloud Vision AI can automate the inspection process, which can save a significant amount of time.
- **Improved accuracy:** Google Cloud Vision AI is very accurate at detecting defects. This can help to ensure that products are of high quality.
- **Reduced costs:** Google Cloud Vision AI is a cloud-based service, meaning there are no upfront costs or hardware requirements. This can help to reduce the overall cost of inspection. As AI technology continues to develop, we can expect to see even more innovative applications in the years to come.

Samsung case study

Samsung, a South Korean electronics giant, was looking for manufacturing process optimization. Leveraging Google Cloud AI, a cloud-based service, Samsung gathered and analyzed sensor data from its manufacturing plants. This data encompassed environmental factors like temperature and humidity, as well as machine performance metrics. Google Cloud AI identified process improvements beyond human capability, leading to heightened efficiency, productivity, and cost reduction.

Here are some of the benefits that Samsung realized by using Google Cloud AI:

- **Increased efficiency:** Google Cloud AI was able to identify ways to improve the manufacturing process, resulted in a significant increase in efficiency. This led to a reduction in the amount of time and resources required to manufacture products.
- **Improved productivity:** Google Cloud AI was also able to identify ways to improve the manufacturing process, resulting in a significant increase in productivity. This led to an increase in the number of products that could be manufactured per unit of time.
- **Reduced costs:** Google Cloud AI identified ways to reduce costs in the manufacturing process. This led to a reduction in the overall cost of manufacturing products.

Samsung is just one example of how AI can be used to optimize manufacturing processes. As AI technology continues to develop, we can expect to see even more innovative applications in the years to come.

Here are some specific examples of how Google Cloud AI helped Samsung to optimize its manufacturing process:

- **Identifying bottlenecks:** Google Cloud AI was able to identify bottlenecks in the manufacturing process. This allowed Samsung to focus its efforts on improving these areas, which led to a significant increase in efficiency.
- **Reducing waste:** Google Cloud AI was able to identify ways to reduce waste in the manufacturing process. This led to a reduction in the number of materials that were wasted, which saved Samsung money.
- **Improving quality:** Google Cloud AI was able to identify ways to improve the quality of products. This led to a reduction in the number of defects, which improved customer satisfaction.

Overall, Google Cloud AI helped Samsung to optimize its manufacturing process in a number of ways. This resulted in a significant increase in efficiency, productivity, and quality, as well as a reduction in costs.

AI in pharmaceutical manufacturing

The pharmaceutical industry is accelerating the adoption of AI technologies, according to *Gartner* research. In a recent study, Gartner surveyed pharma executives and found over 50% of respondents have invested in AI, while 30% plan to increase spending on AI over the next 1-2 years. The top use cases include manufacturing, drug R&D, trial optimization, safety monitoring, and quality management. Gartner predicts increased AI adoption could improve pharmaceutical productivity by up to 10% annually over the next five years. By harnessing the power of AI across their organizations, pharma companies can drive digital transformation, resulting in shorter development timelines, reduced manufacturing costs, and higher quality standards.

Drug discovery using AI-powered language models

Novartis is an innovative pharmaceutical company dedicated to discovering new drugs and improving healthcare worldwide. To accelerate its research and development efforts, Novartis recently started leveraging **large language models** (LLM) and applied them across the drug discovery pipeline.

In one project, Novartis researchers used LLM to help design novel molecules that could effectively inhibit a key cancer cell receptor protein. The team prompted LLM with a description of the drug target and the need for high binding affinity and selectivity. LLM generated molecular graph representations and detailed explanations of how its proposed chemical structures achieve the desired mechanism of action.

By synthesizing these AI-generated compounds in the lab, Novartis obtained promising hit molecules in just a few weeks compared to over a year typically. The firm is now optimizing the lead structures and preparing to enter human clinical trials soon. This showcases the potential to slash drug development timelines by using AI language models early in the R&D process.

In another initiative, Novartis trained LLM to automatically generate technical documents, experimental protocols, and data analysis reports to improve research efficiency. The AI system produces custom protocols using natural language descriptions of the experimental aims and constraints. It also summarizes findings from large volumes of disparate research data through conversational queries.

By leveraging the knowledge and language capabilities of LLM, Novartis is gaining significant productivity improvements in its drug discovery labs. The company aims to continue expanding the applications of AI across its R&D workflows.

Regulatory compliance and documentation improvement

To improve manufacturing quality and compliance, Novartis deployed AI-based solutions across its global production facilities. The company uses computer vision systems to perform real-time inspection of tablets, capsules, and packaging for defects. Novartis has also implemented automated compliance checking.

During tablet compression, AI monitoring enables detecting anomalies and out-of-specification measurements instantly so operators can take corrective actions. This has reduced batch failures and quality deviations by over 40%.

In packaging areas, the AI system scans labels, inserts, and cartons to verify accuracy and completeness as per internal standards and regulatory requirements. Near-miss errors like missing lot numbers are proactively flagged before completion.

For reporting, Novartis configured an AI generator to automatically compile batch records, process data analyses, and quality audit reports tailored to each process. This reduced documentation time by 30%, allowing quality teams to focus on higher-value tasks.

By continuously training its AI systems on new data, Novartis has significantly improved quality and compliance, avoiding regulatory violations. AI has enabled Novartis to scale its manufacturing without increasing its headcount. The company will expand its AI automation initiatives to supply chain and clinical trials next.

Conclusion

The manufacturing industry stands on the brink of a transformative era, driven by the synergy of artificial intelligence and IoT. This chapter has unveiled the potential of combining AI algorithms, IoT connectivity, and big data analytics across the manufacturing value chain. From product design to predictive maintenance, integrating AI and IoT revolutionizes processes, translating vast data streams into real-time insights and automation. To harness these benefits, manufacturers must adopt a strategic approach, including process assessment, infrastructure upgrades, cross-functional teams, and ongoing governance. This journey towards interconnected, intelligent, and self-optimizing production promises efficiency gains, quality control, supply chain agility, and rapid market responsiveness, offering early adopters enduring competitive advantages and a future where factories continually learn, adapt, and excel. IoT represents the next phase in digital manufacturing, building on earlier developments like automation and data analytics.

In the next chapter, we will explore how IoT impacts the key manufacturing processes. We will cover enabling technologies like sensors, connectivity, data analytics, and security that collectively realize the promise of smart, interconnected manufacturing powered by IoT.

Points to remember

- AI and IoT enable predictive maintenance, reducing downtime through data-driven insights and automation.
- Advanced analytics transform production planning, inventory management, and scheduling for optimal efficiency.
- Computer vision AI maximizes quality control, rapidly identifying defects and anomalies.
- Natural language processing facilitates human-machine collaboration on the factory floor.
- Machine learning algorithms optimize complex manufacturing processes in real-time.
- Robotics and automation are enhanced by AI to boost speed, precision and flexibility.
- Edge computing allows real-time analytics and low latency response in distributed environments.
- Digital twins mirror physical assets virtually to model performance and conduct simulations.
- Blockchain facilitates supply chain transparency, automation, and anti-counterfeiting.
- AI and IoT enhance sustainability across product lifecycles and global supply chains.
- Adoption requires upgraded connectivity, sensors, data infrastructure, and security.
- Change management and reskilling workforces smooth the integration of AI capabilities.

- AI should augment human skills rather than replace manufacturing jobs altogether.
- Ongoing model governance prevents algorithmic bias and maintains predictive accuracy.
- Manufacturers must take a strategic approach to realize the full benefits of AI and IoT.

Multiple choice questions

1. **Which technology enables real-time data processing at the edge in an IoT architecture?**
   a. Cloud platforms
   b. MES system
   c. SCADA system
   d. Edge computing
2. **Why is incorporating uncertainty estimates in supply chain demand forecasting essential?**
   a. To automate order placing
   b. To improve inventory management
   c. To consider potential changes in demand
   d. To remove outliers from the data
3. **How can blockchain technology be integrated with IoT systems?**
   a. Enabling transparency
   b. Improving security
   c. Automating processes
   d. All of the above
4. **Which connectivity protocol is commonly used for lightweight M2M communication in IoT?**
   a. OPC UA
   b. MQTT
   c. AMQP
   d. CoAP

5. **How can manufacturers start their AI and IoT journey?**
   a. Pilot projects
   b. Incremental rollout
   c. Process reengineering
   d. All of the above
6. **What business intelligence capability helps monitor manufacturing KPIs?**
   a. OLAP
   b. Data mining
   c. Dashboard
   d. Reporting
7. **How can IoT improve coordination across supply chain partners?**
   a. Automating production
   b. Enabling visibility and information sharing
   c. Robotizing warehouses
   d. 3D printing spare parts
8. **Which advanced analytics method enables optimizing manufacturing processes?**
   a. Diagnostic analytics
   b. Descriptive analytics
   c. Predictive analytics
   d. Prescriptive analytics
9. **How can natural language processing aid human-machine collaboration?**
   a. Speech recognition
   b. Chatbots
   c. Documentation
   d. All of the above
10. **What is one advantage of using GPT in generating purchase orders?**
    a. It only considers current inventory levels
    b. It does not require any input data

c. It can provide real-time insights into supplier negotiations

d. It can recommend the best order quantities and timing

Answer key

1. d.
2. c.
3. d.
4. b
5. d.
6. c.
7. b.
8. d.
9. d.
10. d.

Questions

1. How can predictive maintenance improve equipment uptime?
2. What role does edge computing play in manufacturing IoT systems?
3. How can computer vision improve quality control?
4. What are digital twins and how are they used in manufacturing?
5. How can blockchain enhance supply chain traceability?
6. How does AI optimize production planning and scheduling?
7. What are some challenges in adopting AI in manufacturing?
8. How can manufacturers reskill workers for AI integration?
9. How can natural language processing aid human-machine collaboration?
10. What data infrastructure is required for manufacturing AI?
11. How can AI and IoT enable sustainability initiatives?
12. What business benefits does AI-driven predictive maintenance provide?
13. How can manufacturers ensure AI model accuracy over time?

14. What connectivity protocols are commonly used in industrial IoT?

15. How can manufacturers start their AI and IoT journey?

Key terms

- **Predictive maintenance:** Using data analytics to predict equipment failures before they occur and schedule proactive maintenance.
- **Edge computing:** Processing data locally on distributed devices rather than transmitting to the cloud, enabling real-time insights.
- **Blockchain:** Decentralized ledger providing supply chain transparency, automation, and anti-counterfeiting via distributed consensus.
- **Machine learning:** Algorithms that can learn from data to make predictions or decisions without explicit programming.
- **Computer vision:** AI technology that extracts insights from visual data such as images, video and camera feeds.
- **Natural language processing:** AI that can understand, interpret, and generate human language.
- **OPC UA:** Industry standard IoT communication protocol enabling interoperability between manufacturing devices, systems, and software.
- **MQTT:** Lightweight IoT messaging protocol using publish-subscribe architecture for machine-to-machine communication.
- **Change management:** Strategies for transitioning organizations, processes, and employees smoothly to new working methods.
- **Reskilling:** Teaching employees new skills to work with and complement AI systems.
- **Cloud computing:** On-demand delivery of storage, databases, analytics, and other services over the internet.
- **Data infrastructure:** Integrated hardware and software systems for collecting, storing, and analyzing manufacturing data at scale.
- **Cybersecurity:** Safeguarding connected manufacturing environments and data against threats through policies, controls, and technologies.

Join our book's Discord space

Join the book's Discord Workspace for Latest updates, Offers, Tech happenings around the world, New Release and Sessions with the Authors:

https://discord.bpbonline.com

CHAPTER 8
The Future of IoT

Introduction

The **Internet of Things (IoT)** is transforming the manufacturing industry by connecting physical devices and assets to the internet and each other. This convergence of operations technology with information technology unlocks valuable insights, automation, and communication capabilities. IoT represents the next phase in digital manufacturing, building on earlier developments like automation and data analytics. This chapter explores how IoT impacts key manufacturing processes like equipment maintenance, production planning, quality control, logistics, and supply chain coordination. It covers enabling technologies like sensors, connectivity, data analytics, and security that collectively realize the promise of smart, interconnected manufacturing powered by IoT.

Structure

The chapter covers the following topics:

- AI predictive analysis using IoT
    - IoT predictive analytics with data analysis
    - Predictive modeling process overview
    - Data cleaning, processing, and transformation

  - Manufacturing use cases
  - Predictive models for IoT
  - Case study: IoT strategy for AI-driven predictive analytics
  - Future directions for predictive analytics in IoT
- Intersection of blockchain and IoT
  - Blockchain with IoT
  - Case study: Leveraging blockchain and IoT
  - Future of IoT blockchain
- IoT sustainability in the supply chain
  - Case study: Sustainability efforts powered by IoT
  - Benefits and challenges of green supply chain
  - Future of sustainable IoT supply chain
- 3D printing and IoT
  - Case study: Utilization of IoT in 3D printing
  - Benefits and challenges of IoT and 3D printing
  - Future trends of IoT and 3D printing
- Big data analytics from IoT-generated data
  - Big data analytics for business insights
  - Case study: Big data analytics in healthcare
  - Future trends in big data analytics for IoT

Objectives

By the end of this chapter, you will fully understand how IoT is used in manufacturing. This encompasses a deep dive into IoT system structures, including their essential components and connectivity methods and data analytics' pivotal role. This chapter covers how IoT not only facilitates predictive maintenance and diminishes downtime but also augments production strategies, inventory control, and real-time quality assurance. Furthermore, it highlights IoT's transformative potential in refining supply chain processes. However, it is crucial to acknowledge the challenges in IoT adoption and security concerns and envision a promising future where IoT seamlessly integrates with automation and advanced analytics in manufacturing.

AI predictive analysis using IoT

IoT transforms daily life with interconnected devices sending data without human interaction. It is a revolutionary technology connecting billions of objects worldwide. This chapter explores IoT's future, importance, applications, architecture, and challenges, utilizing quantum and nanotechnology for unprecedented capabilities.

With the advancement of technology, IoT is expected to revolutionize how we live and work. Here are some of the potential developments that we can expect in the future of IoT:

- **Increased connectivity:** IoT devices will become more connected, allowing seamless communication between devices. This will enable more efficient and effective data sharing, leading to better decision-making and improved productivity.
- **Improved security:** As IoT devices become more prevalent, security will become a top priority. The future of IoT will see the development of more secure devices and protocols to protect against cyber threats.
- **Greater automation:** IoT devices will become more intelligent and autonomous, allowing for greater automation in various industries. This will lead to increased efficiency and productivity, as well as cost savings.
- **Enhanced data analytics:** IoT devices generate vast amounts of data, and the future of IoT will see the development of more advanced data analytics tools to understand this data. This will enable better decision-making and improved business outcomes.
- **Integration with AI and ML:** IoT devices will become more integrated with AI and machine learning, enabling them to learn and adapt to changing environments. This will lead to more intelligent and efficient devices, as well as new applications and use cases.

IoT predictive analytics with data analysis

Data analytics encompasses many subfields, one known as **predictive analytics**. This subfield uses historical and real-time data to speculate on what might happen in the future. In the context of IoT, its goal is to extract useful information from the copious amounts of data that are produced by the sensors and devices that make up the IoT, as well as to recognize and anticipate recurring patterns. Businesses and other organizations have the ability to make decisions based on data, increase the efficiency of their processes, and optimize their operations when they use predictive analytics in IoT. Take a look at *Figure 8.1:*

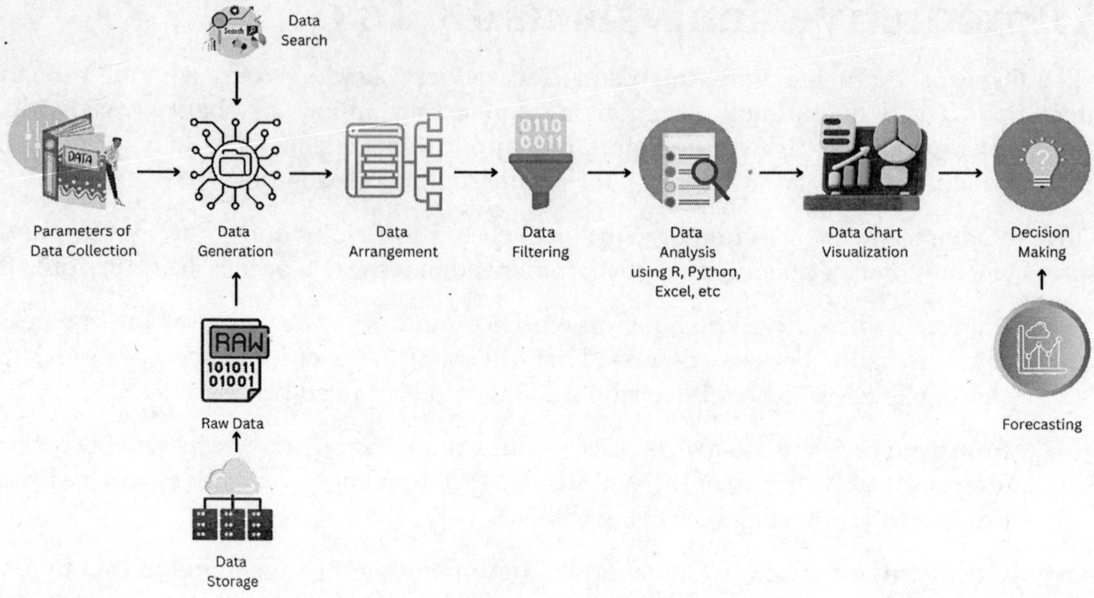

Figure 8.1: Predictive analytics using data analysis

Predictive modeling process overview

To design and deploy predictive models for IoT scenarios in manufacturing and supply chain, several critical processes are included in the predictive modeling process:

- **Data collection:** Data is collected from numerous connected devices and sensors in an IoT-enabled environment. This data could include machine performance, production output, ambient conditions, supply chain movements, and other information.
- **Data preprocessing:** Unprocessed data from IoT devices frequently contains noise, mistakes, and missing information. Data preparation includes cleaning and modifying data to ensure its high quality and suitability for analysis.
- **Feature engineering:** Predictive modeling uses feature engineering to identify or engineer relevant features or variables from preprocessed data. These characteristics have a significant impact on the model's predictions.
- **Model selection:** Predictive modeling approaches such as regression analysis, time series forecasting, decision trees, and machine learning algorithms (for example, random forests, support vector machines, neural networks) are available. The model chosen is determined by the nature of the data and the specific forecasting task.

- **Model training:** Using historical data, the selected predictive model is trained to understand patterns and relationships in the data.
- **Model evaluation:** To guarantee that the trained model is accurate and dependable, its performance is evaluated using evaluation metrics and validation methodologies.
- **Model deployment:** Once the model has been validated, it is deployed in the IoT environment to make real-time predictions based on incoming data.

Data cleaning, processing, and transformation

Data preprocessing, cleaning, and transformation are crucial in preparing manufacturing data for predictive analysis. In manufacturing, IoT-enabled sensors and devices generate massive amounts of data, capturing information from various production processes, machinery, and equipment. This data often requires thorough preprocessing to ensure its quality and suitability for predictive analytics. Take a look at *Figure 8.2:*

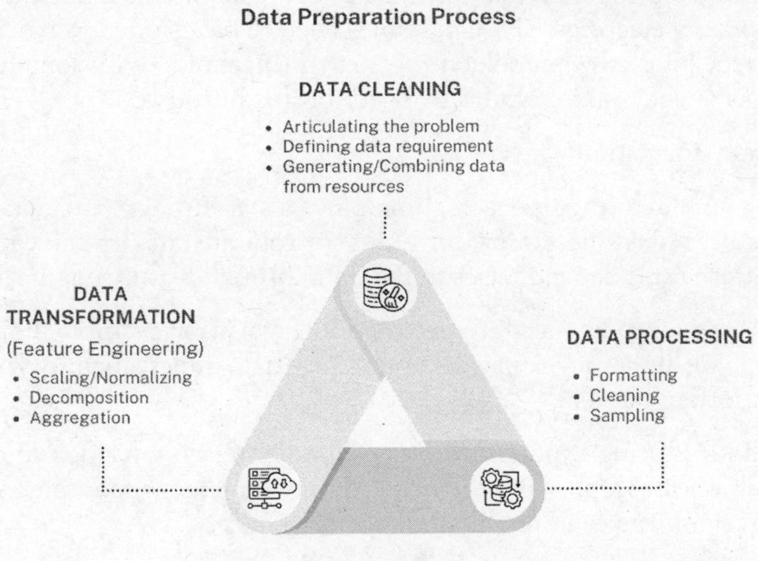

Data Preparation Process

DATA CLEANING
- Articulating the problem
- Defining data requirement
- Generating/Combining data from resources

DATA TRANSFORMATION
(Feature Engineering)
- Scaling/Normalizing
- Decomposition
- Aggregation

DATA PROCESSING
- Formatting
- Cleaning
- Sampling

Figure 8.2: *Data preparation process*

Following are detailed techniques for data preprocessing, cleaning, and transformation in manufacturing use cases:

- **Data cleaning**
    - o Identify and handle outliers in manufacturing data. Outliers can be caused by sensor malfunctions, measurement errors, or other anomalies that may lead to inaccurate predictions. Techniques like Z-score or **interquartile range (IQR)** can be used to detect and remove outliers.

- o Address missing data points, which can occur due to sensor failures or transmission issues. Imputation methods like mean, median, or regression, can be employed to estimate and fill in missing values.
- o Manufacturing data can be noisy due to sensor inaccuracies or environmental factors. Filtering techniques like moving averages or Gaussian filters can be applied to smooth the data and reduce noise.

- **Data processing**
  - o Standardize the data to a common scale to ensure that all features contribute equally to the predictive model. Scaling methods like Min-Max scaling or Z-score normalization can bring data into a specific range or distribution.
  - o In some manufacturing processes, data can exhibit skewed distributions. A log transformation can normalize the data and improve the performance of certain predictive models.
  - o Manufacturing data may contain categorical variables like machine types or product categories. These variables need to be encoded into numerical values for the predictive model to process them. Techniques like one-hot encoding or label encoding are commonly used for this purpose.
- **Data transformation**
  - o In manufacturing use cases, time plays a significant role. Creating time-based features like timestamps, time lags, or rolling statistics can capture temporal patterns and dependencies in the data through feature engineering.
  - o Aggregating data at different time intervals (for example, hourly daily) can provide higher-level insights and reduce data dimensionality while preserving important trends.
  - o Manufacturing experts can contribute domain knowledge to create relevant features that represent specific process parameters or equipment states, which can significantly improve model performance.

Manufacturing use cases

The following are the use cases in the manufacturing industry:

- **Predictive maintenance**
  - o **Data preprocessing:** Cleans and preprocess sensor data from manufacturing equipment to handle outliers and missing values. Feature engineering may include time-based features like lagging sensor values or aggregating data over specific time intervals.

- o **Data transformation:** Scale sensor readings to a common range and apply log transformation if data is skewed. Transform categorical variables, such as equipment types, using one-hot or label encoding.
- o **Feature engineering:** Create features based on historical maintenance records, such as the number of previous breakdowns or repair durations, to improve the predictive maintenance model's accuracy.

- **Quality control**
  - o **Data cleaning:** Detects and handles outliers in product quality data to ensure accurate quality assessment. Address any missing values in the inspection data using appropriate imputation methods.
  - o **Data transformation:** Scale quality metrics to a common range, allowing equal weighting in the predictive model. Transform categorical variables like product categories or defect types into numerical values.
  - o **Feature engineering:** Generate features based on historical quality control data, such as defect rates over time, average quality scores, or variance in quality metrics.
- **Production optimization**
  - o **Data cleaning:** Clean and preprocess data related to production metrics, such as throughput, cycle times, and downtime to ensure reliable insights.
  - o **Data transformation:** Scale production data to a common range and transform categorical variables like machine types or shift schedules.
  - o **Feature engineering:** Create features representing **Overall Equipment Effectiveness** (**OEE**), production efficiency trends, or utilization rates, which can aid in optimizing production processes.

By employing these data preprocessing, cleaning, and transformation techniques, manufacturers can extract valuable insights from their IoT-generated data. This enables them to make data-driven decisions, improve process efficiency, reduce downtime, and enhance product quality.

Predictive models for IoT

Predictive models are algorithms that utilize historical data to make predictions or forecasts about future events or outcomes. These models analyze data generated by sensors and devices to provide valuable insights and support decision-making processes. Here are some common predictive models used in IoT. Take a look at *Table 8.1:*

Model type	Overview	How it works	Strengths	Weaknesses
Regression model	Predicting numerical values based on input features. Used in IoT to establish relationships between variables.	Fit a line (simple linear) or a hyperplane (multiple regression) to data points to minimize the distance between predicted and actual values.	Simple, interpretable, and effective for continuous predictions.	May not capture complex non-linear relationships; performance can degrade with noisy or high-dimensional IoT data.
Time series analysis model	Deals with data collected over time. Involves understanding temporal patterns, trends, and seasonality.	Use past data points (for example, ARIMA, STL) to forecast future values based on observed patterns in the series.	Excellent for data with temporal dependencies.	May not account for external factors or events; accuracy can decrease with irregular or sparse data.
Machine learning model	Encompasses a range of techniques applied in IoT for predictive modeling. Includes decision trees, random forests, SVM, neural networks, and so on.	Learn patterns and relationships during the training phase and make predictions on new data during the testing phase.	Can handle complex relationships; versatile for anomaly detection, classification, and regression.	Some models, like deep neural networks, need significant computational resources and large training datasets; challenging for constrained IoT devices.
Anomaly detection model	Aims to identify rare or abnormal events in the data that deviate significantly from the norm.	Based on statistical techniques or machine learning algorithms that learn normal behavior from data and flag unusual patterns.	Valuable for identifying faults, defects, or irregularities in processes, maintenance, or cybersecurity.	Can produce false positives or negatives; requires tuning for balance between sensitivity and specificity in complex IoT environments.

Table 8.1: Common predictive models used in IoT

Take a look at *Figure 8.3* for the ML model:

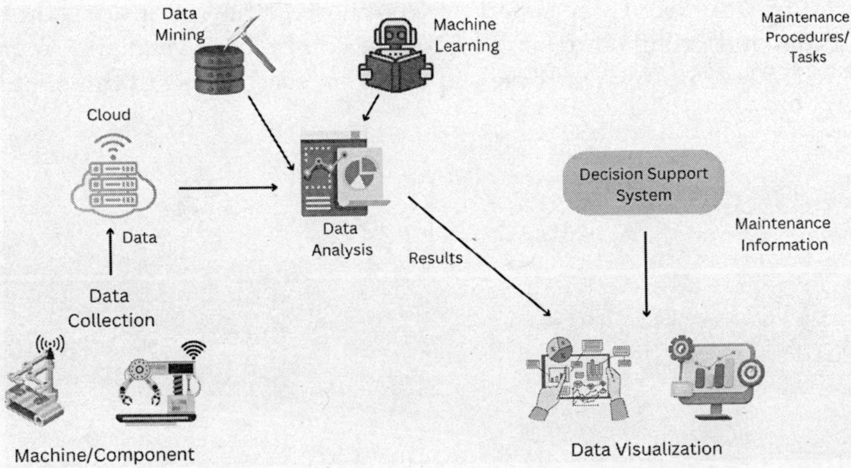

Figure 8.3: *Machine learning algorithm model*

Take a look at *Figure 8.4* for the anomaly detection model:

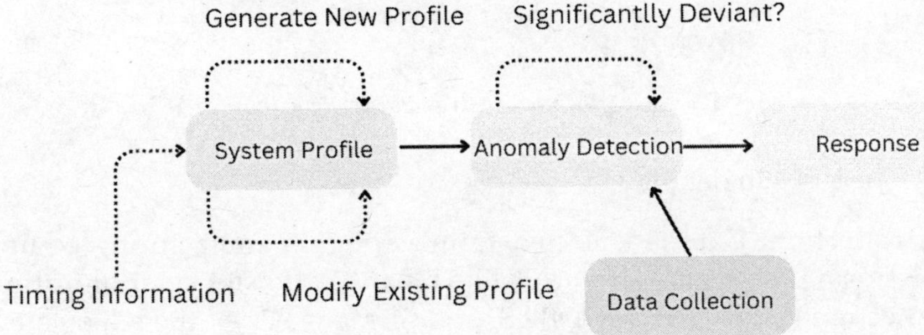

Figure 8.4: *Anomaly detection model*

The choice of a predictive model depends on the specific use case, the nature of the data, and the intended prediction task. Frequently, a combination of multiple models or ensemble techniques can be used to capitalize on the strengths of each model and compensate for their shortcomings. To ensure accurate predictions and maximize the value of IoT data-driven insights, it is crucial to evaluate and fine-tune the models thoroughly. In addition, as IoT technologies continue to advance, newer and more specialized predictive models tailored to address the unique challenges and opportunities presented by the IoT ecosystem may emerge.

Case study: AI-driven predictive analytics

This case study explores the integration of advanced technologies: the use of virtual duplicates of actual assets, machinery, and systems, to facilitate predictive insights for improved maintenance strategies. The optimization of manufacturing processes is revolutionized by a series of steps, starting from data gathering at the shop floor using legacy protocols and culminating in access to a comprehensive digital representation facilitated by REST APIs. Each of these steps plays a crucial part in this transformation. Take a look at *Figure 8.5:*

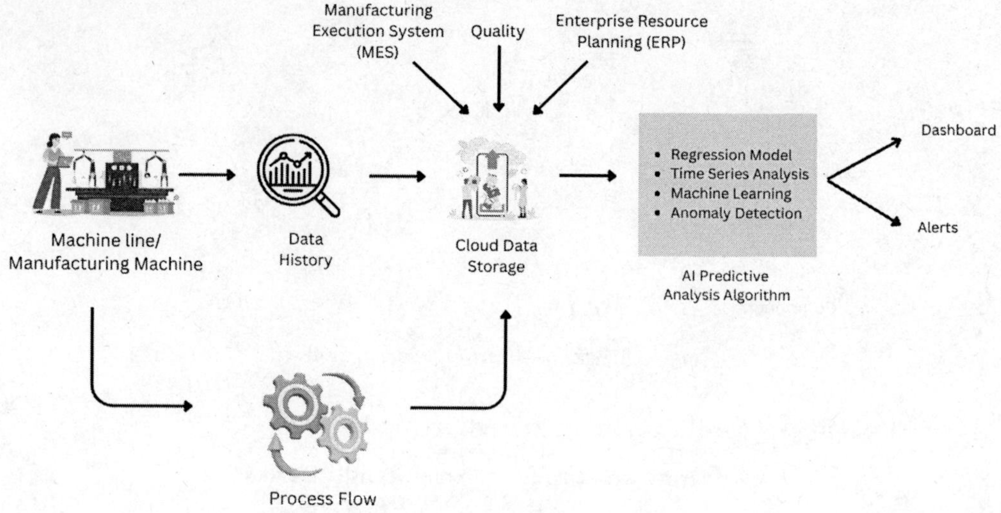

***Figure 8.5:** AI predictive analytics algorithm*

Let us discuss the steps in detail:

1. **Data collection:** Data is collected from various manufacturing equipment and sensors using IoT legacy protocols like **Open Platform Communications United Architecture (OPC UA)**, MODBUS, and Siemens S7. At the edge gateway, these protocols are translated into standard shop-floor protocols such as MQTT or OPC UA for seamless data communication.

2. **Data flow and aggregation:** The data flows through the shop floor using standard protocols like MQTT and OPC UA, facilitated by new-generation equipment or edge gateways. This process ensures the transformation of legacy protocols into standard ones and vice versa.

3. **Data arrival at central data collection:** The data is collected at the **Plant Service Bus (PSB)**, aggregated, and sent to the central data collection. The aggregated data from different plants arrives at the central data collection point through the PSB, typically using MQTT for efficient data transmission.

4. **Data integration into central data lake:** The collected data is then pushed into the central data lake, which serves as a repository for all the incoming data.

5. **Central digital twin data model:** The central digital twin data model, represented by **keep IoT trivial (KITT)**, references the raw data from the central data lake. This

data model serves as a virtual representation of the physical assets and processes in the manufacturing environment.

6. **Data access via REST APIs:** Access to the digital twin's information is provided through REST APIs. The data from the digital twin is accessed based on its representation in the data model, which references the raw data stored in the data lake. This approach ensures a consistent enterprise-wide data representation, such as equipment hierarchy or production records.
7. **Integration with central applications:** The digital twin is seamlessly integrated with central applications using the capabilities of an **enterprise service bus** (**ESB**). The ESB handles routing, transformation, and mediation, allowing smooth data exchange between the digital twin and other applications.

By following these steps, the digital twin for predictive analysis facilitates efficient data collection, integration, and representation of the manufacturing processes. This integrated approach enables businesses to make informed decisions, optimize operations, and enhance predictive maintenance strategies for increased productivity and efficiency.

Future directions for predictive analytics in IoT

AI and predictive analytics are significant presences in the world of IoT. They are changing how we make decisions and are especially useful in things like predictive maintenance, where we can keep machines running smoothly. As advanced technologies become more common, businesses can save money and make things work better by using edge computing and 5G for faster data processing, especially in smart cities where they can keep everything running smoothly and safely.

Intersection of blockchain and IoT

Understanding the fundamental aspects and characteristics that identify and differentiate Blockchain Technology and IoT is critical as we explore these fascinating domains. Blockchain and IoT can potentially transform many industries by providing unique approaches to data interchange, security, automation, and real-time answers.

The blockchain is a distributed digital ledger system that secures transactions over a network of computers known as nodes. Although its original purpose was to allow virtual currencies such as Bitcoin, its uses have since expanded to include many other digital assets.

A blockchain can be thought of as a series of discrete blocks. Within each block, all completed transactions are recorded in a log. This category includes the purchase and selling of cryptocurrencies, the transfer of digital assets, and the storage of any other data or information. A connected series of blocks exists when each block in a sequence has its unique identity, a timestamp, and a pointer to the block preceding it. Take a look at *Figure 8.6*:

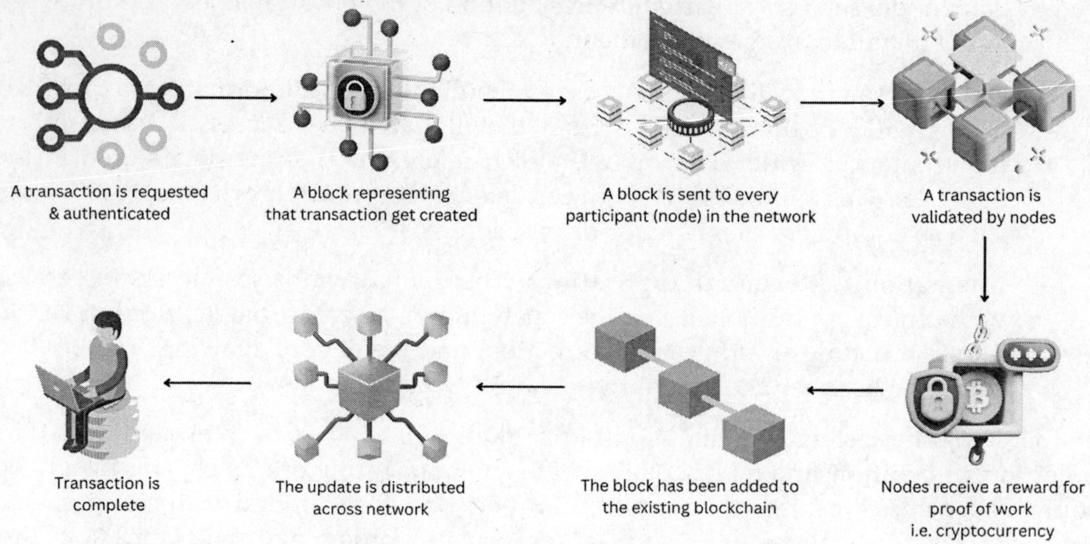

Figure 8.6: Blockchain transaction process

Blockchain with IoT

The convergence of blockchain and IoT has the potential to bring about a range of benefits, addressing several challenges currently faced by IoT systems. Here are some key areas where this integration could be beneficial. Take a look at *Figure 8.7*:

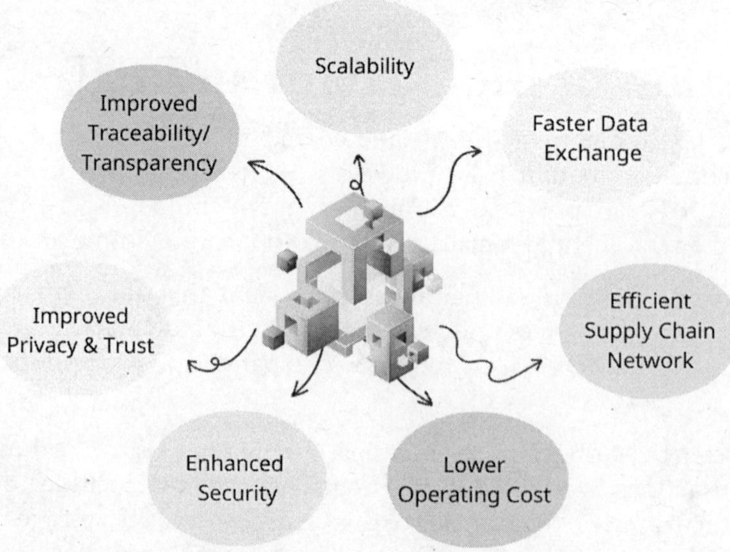

Figure 8.7: Blockchain with IoT

The benefits of blockchain technology with IoT integration are as follows:

- **Accelerated data exchange:** Blockchain removes intermediaries, enabling faster data exchange among IoT devices, and enhancing network efficiency.
- **Efficient supply chains:** Real-time data on goods' location, condition, and status improves supply chain transparency, traceability, and efficiency, aiding tracking, authenticity verification, and reducing inefficiencies.
- **Resilience:** Blockchain's decentralized architecture ensures network resilience, vital for distributed device networks.
- **Cost reduction:** IoT paired with blockchain minimizes operational expenses by eliminating intermediaries, enhancing security, and streamlining processes through automation, reducing administrative costs.
- **Enhanced security:** Blockchain's cryptographic security safeguards IoT networks, preventing data breaches and unauthorized access.
- **Improved data privacy and trust:** Immutable blockchain records ensure data integrity and user privacy.
- **Enhanced device autonomy:** IoT devices can autonomously verify data and execute actions, fostering efficiency.
- **Improved transparency:** Blockchain enables traceability, benefiting supply chain management.
- **Scalability:** Blockchain efficiently manages data and network operations as IoT device numbers grow.

Case study: Leveraging blockchain and IoT

Track and trace in the supply chain industry refers to the ability to monitor and record the entire journey of a product, from its origin through each stage of the supply chain until it reaches the end consumers. This process involves tracking the movement and custody of products, as well as recording important data related to the product's manufacturing, handling, and transportation. Take a look at *Figure 8.8*:

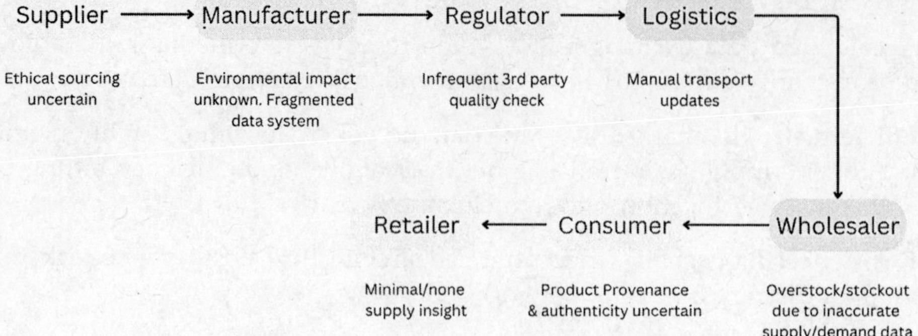

Figure: 8.8: *Traditional supply chain process*

Traditionally, track and trace processes have been challenging due to the reliance on outdated paper-based systems and disjointed data management systems. These limitations result in visibility gaps, slow communication, inaccuracies, and potential issues like counterfeiting and compliance violations. Take a look at *Figure 8.9:*

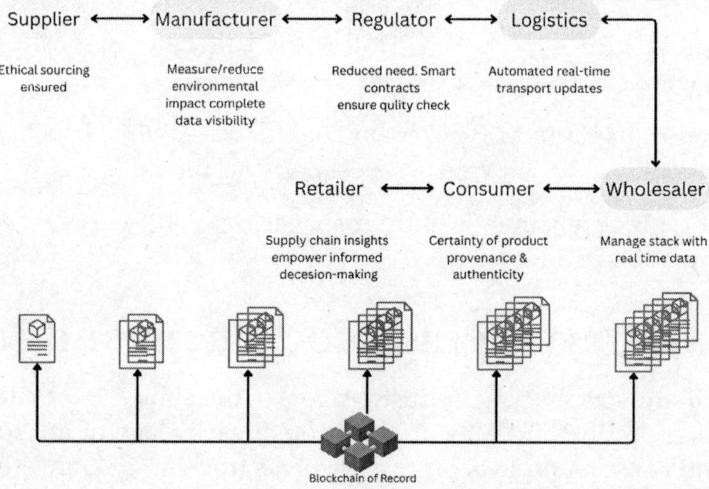

Figure 8.9: *IoT blockchain-enabled supply chain*

Blockchain technology offers a promising solution to enhance track and trace capabilities in the supply chain. By utilizing blockchain, multiple parties involved in the supply chain can transact directly through a decentralized and transparent network without relying on a central authority. The blockchain acts as a shared and immutable ledger, where all transactions are cryptographically recorded and time-stamped, ensuring data integrity and transparency. Take a look at *Figure 8.10*:

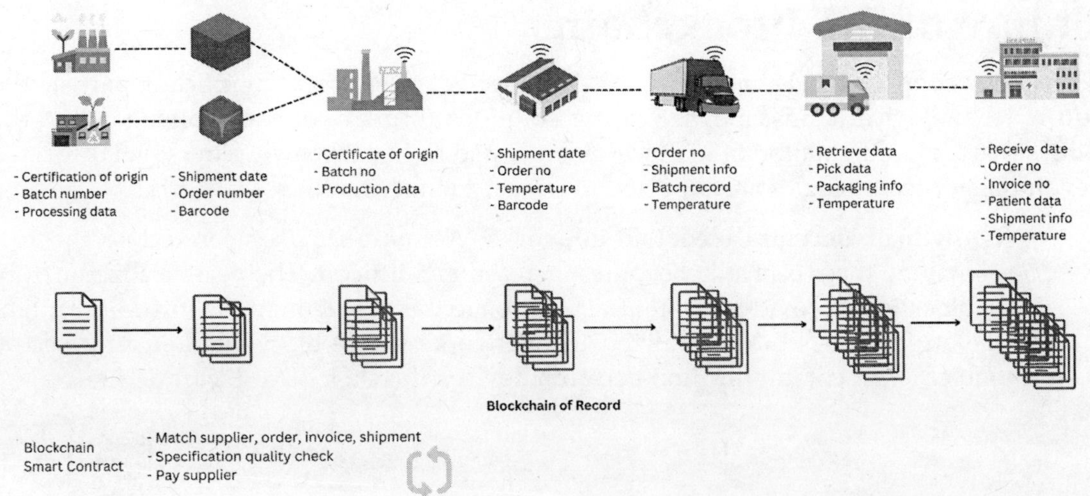

Figure 8.10: *IoT track and trace using blockchain*

The key benefits of using blockchain for track and trace in the supply chain include:

- **Data visibility:** All participants in the supply chain have access to a single source of truth, providing complete visibility into the product's status and location at any given point in time.
- **Provenance and authenticity:** The immutable nature of blockchain ensures that the product's origin, manufacturing details, and custody history are securely recorded, making it easier to verify product authenticity and combat counterfeiting.
- **Real-time updates:** With blockchain's time-stamping and up-to-date records, companies can obtain real-time information on product movements and status, facilitating faster decision-making and responsiveness.
- **Improved compliance:** The blockchain's audit trail helps ensure regulatory compliance, making it easier to demonstrate adherence to industry standards and regulations.
- **Automation and smart technology:** Integrating blockchain with smart technologies like IoT enables automated tracking of product conditions during production and transportation, improving quality control and reducing manual errors.
- **Enhanced emergency response:** In cases of emergencies or product recalls, the immediate and transparent nature of blockchain data allows for quick action and resolution.
- **Ethical supply chain practices:** Companies can choose to share track and trace data with customers, providing them with information on the product's journey and verifying ethical supply chain practices.

Future of IoT blockchain

The intersection of blockchain and IoT is expected to shape a significant part of the future technological landscape, providing solutions to many of the challenges that the widespread implementation of IoT faces. Here are some key takeaways in which these two revolutionary technologies are expected to influence the future:

- **Growth of decentralized IoT networks:** As more devices connect to the IoT, managing them centrally becomes increasingly difficult. The decentralized nature of blockchain provides a potential solution to this problem. In the future, we might see an increase in decentralized IoT networks where blockchain ensures secure and efficient communication between devices. Take a look at *Figure 8.11*:

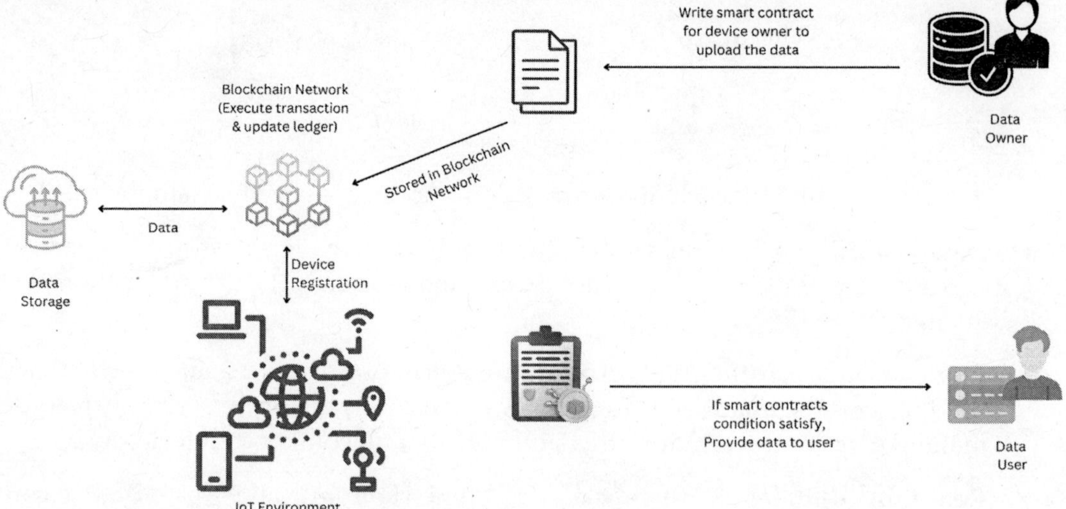

Figure 8.11: *Future of IoT blockchain*

- **Advanced security measures:** Security remains a significant concern for IoT implementations. The cryptographic security measures inherent in blockchain can help to address this issue. Future IoT networks may widely incorporate blockchain to ensure the security and integrity of data exchange between devices.
- **Development of smart cities:** Smart cities leverage IoT devices to optimize services and enhance the quality of life for their residents. Integrating blockchain within smart cities can enhance data security, provide transparent governance, and create a more efficient, automated environment. This concept is already being explored in various pilot projects worldwide.
- **Streamlined supply chains:** Using blockchain and IoT in supply chain management can revolutionize the industry by providing full transparency, improved traceability, and increased efficiency. The future might see more widespread adoption of these technologies in supply chains across various industries.

- **Emergence of blockchain-as-a-service:** As more companies seek to leverage blockchain within their IoT networks, there is likely to be a rise in the development of **blockchain-as-a-service (BaaS)** platforms. BaaS providers handle the complex backend operations of blockchain, allowing businesses to focus on their core operations while reaping the benefits of blockchain technology.
- **Regulatory development:** As blockchain and IoT continue to evolve and intersect, there will be a need for new regulations to manage these technologies. Governments and regulatory bodies worldwide will need to develop frameworks that protect consumers, ensure privacy, and promote innovation in this space.

While these potential developments are exciting, they also come with challenges. Issues around scalability, energy efficiency, interoperability, and data privacy must be effectively addressed for the full potential of the blockchain and IoT intersection to be realized.

IoT sustainability in the supply chain

Modern supply chains are evolving with a strong focus on customer satisfaction, increased margins, and sustainable practices. Notably, IoT spending in the logistics market has already reached $39.6 billion as of 2022 and is projected to soar to $114.7 billion by 2032.[1]

The IoT holds significant potential to transform global supply chains, particularly in achieving sustainability objectives. As climate change becomes an unavoidable concern, governments, businesses, and consumers prioritize sustainable practices. An *Accenture* report highlights that 45% of customers now purchase based on green concerns, making sustainable practices vital for customer retention and compliance with climate action laws.[2]

Secondly, IoT-embedded sensors play a crucial role in reducing waste. They provide valuable insights into using critical materials, tracking purchase patterns in real-time, and monitoring factors affecting product quality like heat, humidity, temperature, and shock. Armed with critical data, companies can eliminate defective products and prevent further damage, resulting in substantial waste reduction.

Following are the guiding principles for IoT sustainability in the supply chain:

- **Ethical practices:** The social and ethical consequences of a supply chain's actions are considered by one that is truly sustainable. It safeguards equitable working conditions, upholds human rights, and encourages a welcoming and diverse workplace.

---

1 IoT Spend by Logistics Industry Market Outlook (2022-2032) - **https://www.futuremarketinsights.com/reports/iot-spend-by-logistics-industry-market**

2 Pandemic accelerating digital adoption and likely to cause long-term changes in consumer behaviors - **https://newsroom.accenture.com/news/covid-19-increasing-consumers-focus-on-ethical-consumption-accenture-survey-finds.htm**

- **Environmental responsibility:** A sustainable supply chain is conscientious about its impact on the planet. Greenhouse gas emissions are a primary target, along with resource conservation, waste management, and the utilization of renewable energy.
- **Transparency and traceability:** Transparency all the way through the supply chain is essential for long-term viability. Throughout the supply chain, items and materials are tracked and recorded for information on their origin, movement, and impact.
- **Collaboration and partnerships:** Suppliers, customers, and other stakeholders in sustainable supply chains all work together to effect good change through collaboration and partnerships. Together, they pool their knowledge, expertise, and resources to boost their sustainability efforts.
- **Continuous improvement:** A sustainable supply chain is one that is dedicated to constant development and enhancement. To improve sustainability over time, it establishes objectives, monitors progress, and executes measures.
- **Risk management:** Sustainable supply chains proactively recognize and address threats posed by environmental, social, and economic factors. They train themselves to be tough and flexible to deal with setbacks better.
- **Innovation and technology:** To optimize operations, increase efficiency, and boost sustainability performance, emerging technologies like IoT, blockchain, and data analytics are used in sustainable supply chains.
- **Compliance and standards:** A sustainable supply chain is one that complies with all applicable rules and regulations. The ESG requirements are met, meaning the environment, society, and governance are all considered.

Businesses may improve their image, gain more environmentally conscientious customers, and lessen their negative impact on the planet by implementing sustainable supply chain policies.

Case study: Sustainability efforts powered by IoT

Unilever, a leading company in **consumer packaged goods** (**CPG**), has been actively embracing advancements to improve their business processes. With a fleet of over 10,000 vehicles, Unilever recognized the potential of IoT technology to revolutionize its supply chain management system.[3]

The collected data played a role in driving optimizations. By analyzing the gathered information, Unilever was able to improve truck loading and routing resulting in a

[3] How Unilever is leveraging AI, cloud and IoT to take data-driven decisions - **https://cio.economictimes.indiatimes.com/news/strategy-and-management/how-unilever-is-leveraging-ai-cloud-and-iot-to-take-data-driven-decisions/71299395**

reduction of travel by 15%. This meant fewer *empty miles* where trucks are without cargo, which led to fuel savings and a decrease in carbon emissions showcasing Unilever's commitment to responsibility. Additionally, Unilever successfully decreased the energy usage of their refrigeration units in trucks by 20% by monitoring temperature and humidity. This accomplishment was made possible through data monitoring, making prompt adjustments to maintain optimal energy levels.

The real-time data provided by the solution played a role in revolutionizing Unilever's packaging process. By understanding how their products were affected during transportation due to vibration, shocks, and temperature changes, the company redesigned its packaging to withstand these factors better. This proactive measure reduced damages and subsequent waste of products, highlighting the impact of IoT on supply chain sustainability. Take a look at *Figure 8.12*:

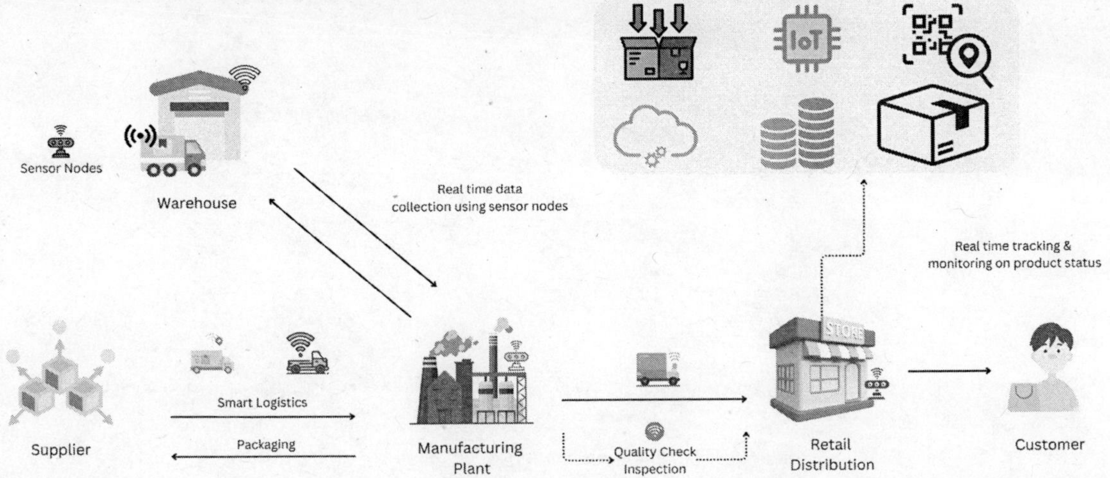

Figure 8.12: *Carbon footprint reduction using IoT*

These combined efforts have yielded results. In one year, Unilever's implementation of technology resulted in a reduction of over 50,000 metric tons of CO_2 emissions, from transportation alone. Moreover, the company avoided product losses worth €200 million. These savings can largely be attributed to the data gathered by sensors that identified inefficiencies and overlooked issues within the supply chain.

This case study demonstrates how the use of sensors and connectivity for real-time monitoring, tracking, and data analytics can lead to sustainability enhancements in supply chain operations. Unilever experienced advantages from this investment, including decreased emissions, reduced waste, cost savings, and enhanced asset monitoring and planning.[4] It showcased the effectiveness of technology in achieving a sustainable and efficient supply chain, serving as an example for other organizations to emulate.

4 Reducing emissions from the use of our products - **https://www.unilever.com/planet-and-society/climate-action/reducing-emissions-from-the-use-of-our-products/**

Benefits and challenges of green supply chain

In today's world, there is a growing concern for the environment and businesses need to adopt practices in supply chain management to stay competitive. Companies are now focusing on reducing their carbon footprint, minimizing waste, and meeting the increasing demand for eco products. IoT plays a role in transforming the supply chain into an ecosystem. By using interconnected devices and sensors, IoT offers opportunities to improve visibility, optimize resource usage, and enhance efficiency throughout the supply chain. Take a look at the *Figure 8.13*:

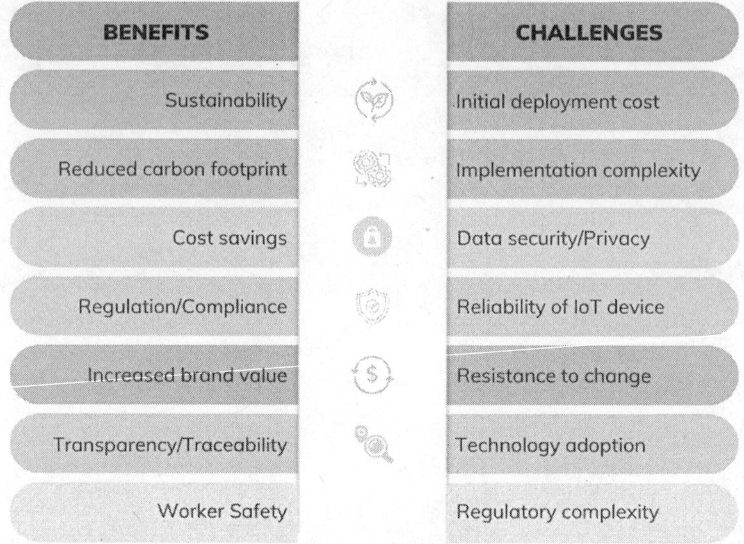

***Figure 8.13:** Benefits and challenges of green supply chain*

Benefits

Here are the benefits of sustainability in the supply chain:

- **Sustainability of resources:** IoT enables real-time resource monitoring and management, reducing waste and promoting eco-friendly practices for long-term sustainability.
- **Carbon footprint reduction:** IoT optimizes transportation routes, enhancing fuel efficiency and lowering emissions for a smaller carbon footprint.
- **Cost savings:** IoT-driven supply chain management boosts productivity, reduces waste, and optimizes energy use, resulting in cost savings.
- **Compliance with regulations:** Real-time IoT data aids businesses in complying with environmental regulations, ensuring accurate reporting of emissions and waste levels.

- **Brand value increase:** Green supply chain practices improve brand value, aligning with consumer and corporate expectations for sustainability and social responsibility.
- **Better transparency and traceability:** IoT enhances supply chain visibility, enabling early issue detection and response, from goods movement to condition monitoring.
- **Enhanced worker safety:** IoT sensors enhance workplace safety by monitoring potential hazards like high temperatures or dangerous chemicals and sending immediate notifications.

Challenges

Here are the challenges of sustainability in the supply chain:

- **Initial deployment cost:** While implementing green practices can lead to long-term cost savings, businesses often face the challenge of making significant upfront investments in eco-friendly technologies and processes, which may strain financial resources.
- **Complexity of implementation:** Adopting IoT in supply chain management can be intricate, requiring expertise in both technology and process adjustments, particularly for less IoT-savvy businesses.
- **Data security and privacy:** Managing the vast data generated by IoT devices requires robust security measures, including secure transmission, storage, and data protection adherence.
- **Reliability of IoT devices:** Ensuring IoT devices' durability and performance in diverse supply chain conditions can be tested, necessitating devices built to withstand varying environments.
- **Resistance to change:** Employees and suppliers may be resistant to changes in established processes, particularly when transitioning to more sustainable practices, requiring effective change management strategies and communication.
- **Technology adoption:** Adopting new sustainability technologies can be a hurdle due to factors like compatibility with existing systems, integration challenges, and the need for employee training.
- **Regulatory complexity:** Navigating the complex landscape of evolving environmental regulations can be daunting for companies, requiring dedicated resources for compliance and risk mitigation.

IoT has the potential to improve environment-friendly supply chain management by means of increased efficiency, decreased carbon emissions, and promotion of long-term viability. To fully reap the benefits of IoT in their supply chain operations, firms must overcome a number of obstacles, including the complexity of implementation, data security concerns, and scalability constraints.

Future of sustainable IoT supply chain

The potential application of IoT in enhancing sustainable supply chains appears highly encouraging. IoT has the capacity to revolutionize global supply chains in numerous ways, facilitating corporations in accomplishing their sustainability objectives. It is projected that expenditure on IoT in the logistics sector will ascend to approximately $114.7 billion by 2032.[5] Here are several crucial methods in which IoT can contribute to sustainable supply chain management:

- **Asset tracking:** IoT facilitates real-time monitoring and location identification of assets and shipments, thereby enhancing agility and decision-making processes in fluctuating scenarios.
- **Inventory management:** Equipment incorporating IoT technology can augment inventory transparency and optimize energy utilization.
- **Data analysis:** IoT platforms process data procured from interconnected devices, empowering organizations to enhance delivery routes, diminish waste, and ascertain efficient transactions with suppliers.
- **Predictive maintenance:** IoT technology can aid in the scheduling of equipment maintenance and forestall machine malfunctions, mitigating downtime and augmenting operational efficiency.
- **Greenhouse gas emissions reduction:** Enterprises can leverage IoT, AI, and blockchain technologies to reduce greenhouse gas emissions, thereby fostering a more sustainable supply chain.
- **Energy efficiency:** Systems powered by IoT can utilize renewable energy sources such as solar energy, minimizing greenhouse gas emissions and conserving financial resources.
- **Real-time visibility:** IoT devices facilitate enhanced visibility and transparency regarding the transportation of goods throughout the supply chain, allowing supply chain managers to identify discrepancies and inefficiencies promptly.
- **Collaboration:** IoT promotes improved collaboration among diverse participants in the supply chain, eliminating data compartmentalization and boosting overall productivity.
- **Demand forecasting:** IoT technology can assist in forecasting consumer demand, aligning supply with demand, and adjusting prices and promotions accordingly.

---

[5] How the IoT Can Drive Sustainable Supply Chains - **https://www.supplychainbrain.com/blogs/1-think-tank/post/36238-how-the-iot-can-drive-sustainable-supply-chains**

- **Sustainability:** IoT innovations can stimulate efficiency and sustainability in supply chain procedures, assisting corporations in transitioning from cost reduction to carbon reduction strategies.

Traditionally, supply chains aimed at cost reduction, but now there is a shift towards sustainability. IoT helps strike a balance between cost efficiency and environmental impact. For example, it aids in optimizing transportation routes, reducing fuel consumption, and monitoring emissions. IoT also supports the adoption of renewable energy sources. This shift towards sustainability ensures that businesses minimize their carbon footprint while maintaining efficiency.

3D printing and IoT

Manufacturing robotics involves incorporating autonomous machines and computer systems into industrial operations, boosting precision and efficiency. These robots handle various tasks, streamline processes, reduce errors, save time, and enhance resource management, transforming manufacturing for improved productivity, cost efficiency, and adaptability.

Additive manufacturing (**AM**), or 3D printing, is a revolutionary manufacturing technique that uses digital 3D models to create physical objects by adding material layer by layer. Then, the items can be used in fields as diverse as medicine, construction, and even the arts.

One must first create or acquire a **computer-aided design** (**CAD**) model before beginning the process of 3D printing. After that, specialized software is used to slice the digital model into several thin layers horizontally. After reading these slices, the 3D printer builds the final thing by depositing or fusing material in successive layers. The versatility of 3D printing allows for a wide range of materials to be used, including plastics, metals, ceramics, resins, and even culinary ingredients. Take a look at *Figure 8.14*:

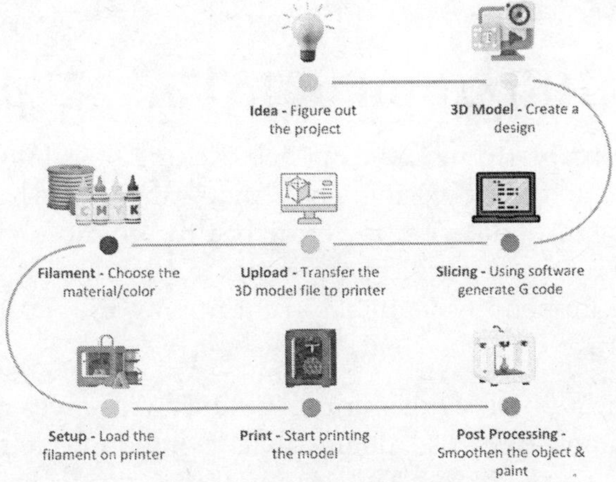

Figure 8.14: *3D printing process*

Here are the main steps of 3D printing in manufacturing:

1. **Design:** The process of designing something begins with creating a 3D model. This is often done using CAD software, although it is also possible to scan existing models or download them from databases.
2. **Slicing:** After creating the 3D model, it is fed into software that divides the object into individual layers. This slicing program generates a set of instructions called **G code** which the 3D printer will use to build the object layer by layer.
3. **Printing:** Next, the G code is read by the 3D printer initiating the printing process. The printer utilizes a chosen printing material, such as filaments, powders, or liquid resins, depending on the technology being used.
4. **Layer-by-layer building:** By following the instructions provided in the G code, the 3D printer adds material layer-by-layer and constructs the object. The computer model guides the printer's nozzle or laser to place and solidify each layer of material precisely.
5. **Post processing:** After printing is complete, certain items may require steps such as cleaning, curing, polishing, or painting to achieve the desired finish and properties as intended by the designer.

The fusion of 3D printing and IoT is set to revolutionize manufacturing, ushering in a data-driven production era. This synergy between Industry 4.0 and AM creates opportunities for collaboration among sellers, producers, and end users.

The benefits of AM, like mass customization and lightweight design, combined with IoT in Industry 4.0, can enhance productivity, functionality, and sustainability. The future of 3D printing hinges on the synergy of materials science, manufacturing techniques, and driven processes. 3D printing will likely become prevalent for producing certified end-use parts, while smart distributed manufacturing evolves into a long-term solution for global supply chain challenges.

Case study: Utilization of IoT in 3D printing

Cloud-based 3D printing platforms have opened exciting possibilities in the medical field, particularly in medical image processing. These platforms enable the efficient management and visualization of medical data, empowering healthcare professionals to create patient-specific 3D printed models for surgical planning and medical research. This innovative approach has proven immensely valuable in improving diagnosis, treatment decisions, and surgical procedures.

One compelling application of 3D printing in medicine involves crafting patient-specific organ replicas. Surgeons now use detailed 3D-printed models to rehearse complex operations before actual surgery. This groundbreaking technique has significantly accelerated procedures and reduced trauma for patients, benefiting surgeries from full-face transplants to delicate spinal procedures. 3D printing extends beyond surgical planning. Medical education and training have also witnessed a revolution with intricately designed replicas aiding medical professionals in understanding complex anatomical structures and pathologies more effectively. These models are valuable resources for procedural simulation training, enhancing medical practitioners' skills. Take a look at *Figure 8.15*:

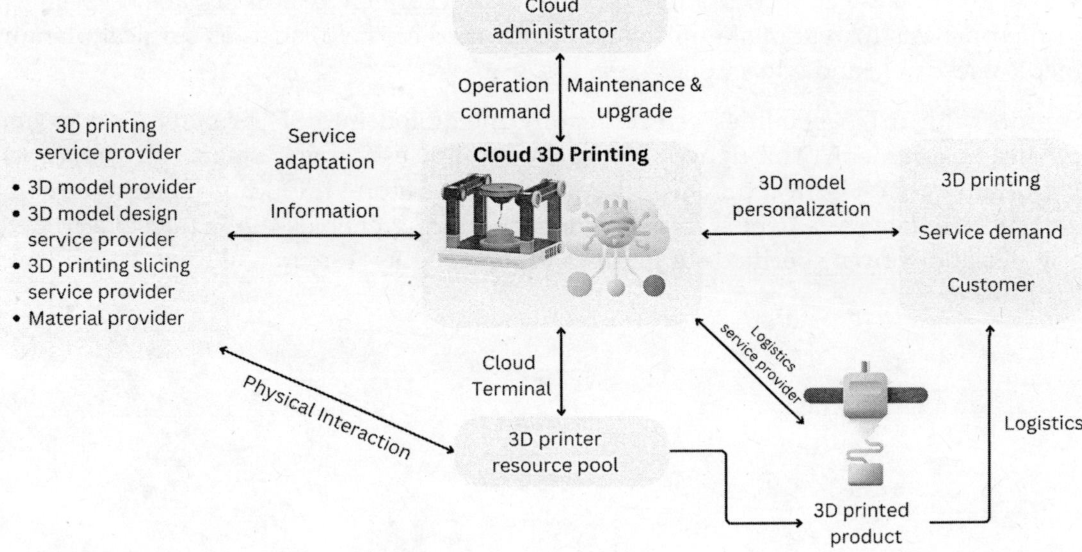

***Figure 8.15:** IoT 3D printing*

Cloud computing improves medical image processing for 3D printing by offering several advantages, including:

- **Scalability:** Cloud computing platforms can handle large volumes of medical imaging data, allowing for efficient storage, processing, and analysis of images at a large scale.
- **Accessibility:** Cloud-based platforms enable medical professionals to access and share medical images and 3D models from anywhere, facilitating collaboration and streamlining the design-to-production process.
- **Speed:** Cloud computing platforms can process medical images more quickly than traditional methods, reducing the time it takes to create patient-specific 3D printed models for surgical planning, medical research, or education.
- **Integration:** Cloud computing platforms can integrate various resources, such as hardware (3D printers and materials) and software (data management and visualization tools), enabling seamless collaboration among different stakeholders in the 3D printing ecosystem.

- **AI and ML:** Some cloud-based platforms leverage AI and ML algorithms to optimize the medical image processing and 3D printing process, improving efficiency and accuracy.

Cloud computing improves medical image processing for 3D printing by offering scalability, accessibility, speed, integration, and the potential for AI and ML enhancements. These advantages can lead to more efficient and accurate creation of patient-specific 3D printed models for various applications in the medical field, such as surgical planning, medical research, and education.

Sensors with IoT capabilities can be readily integrated into 3D printers used to make medical equipment. Throughout the printing process, these smart sensors capture important data on critical parameters such as temperature, humidity, material flow rate, and other relevant elements. This constant monitoring enables the IoT system to detect any deviations from specified standards and inform operators in real time. Take a look at *Figure 8.16*:

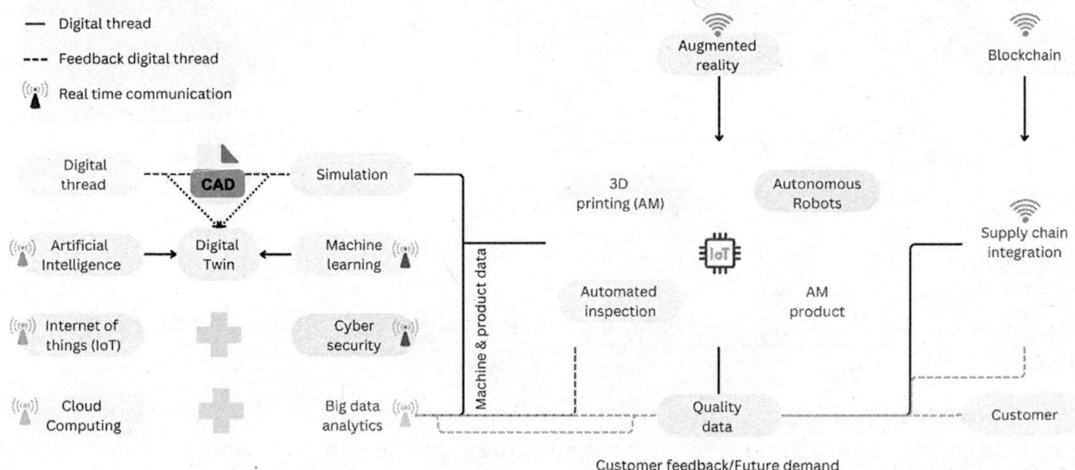

Figure 8.16: *IoT 3D printing architecture*

In a hypothetical situation, if the 3D printing process for medical equipment encounters abnormal temperature levels, IoT technology notifies the operator, enabling quick intervention. To ensure the final product meets requirements, the operator can take corrective actions like modifying temperature settings or adjusting printing parameters. The extensive data gathered by IoT sensors can undergo advanced data analysis to uncover patterns, helping manufacturers enhance the 3D printing process, enhance quality control, and create more reliable medical products.

Benefits and challenges of IoT and 3D printing

Integrating IoT and 3D printing in manufacturing holds immense promise, offering many benefits along with some notable challenges.

Benefits

The benefits of IoT and 3D printing in manufacturing are as follows:

- **Enhanced efficiency:** Combining IoT with 3D printing allows real-time data gathering from IoT-enabled sensors during printing. These sensors monitor crucial parameters like temperature, humidity, and material flow rate, enabling precise insights into the printing environment. Manufacturers can use this data to optimize printing parameters, reduce waste, enhance productivity, and save costs.
- **Customization and personalization:** IoT and 3D printing enable mass customization by translating individual preferences and requirements into unique 3D-printed objects. This empowers manufacturers to produce tailored items swiftly, reducing the need for large inventories and promoting sustainable and responsive production.
- **Remote monitoring and control:** IoT connectivity in 3D printing enables remote oversight, issue detection, and resolution, enhancing quality control and operational efficiency. This flexibility allows manufacturers to adapt to changing demands and optimize workflows.
- **Supply chain optimization:** IoT-enabled 3D printing transforms supply chain management by offering real-time inventory tracking, equipment monitoring, and automated replenishment. On-demand production minimizes inventory needs and streamlines logistics, making supply chains more responsive and cost-effective.

Challenges

The challenges of IoT and 3D printing in manufacturing are as follows:

- **High-quality digital files:** Accurate design files are crucial for precise 3D printing. Inaccurate or unreliable files can lead to subpar products.
- **Cost and training:** Investment in 3D printing technology and staff training is required, making initial costs prohibitive for some manufacturers.
- **Safety and intellectual property:** Increased connectivity raises concerns about protecting intellectual property and data security.
- **Material limits:** Current 3D printing technologies have limitations in terms of compatible materials, necessitating ongoing advancements in material science.

IoT and 3D printing hold immense promise in manufacturing, offering efficiency, customization, remote monitoring, and supply chain optimization. Addressing challenges related to digital file quality, costs, security, and materials is vital for widespread adoption and innovation in the manufacturing industry. These technologies are poised to transform manufacturing processes and drive future advancements.

Future trends of IoT and 3D printing

Future 3D printing and IoT trends in advanced manufacturing promise breakthroughs and applications:

- **Smart factories enabled by IoT:** Integration of 3D printing and IoT enables smart factories for real-time monitoring, automation, efficiency, and reduced downtime.
- **Digital twins:** 3D printing, when integrated with IoT, enhances digital twins by enabling real-time updates of physical assets' digital representations. IoT sensors collect data from the 3D-printed objects, allowing continuous monitoring, simulation, and optimization.
- **IoT-enabled supply chain:** 3D printing contributes to real-time insights and coordination in IoT-enabled supply chains by manufacturing parts and products on-demand. This allows for agile responses to changing demand, reduced inventory, and improved supply chain flexibility.
- **On-demand manufacturing:** IoT and 3D printing enable efficient, customized on-demand manufacturing, reducing inventories.
- **Sustainability:** Integration drives sustainability through localized production, resource optimization, and the ongoing development of eco-friendly 3D printing materials. This combination of factors promotes environmentally responsible practices within manufacturing processes.

However, before 3D printing and IoT can be widely adopted in the field of advanced manufacturing, several challenges must be overcome. These issues include the preservation of intellectual property and data security, the provision of high-quality digital files, the cost of 3D printers and training, the expansion of the range of printable materials, and the affordability of 3D printers.

Big data analytics from IoT-generated data

Data represents raw information collected from sources like IoT devices, often including unprocessed content that requires further analysis and organization to become valuable information. Big data involves intricate datasets surpassing traditional analysis capabilities, defined by the *Four V's*: volume, velocity, variety, and veracity, specifying these data collections. Take a look at *Figure 8.17*:

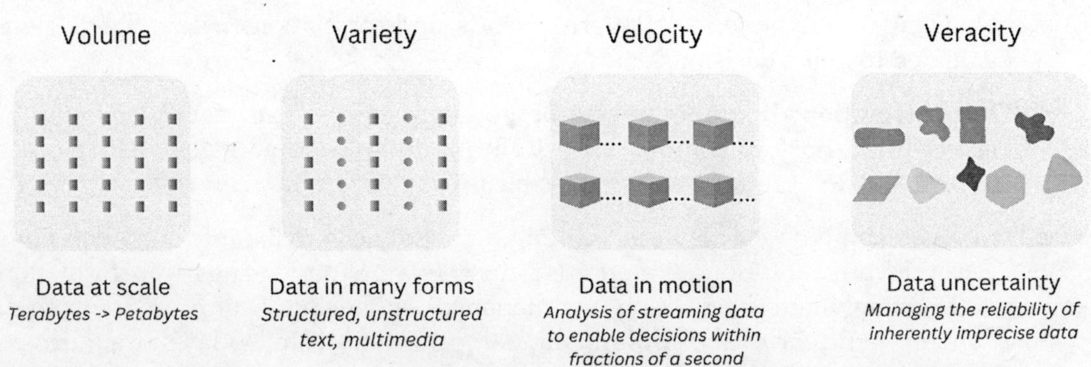

Figure 8.17: *Four V's of big data*

Here is the differentiation of four aspects of big data analytics:

- **Volume:** Big data consists of volumes of data ranging from terabytes to petabytes and beyond. Various sources including social media interactions, sensor readings, and transaction records contribute to this dataset.
- **Velocity:** The speed at which big data is generated necessitates analysis in order to derive insights. Time or near real-time analysis is often required to keep up with the stream of data.
- **Variety:** Big data encompasses a range of formats spanning from structured databases to semi-structured XML files and even unstructured content, like text documents, photos, and videos.
- **Veracity:** Big data can be noisy, uncertain, and insufficient, making it difficult to ensure the accuracy and dependability of the insights derived from them.

Here are a few examples that demonstrate how the convergence of IoT and big data is taking place:

- **Data collection:** IoT generates an abundance of information from devices. Real-time sensor readings, event logs, and user interactions contribute to the volume and speed at which big data grows.
- **Data storage:** To handle the quantities of data produced by devices, technologies like distributed databases and data lakes are employed within big data systems. These advancements allow for cost-effective storage solutions for data.
- **Data processing:** The tools and techniques used in big data analytics are applied to process the amounts of data. Real-time processing enables analysis and response to information.
- **Data analysis:** By employing big data analytics on data, organizations can gain intelligence for improving operations, predicting maintenance needs, and

enhancing user experiences. Patterns, trends, and correlations within the data are evaluated to make decisions.

- **Data integration:** To obtain a view of a system and perform device analytics, it becomes necessary to combine data from multiple IoT devices as well as other sources. This integration is made possible through big data platforms.

When businesses combine IoT devices with big data, they can make informed decisions and generate innovative solutions. Numerous industries are experiencing a transformation thanks to this combination, enabling maintenance, enhancing healthcare outcomes, boosting energy efficiency, and optimizing supply chains. In today's data-driven companies, the convergence of the ecosystem is becoming increasingly vital as it expands in scale and complexity.

Big data analytics for business insights

Utilizing the power of big data analytics to gain business insights and make informed decisions has become a strategy for organizations aiming to stay in the market. Here are some key takeaways in which businesses can effectively harness the potential of big data analytics:

- **Data collection and integration:** Businesses gather data from diverse sources like customer interactions, sales, websites, social media, and IoT devices. This data needs consolidation for a comprehensive view.
- **Storage and processing:** Handling big data requires storage solutions like data warehouses, data lakes, and cloud storage. High-performance engines such as Hadoop and Spark aid data analysis.
- **Real-time analytics:** Competitive businesses rely on real-time insights to respond swiftly to market changes. big data analytics combined with real-time data empower timely decision-making.
- **Predictive analytics:** Going beyond analysis, big data employs machine learning and statistical models for predicting trends, customer behavior, and outcomes, aiding in planning and risk management.
- **Customer insights:** Big data unlocks customer preferences and behaviors, enabling tailored marketing strategies to enhance customer experiences and loyalty.
- **Supply chain optimization:** Analyzing supply chain data optimizes inventory, and logistics, and identifies bottlenecks, improving efficiency and reducing costs.
- **Fraud detection and security:** Big data detects fraud, cyber threats, and security breaches through real-time pattern analysis, enhancing data protection.
- **Business process optimization:** Analyzing data patterns identifies inefficiencies, streamlining operations for increased productivity.

- **Market and industry analysis:** Big data helps businesses stay ahead by monitoring market trends, competitors, and industry advancements for informed decision-making and growth.

Using big data analytics to gain business insights and make business decisions is a game-changer for groups in all fields. Businesses can find useful insights, improve customer experiences, and make well-informed decisions that lead to success in a data-driven world when they can process and analyze large amounts of data in real-time. Big data analytics will continue to be important for businesses aiming to thrive in a market that is constantly changing and becoming more complex. Take a look at *Figure 8.18*:

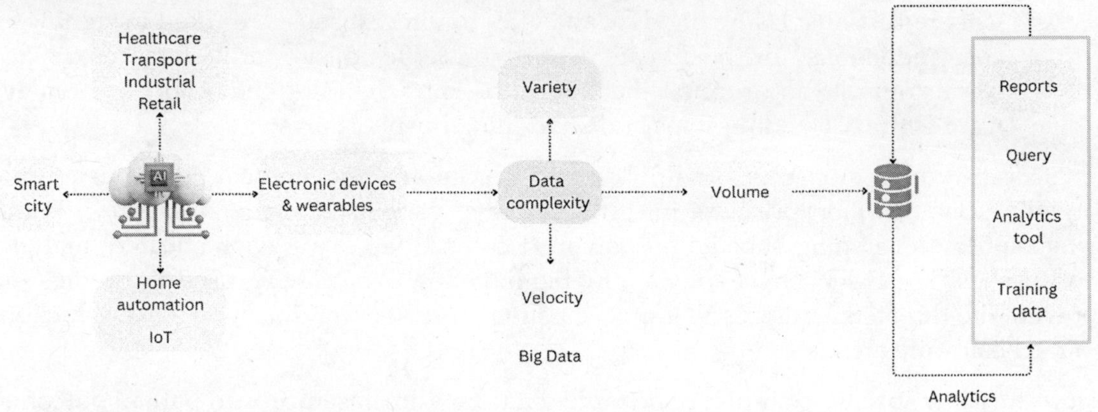

Figure 8.18: Big data for business insights

Case study: Big data analytics in healthcare

Penn Medicine's pioneering **Predictive Analytics for Healthcare** (**PATH**) effort is an illuminating case study demonstrating the application of big data analytics in healthcare.[6] The major goal of the PATH program was to construct a predictive model capable of detecting individuals at high risk of developing sepsis, a potentially fatal infection-related illness.

Big data analytics was critical in evaluating the **Electronic Health Records** (**EHR**s) of patients in real time as part of the PATH initiative. The team collected and methodically examined massive amounts of patient data, such as vital signs, laboratory results, medication history, and clinical notes. They used machine learning algorithms to identify patterns and signs that could predict the beginning of sepsis.

Using big data analytics, the PATH initiative achieved numerous outstanding results, which are as follows:

6 Data Analytics in Healthcare: 7 Real-World Examples and Use Cases - **https://www.altexsoft.com/blog/analytics-in-healthcare/**

- **Early sepsis detection:** The PATH initiative's predictive model demonstrated its capacity to identify high-risk patients up to 24 hours before the onset of sepsis symptoms. This early discovery allowed healthcare providers to intervene quickly and give appropriate treatment, potentially saving lives and improving patient outcomes.
- **Reduced mortality rates:** The prediction model's application resulted in a significant decrease in sepsis-related mortality rates. Healthcare personnel successfully halted the course of sepsis by rapidly identifying high-risk patients and prompt therapies, ultimately boosting patient survival rates.
- **Cost reductions:** Using big data analytics to forecast sepsis resulted in significant cost reductions for healthcare institutions. Healthcare providers maximized resource usage and reduced healthcare costs by avoiding the need for **Intensive Care Unit** (**ICU**) admissions and shortening hospital stays.

This case study demonstrates the power of big data analytics in healthcare. Healthcare organizations can gain priceless insights, improve patient care, and optimize resource allocation by leveraging substantial patient data and deploying sophisticated analytics approaches. The PATH effort shows how big data analytics may be used to predict and prevent life-threatening illnesses, improve patient outcomes, and usher in cost reductions in the healthcare arena.

Here are a few specific examples of how big data analytics has improved patient outcomes in healthcare:

- **Personalized medicine**[7]**:** Big data analytics enables the analysis of large volumes of patient data, including genetic information, to identify optimal treatments for individual patients. This personalized approach improves treatment efficacy and patient outcomes.
- **Reducing hospital readmissions:** Big data analytics can identify patterns and risk factors associated with hospital readmissions. By analyzing patient data, healthcare providers can develop interventions and care plans to reduce readmission rates and improve patient outcomes.
- **Real-time monitoring and alerts**[8]**:** Big data analytics enables real-time monitoring of patient data, such as vital signs and sensor data from wearable devices. This allows healthcare providers to detect and respond to changes in patient conditions promptly, leading to improved patient outcomes and reduced adverse events.
- **Population health management**[9]**:** Big data analytics helps identify trends and risk factors at the population level. By analyzing large datasets, healthcare providers

[7] 6 Use Cases for Big Data and Analytics in Healthcare - **https://www.itconvergence.com/blog/6-use-cases-for-big-data-and-analytics-in-healthcare/**

[8] The use of Big Data Analytics in healthcare - **https://journalofbigdata.springeropen.com/articles/10.1186/s40537-021-00553-4**

[9] Big Data Healthcare Analytics - **https://www.foreseemed.com/blog/big-data-analytics-in-healthcare**

can develop targeted interventions and preventive strategies to improve the overall health of a population, leading to better patient outcomes.

- **Improving patient experience[10]:** Big data analytics allows healthcare providers to capture and analyze data to gain insights into patient experience. By understanding patient preferences and needs, healthcare providers can tailor care plans and interventions, improving patient satisfaction and outcomes.

These examples demonstrate how big data analytics has been successfully applied in healthcare to improve patient outcomes. By leveraging large volumes of data and advanced analytics techniques, healthcare providers can make data-driven decisions, personalize treatments, detect risks early, and improve overall patient care.

Future trends in big data analytics for IoT

Within the expansive realm of technical progress, a significant shift is occurring as a result of the notable intersection of big data analytics and IoT. As we find ourselves on the verge of this era characterized by data utilization, there exists a remarkable opportunity to access hitherto unattainable knowledge and prospects. The future of big data analytics for IoT holds the potential to significantly transform industries, provide decision-makers with enhanced capabilities, and foster innovation on an unprecedented level. This transformation is anticipated to be driven by advancements in cloud and edge computing, as well as the integration of real-time monitoring and artificial intelligence.

Following is a list of future trends in IoT:

- **Cloud and edge computing:** They provide flexibility and cost-effectiveness in IoT's big data analytics, with cloud storage offering scalability and edge computing enabling real-time data processing.
- **Real-time monitoring and data processing:** IoT enhances real-time monitoring and data processing for predictive maintenance and improved customer service.
- **Non-database sources and IoT devices:** IoT's diverse data sources require stream processing and event-driven architectures for efficient data management.
- **Data storage innovation:** Innovative solutions like cloud platforms, data lakes, and hybrid cloud address the growing volume of IoT data.
- **Data as a service:** DaaS promotes data sharing and collaboration through cloud platforms, fostering informed decision-making.
- **Low-code/no-code solutions:** These tools make it easier to create and deploy AI and machine learning models, increasing accessibility and decreasing the requirement for technical expertise.

---

[10] How big data in Health Care Influences Patient Outcomes - **https://publichealth.tulane.edu/blog/big-data-in-healthcare/**

The future of big data analytics for IoT offers growth and transformation. Cloud, real-time monitoring, and data solutions empower data-driven decisions. AI and DaaS drive innovation for competitive advantages.

Conclusion

IoT delivers transformative capabilities across the manufacturing value chain by connecting assets, processes, and systems to provide real-time visibility, data-driven analytics, and digital optimization. IoT unlocks new potential in predictive maintenance, production planning, quality control, logistics, and supply chain coordination. While bringing enhanced efficiency, flexibility, and precision, IoT also raises concerns around data security, infrastructure readiness, and systems integration that must be addressed. Manufacturers embracing IoT, advanced analytics, and digital transformation will gain long-term competitiveness. However, success requires an integrated IT/OT approach spanning sensors, connectivity, platforms, insights, and security. As manufacturing evolves, IoT will become integral in enabling the next level of intelligent, interconnected, and highly automated smart factories.

In the next chapter of the book, we will bring together the key takeaways from each chapter, providing a comprehensive recap of the IoT revolution in manufacturing and supply chain. We will reflect on the transformative journey we have explored, including real-world case studies, practical insights, and the influence of emerging technologies like predictive analytics, blockchain, sustainability, artificial intelligence, and 3D printing.

Points to remember

- IoT refers to a network of interconnected physical objects and devices that can collect and share data through embedded sensors and software.
- The key components of an IoT architecture include sensors, controllers, cloud platforms, data analytics tools, and communication protocols.
- IoT allows real-time monitoring and predictive maintenance by analyzing sensor data to forecast equipment failures before they occur.
- IoT improves production planning by providing real-time visibility into inventory, orders, machine performance, and other factors.
- IoT enhances quality control by rapidly identifying defects using inline sensor data and analytics during production.
- IoT offers wide visibility across supply chains by connecting assets, inventory, shipments and partners for coordination.
- IoT analytics including predictive modeling and machine learning help identify trends and opportunities to optimize manufacturing.

- Data security, infrastructure readiness, system integration, and managing change are key IoT adoption challenges.
- Critical IoT security measures include encryption, access control, device authentication, network segmentation, and audits.
- MQTT, CoAP, OPC-UA, and AMQP are common IoT communication protocols for device connectivity and data exchange.
- Long-term IoT benefits include increased speed, flexibility, accuracy, and responsiveness across integrated, intelligent operations.
- Edge computing provides localized, real-time data processing while cloud platforms offer storage and computing capabilities.

Multiple choice questions

1. **Which protocol enables lightweight M2M communication for IoT devices?**
   a. MQTT
   b. OPC UA
   c. AMQP
   d. CoAP
2. **What provides short-range wireless communication between IoT devices?**
   a. Wi-Fi
   b. LoRaWAN
   c. 3G/4G
   d. LiFi
3. **How can data analytics help optimize quality in manufacturing?**
   a. Identifying defects rapidly
   b. Improving production planning
   c. Enhancing equipment performance
   d. Reducing operating costs
4. **Which technology enables tracking and localization of assets in an IoT system?**
   a. PLCs
   b. Robotics
   c. RFID
   d. GPS

5. **What enables real-time data processing at the edge in an IoT architecture?**
   a. Cloud platforms
   b. MES systems
   c. SCADA systems
   d. Edge computing
6. **IoT allows manufacturers to shift from _______ to ________ maintenance strategies.**
   a. corrective, preventive
   b. preventive, predictive
   c. reactive, proactive
   d. digital, analytical
7. **Which data analytics method can help forecast equipment failures in manufacturing plants?**
   a. Prescriptive analytics
   b. Descriptive analytics
   c. Diagnostic analytics
   d. Predictive analytics
8. **How can IoT improve coordination across supply chain partners?**
   a. Automating production
   b. Enabling visibility and information sharing
   c. Robotizing warehouses
   d. 3D printing spare parts
9. **What long term impact will IoT have on manufacturing operations?**
   a. Reduced automation
   b. Lower costs
   c. Decreased data visibility
   d. Highly interconnected and intelligent processes

10. Which technologies support centralized storage and compute for IoT platforms?

a. Cloud computing

b. Blockchain

c. Edge computing

d. Virtualization

Answer key

1. a.
2. a.
3. a.
4. c.
5. d.
6. b.
7. d.
8. b.
9. d.
10. a.

Questions

1. What is IoT and how does it impact manufacturing operations?
2. What are the key components of an IoT system architecture?
3. How can IoT enable predictive maintenance in manufacturing?
4. How does IoT improve production planning and inventory management?
5. How can IoT enhance quality control in manufacturing processes?
6. How does IoT provide supply chain visibility and coordination?
7. What role does data analytics play in generating insights from IoT data?
8. What are some key challenges in adopting IoT systems in manufacturing?
9. What communication protocols are commonly used in IoT systems?
10. What are the long-term benefits of implementing IoT in manufacturing?
11. How does edge computing support IoT platforms and applications?

12. How can blockchain technology be integrated with IoT systems?
13. How can IoT enable sustainability across supply chains?
14. What are the benefits of combining 3D printing and IoT in manufacturing?
15. How can big data analytics generate business insights from IoT data?

Key terms

- **Open Platform Communications Unified Architecture:** An industrial IoT communication protocol that enables interoperability between devices and systems.
- **Blockchain:** Distributed ledger technology that provides secure, transparent transaction records across a decentralized network of participants. It can be integrated with IoT.
- **Predictive analytics:** A subfield of data analytics that uses historical and real-time data to make predictions about the future.
- **Dashboard:** A visual representation of KPIs is used to track and monitor the performance of a business or organization.
- **Smart contracts:** Self-executing contracts on a blockchain network whose terms get fulfilled when pre-defined conditions are met. It can automate IoT processes.
- **Digital twin:** Virtual representation of a physical asset or process, mirrored throughout its lifecycle via integrated IoT sensors, data, and analytics.
- **Data as a service:** Delivery model that provides access to data storage, management, processing, and analytics as an on-demand service via the cloud. It applies to IoT data.
- **Constrained application protocol:** A web transfer protocol designed for machine-to-machine communication in resource-constrained IoT devices.
- **Data security:** Protecting confidentiality, integrity, and availability of IoT data through encryption, access control, authentication, and so on, against cyber threats.
- **Graphical user interface:** Visual interface allowing users to interact with software or systems. Used to access, analyze, and visualize IoT data.
- **Latency:** The delay or lag in data communication over IoT networks. Lower latency enables real-time analytics.
- **Load balancing:** Distributing network traffic across multiple servers to optimize resource use, minimize response time, and prevent overload. Crucial for IoT data traffic.
- **System integration:** Integration of IoT systems with legacy networks, software and hardware infrastructure.

CHAPTER 9
Key Takeaways

Introduction

This chapter discusses the **Internet of Things** (**IoT**) for manufacturing, infrastructure, and business aspects in a summarized way. This will also cover an overview of future trends of IoT, the IoT revolution in manufacturing and supply chain, and the role of emerging technologies in IoT.

Structure

The chapter covers the following topics:

- Overview
- Future trends of IoT
- Role of emerging technologies in the IoT

Overview

The IoT is poised to revolutionize the manufacturing and supply chain industries. By connecting machines, sensors, and devices across the entire value chain, IoT enables businesses to achieve unprecedented levels of visibility, efficiency, and agility.

In manufacturing, IoT is used to:

- **Optimize production processes:** By collecting real-time data from sensors on machines and throughout the production line, manufacturers can gain insights into how to improve efficiency and reduce waste. For example, IoT-enabled sensors can monitor machine performance, identify potential problems before they cause downtime, and optimize production schedules.
- **Enhance product quality:** IoT sensors can track product quality throughout the manufacturing process, ensuring that products meet strict standards. For example, they can monitor temperature, humidity, and other critical parameters during the manufacturing process, identifying any deviations that could impact product quality.
- **Automate tasks:** IoT-enabled robots and other machines can automate a wide range of tasks in manufacturing, improving safety, productivity, and consistency. For example, IoT-enabled robots can perform tasks such as welding, painting, and material handling.
- **Enhance worker safety:** IoT devices can monitor the safety of workers in manufacturing environments. For instance, wearable IoT devices can track vital signs, detect potential hazards, and alert workers and supervisors in real time, contributing to a safer work environment.
- **Enable just-in-time production:** IoT data can be leveraged to implement just-in-time production strategies more accurately, ensuring that materials and components are delivered precisely when needed, reducing inventory costs and waste.

In the supply chain, IoT is used to:

- **Improve demand forecasting:** By collecting data on consumer behavior and market trends, IoT can be used to improve demand forecasting. This allows businesses to optimize inventory levels and avoid stockouts or overstocks. For example, IoT-enabled sensors can track sales data, monitor product usage, and gather information from supply chain partners, providing a comprehensive view of demand.
- **Enhance inventory management:** By tracking the location and condition of goods in real-time, IoT can help businesses improve inventory management. This can reduce the risk of loss or damage and ensure that the right products are available in the right place at the right time. For example, IoT-enabled sensors can track the location of goods in transit, monitor temperature and humidity levels, and detect any signs of damage.
- **Optimize logistics:** By providing real-time visibility into the movement of goods, IoT can help businesses optimize logistics operations. This can reduce

transportation costs and improve delivery times. For example, IoT-enabled tracking devices can track the location of goods in transit, identify potential delays, and optimize shipping routes.

- **Automate warehouse operations:** IoT-enabled robots and other machines can automate a wide range of tasks in warehousing, improving efficiency and accuracy. For example, IoT-enabled robots can perform tasks such as picking, packing, and palletizing.

The impact of IoT on manufacturing and supply chain is beginning to be realized. As IoT technology evolves, we expect to see even more innovative and transformative applications emerge. Businesses that can successfully leverage IoT will be well-positioned to gain a competitive advantage in future years.

Future trends of IoT

Here are some of the key future trends of IoT for supply chain and manufacturing:

- **Enhanced supply chain visibility:** IoT sensors, including those for indoor positioning, can be used to track the location and condition of goods not only in outdoor supply chain areas but also inside warehouses and facilities. It provides a real-time view of inventory levels and transit times indoors and outdoors. This information can be used to optimize logistics operations, identify potential disruptions, and improve customer service.

- **Predictive maintenance:** IoT sensors can monitor the health and performance of machines and equipment, enabling predictive maintenance that can prevent downtime and costly repairs. This can significantly improve asset utilization and reduce maintenance costs.

- **Improved quality control:** IoT sensors can be used to monitor the quality of products during the manufacturing process, identifying defects early on and preventing them from reaching the customer. This can improve product quality, reduce waste, and enhance brand reputation.

- **Automated logistics and warehousing:** IoT technologies can be used to automate tasks such as inventory management, order picking, and packaging, improving efficiency and reducing labor costs. This can also reduce errors and improve safety in warehouses.

- **Personalized manufacturing:** IoT data can be used to personalize products and services based on customer preferences, enabling mass customization and a more responsive supply chain. This can lead to increased customer satisfaction and loyalty.

- **Augmented reality (AR) and digital twin:** The integration of AR with digital twin technology is set to change the supply chain and manufacturing processes. AR adds digital information to the real world, making it easier to monitor and fix things. Combined with digital twin simulations, it allows us for advanced scenario testing and immediate adjustments to optimize operations.

In addition to these trends, IoT is also enabling the development of new and innovative supply chain and manufacturing applications. For example, IoT can be used to create digital twins of physical assets, which can be used to simulate and optimize operations. IoT can also be used to develop autonomous vehicles and robots, which can further automate supply chain and manufacturing processes.

The adoption of IoT in supply chain and manufacturing is still in its early stages, but the potential benefits are significant. As IoT technologies continue to mature and become more affordable, we can expect to see even more innovative applications that will transform the way we manufacture and deliver goods.

Role of emerging technologies in IoT

IoT has revolutionized how industries operate, and manufacturing and supply chains are no exception. Emerging technologies are further transforming the IoT landscape, enabling manufacturers and supply chain operators to achieve new levels of efficiency, productivity, and sustainability.

The key emerging technologies in the IoT landscape for manufacturing and supply chain are:

- **Artificial intelligence and machine learning: artificial intelligence (AI)** and **machine learning (ML)** are transforming IoT data into actionable insights. AI algorithms can analyze vast amounts of sensor data to identify patterns, predict trends, and make informed decisions. This enables manufacturers to optimize production schedules, predict equipment failures, and improve quality control. In supply chains, AI can optimize logistics routes, manage inventory levels, and predict demand fluctuations.
- **Edge computing:** Edge computing brings data processing and analysis closer to the source, reducing latency and improving real-time decision-making. This is particularly critical in manufacturing, where real-time insights from IoT sensors can be used to adjust production parameters, prevent downtime, and ensure product quality. In supply chains, edge computing enables real-time tracking of goods, optimizing transportation routes, and responding to disruptions promptly.
- **Digital twins:** Digital twins are virtual representations of physical assets, such as machines, equipment, or entire supply chains. These digital twins are continuously updated with real-time data from IoT sensors, providing a holistic view of asset performance and enabling predictive maintenance, process optimization, and supply chain simulations.

- **Blockchain:** Blockchain technology provides a secure and transparent way to share data among supply chain partners. This can streamline collaboration, improve traceability, and enhance trust within the supply chain. Blockchain can also be used to track the provenance of raw materials, ensuring authenticity and sustainability.
- **5G and advanced connectivity:** 5G networks offer increased bandwidth, lower latency, and massive device connectivity, enabling the deployment of more complex IoT applications. This will support the growth of IoT-enabled manufacturing and supply chain operations, enabling real-time data exchange, remote monitoring, and autonomous operations.

Conclusion

IoT is revolutionizing the manufacturing and supply chain industries, driving unprecedented levels of efficiency, productivity, and sustainability. Emerging technologies, such as AI, ML, edge computing, digital twins, blockchain, and advanced connectivity, further accelerate this transformation.

Manufacturers and supply chain operators that embrace the IoT revolution will gain a competitive edge and achieve long-term success. This involves investing in IoT infrastructure and technologies, developing data analytics capabilities, skilling up the workforce, collaborating with partners, and adopting a mindset of continuous improvement and innovation.

By embracing the IoT revolution, manufacturers and supply chain operators can transform their operations, enhance customer satisfaction, and achieve new levels of success in the digital era.

Join our book's Discord space

Join the book's Discord Workspace for Latest updates, Offers, Tech happenings around the world, New Release and Sessions with the Authors:

https://discord.bpbonline.com